Kentucky Remembered

An Oral History Series

JAMES C. KLOTTER and
TERRY L. BIRDWHISTELL
General Editors

BARRY BINGHAM

A Man of His Word

Samuel W. Thomas, Editor

THE UNIVERSITY PRESS OF KENTUCKY

Publication of this book was assisted by a grant from
the Mary and Barry Bingham, Sr. Fund.

Frontispiece: Portrait of Barry Bingham by Harvard classmate
Gardner Cox, 1970. Courtesy of Mary Caperton Bingham.

Scholarly publisher for the Commonwealth,
serving Bellarmine College, Berea College, Centre
College of Kentucky, Eastern Kentucky University,
The Filson Club, Georgetown College, Kentucky
Historical Society, Kentucky State University,
Morehead State University, Murray State University,
Northern Kentucky University, Transylvania University,
University of Kentucky, University of Louisville,
and Western Kentucky University.

Editorial and Sales Offices: Lexington, Kentucky 40508-4008

Library of Congress Cataloging-in-Publication Data

Bingham, Barry. 1906–1988.
    Barry Bingham : a man of his word / edited by Samuel W. Thomas.
        p.   cm.—(Kentucky remembered)
    Includes bibliographical references and index.
    ISBN 0-8131-1835-2
    1. Bingham, Barry, 1906–1988—Interviews.   2. Journalists—
Kentucky—20th century—Biography.   3. Publishers and publishing—
Kentucky—Biography.   I. Thomas, Samuel W., 1938–   .   II. Title.
III. Series.
PN4874.B48A3   1993
070.5′092—dc20   93-18678
[B]

Contents

[Illustrations follow pages 38 and 102]

General Editors' Preface

In the field of oral history, Kentucky is a national leader. Over the past several decades thousands of its citizens have been interviewed. *Kentucky Remembered* will bring into print the most important of those recollections, with each volume focusing on a particular subject.

Oral history is, of course, only one type of source material. Yet by the very personal nature of recollection, hidden aspects of history are often disclosed. Oral sources provide a vital thread in the rich fabric that is Kentucky history.

This volume is the second in the series and, like the first, focuses on the life and career of an individual. Barry Bingham, Sr., was a many-faceted man whose influence covered several fields. Best known for his career as a newspaper publisher and broadcasting executive, he had a significant impact on his native state through those endeavors. But he also touched the lives of many people in many other ways.

This engaging and important man has been the focus of earlier studies, but none capture the spirit of Barry Bingham to the extent this approach does. Editor Samuel W. Thomas has combined Bingham's recollections with some of his writings. The result is a work that enlightens, while we enjoy and savor the story of a man who was highly respected and will be long remembered.

Acknowledgments

I am indebted to Mary Caperton Bingham for her counsel and support of this project, undertaken as part of the preparation of her late husband's papers for donation to the Filson Club. Her answers to questions of clarification and her critical guidance and encouragement have been invaluable.

The general editors of this oral history publication series—James Klotter, state historian and director of the Kentucky Historical Society, and Terry Birdwhistell, University of Kentucky archivist and director of its Oral History Program—have been most helpful in shaping this manuscript. John Ed Pearce, longtime *Courier-Journal* editorial writer and columnist, and now also a contributor to *The Herald-Leader,* and Keith L. Runyon, editor of *The Courier-Journal*'s Opinion Pages, both offered insight and penetrating evaluation.

Catherine Esary, Ann Cunningham, and Patti Vance diligently prepared the transcriptions and manuscript drafts, and their efforts are appreciated. I also acknowledge the particular assistance of William E. Ellis, director of the Oral History Center at Eastern Kentucky University, who interviewed Barry Bingham extensively in connection with scholarly articles he wrote about the Bingham family. The cooperation of the following was also essential: Kim Lady Smith, director, and Cary Wilkins, former project archivist, of the Kentucky Oral History Commission; Carl Ryant and Dale Patterson, codirectors of the Oral History Program, University of Louisville; Wade Hall, professor of English, Bellarmine College; David Shedden, archivist, Poynter Institute for Media Studies, St. Petersburg, Florida; and C. Thomas Hardin, director of photography, *The Courier-Journal*.

Samuel W. Thomas

Introduction

At a glittering occasion marking the reopening of the Brown Hotel in January 1985, Barry Bingham made a few remarks. He recalled some words his father, Robert Worth Bingham, had spoken when the hotel first opened sixty-two years before. "When my father was speaking at the earlier occasion, he said: 'Success is never an accident. It is a result of courage, character, judgment, and hard work.' I add one more word to what he said: it's also a result of vision." Perhaps vision, or long-term direction, is also what most clearly delineated the son from his father.

Barry Bingham was only seventeen when the Brown was dedicated in 1923. His father had been a successful lawyer, interim mayor and circuit court judge, and for five years owner of *The Courier-Journal* and *The Louisville Times*. He would be named by President Franklin Roosevelt ambassador to Great Britain in 1933. By then, Barry Bingham had graduated from Harvard University and had worked for a year at WHAS radio. He was newly married and was beginning to wend his way into management of the newspapers.

For a 1983 *Kentucky Post* series entitled "Soul of Kentucky," David Wecker described coming to Sixth and Broadway for an interview.

Barry Bingham, Sr. takes light, quick, forward-leaning strides through the lobby of The Courier-Journal and Louisville Times Building. His bulky briefcase seems to have no drag on his headway. Thirty-eight years as editor and publisher of the two largest newspapers in Kentucky taught him to move fast. He blurs through the lobby like a man on a deadline.

He greets the woman at the reception desk with a smile and a quick salute as he swoops into the elevator and punches the button for the third floor. He arrives in his office and flops his briefcase down on his desk. He's just returning from a morning spent tape recording textbooks for blind students, and he's eager to scan the copy of today's paper waiting in front of a portrait of his grandchildren. . . .

Barry Bingham was twelve years old when the Judge bought controlling interest in *The Courier-Journal* and *The Louisville Times. The Courier-Journal,* widely regarded as the more powerful of the two, was first published in 1868—although it was the product of a merger of two papers that dated back to 1826. "My father had a strong feeling that these papers, particularly *The Courier-Journal,* which had a famous old name, had run down very badly," he said.

The Judge's son wasn't very much interested in the newspaper business. He preferred writing poetry to headlines, and in 1928, was graduated from Harvard University with a degree in literature. "I was at that point thinking I wanted to write the great American novel," he said. "I was very interested in what is now called creative writing, having done a great deal of it in college. And it took me the better part of a year to finish the great American novel. It was called 'Battle in the Dark,' after a Walt Whitman quotation, but it was not a great novel. Fortunately for me, it was not published."

When Judge Bingham died in 1937, his son had already begun to formulate a vision of the newspapers that would make them eminently successful, respected, and admired. John Ed Pearce, who worked for *The Courier-Journal* for more than forty years as a reporter, editorial writer, and columnist, made the following assessment for *The Lexington Herald-Leader* after Barry Bingham's death:

As part of his dedication to quality and his state, Barry Bingham, for fifty years, gave Kentucky the best newspapers he could produce, bringing in the best men he could find, curbing profit to take the papers and their coverage to every corner of the state. The pages were designed to inform more than entertain the reader, and their content was not always welcomed. . . .

Barry Bingham was a strong, active, athletic man who loved the outdoors, a game of cards, an occasional drink or earthy story, but except for a few close friends, he was seldom seen as one of the boys. His seeming English mannerisms (he was a great Anglophile), his gracious manners and precise grammar (he loved the language and wrote and spoke it beautifully) seemed a little dandified for many Kentuckians. He had sophisticated tastes in music, art and literature. He loved nice clothes, and wore them as he wore his life, with elegance. With such tastes, shaped by Harvard and travels on the continent, Barry Bingham might well have spent his years and his millions in the casinos, marinas and society playgrounds of the world, as have so many heirs to publishing fortunes. Instead, he chose to devote his life and fortune to Kentucky. [21 Aug. 1988]

The Washington Post commented further: "His newspapers, reflecting his values and commitment to public service, gained a wide reputation for fairness, forthrightness and independence. They were not afraid to espouse unpopular issues that they believed to be right, and through the years they won eight Pulitzer Prizes and many other honors" (17 Aug. 1988).

Pulitzer Prizes are awarded by Columbia University in journalism, letters, and music. From 1956 to 1968 Bingham was a member of the board of advisers that made the final recommendations for prizes. He chaired the biography jury in 1980, when, coincidentally, a *Courier-Journal* reporter and photographer won the Pulitzer Prize for international reporting. Although this was gratifying to the chairman of the board who had conscientiously brought the world scene to local readers, Bingham took particular pride in the newspaper's 1967 Pulitzer for its coverage of strip mining that led to stricter environmental controls.

The Courier-Journal had the distinction of being the smallest newspaper among the ten best American dailies selected by *Time* in 1964 and in 1974. When *Fortune* assessed the newspaper field in August 1950, it remarked: "The newspaper business, being so often a family affair, abounds with rich men's sons, an ignominy that forty-four-year-old Barry Bingham, owner-editor of *The Courier-Journal,* has quietly lived down in the course of making a great newspaper out of the 'good property' he inherited from his father, former ambassador to Great Britain, in 1937."

To make his vision a reality, for more than fifty years Bingham assembled and nurtured the talents necessary. Even through personal tragedy—the accidental deaths of two sons, Worth and Jonathan—he maintained an optimism that was contagious. Some readers did not appreciate his liberal opinions, but still they viewed him with respect. He told Professor William E. Ellis in a 1979 interview: "I notice that candidates who talk about the kiss of death—the endorsement of the papers—are nearly always eager to be kissed."

When *The Reporter* looked at Louisville newspapers, managing editor Llewellyn White found "a quality of writing, particularly on the editorial pages, not to be matched by any newspaper today; it is reminiscent of the old New York *Evening Post* and *World,* the London *News-Chronicle,* and the Paris *Intransigeant* in their best days, and infinitely better than Watterson in his prime" (31 Jan. 1950). White also noted Bingham's unique working relationship with Mark Ethridge.

Mark Foster Ethridge joined the newspapers in 1936 and served as publisher for much of his tenure, until his retirement in 1963. When

Bingham retired in 1971, Ethridge wrote him: "You can never retire, of course, as long as you live, but you are wise, as your father was, to turn over the operation to young Barry, for it gives him a chance, under your guidance, to become the publisher that I am confident he will be. You were only thirty-one when Judge Bingham 'changed the guard' at the luncheon at the Brown. Under your direction the papers have become nationally recognized institutions, among the very best in the country."

In 1950, when *Fortune* had looked nationally at the "gentlemen of the daily press" who "must practice shrewd business as well as an honored craft," it commented: "Though the evening *Times* is gossipy and parochial, the morning *Courier-Journal* lays in with a will on national and worldwide news and comment. Of course, few papers have the topside-inside familiarity with the world of affairs that this organization has."

The world was Barry Bingham's universe, and Louisville, Kentucky, was his home. He witnessed the need for a local understanding of global politics and envisioned a community of nations tied by economics, resources, and an appreciation of diverse cultures. He tried to bring to the commonwealth and the region such an appreciation. The front section of *The Courier-Journal,* with many articles bearing foreign datelines, reflected his obsession with world events. He recognized early on the significance of cooperation within a community of nations. He had been instilled with a belief in the value of the League of Nations by his father, who championed its goals and purposes. Barry Bingham saw the value of cooperation himself as chief of mission to France, administering Marshall Plan aid in 1949-50. He also saw England during World War II from 1942 to 1945; he was present at the Japanese surrender in Tokyo Bay: he made two inspections with other editors of the programs of U.S. occupying forces in Germany, Austria, and Trieste in 1947 and 1948 at the behest of the secretary of the army; and he traveled with Adlai Stevenson during the Far East phase of his world tour in 1953. The Asia Foundation was established in 1954 to further educational and cultural development through joint Asian-American efforts, and Barry Bingham served on its board, from its inception until his death. In 1955 he presented a series of lectures at the fourth Fulbright Conference on American Studies held at University College, Oxford.

Following Bingham's death, John Ed Pearce reminisced with his colleague Al Smith during a special tribute on Kentucky Educational Television.

A lot of people did not realize what a Renaissance man Barry was. His knowledge was so great. He was the best-educated man I ever ran into—not just at Harvard or in Europe, but through his voracious reading, and his enormously assimilative and quick mind. He knew art, he knew religion, he knew theater, he knew politics, and he knew history—all important. So he brought to the paper a great grasp of news. He could see what news meant. And he hired people who reflected this interest in the world—in the whole world, everything in it, and who wanted the whole world presented in that paper every day, so that everybody in Kentucky would have access to all the information they needed.

Bingham had stated as early as 1939, in accepting the University of Missouri's prestigious journalism award on behalf of *The Courier-Journal,* that "absolute honesty in the handling of the news is the key to perpetual freedom for our press." The award read in part, "For independent and intelligent emphasis upon news coverage in its later years, and for recent progressive development of, and leadership in, graphic and pictorial journalism."

At the newspapers Bingham surrounded himself with people with interest and expertise in world news, such as Herbert Agar (England and Europe), Tom Wallace (Latin America), Molly Clowes (Canada and France), and Mark Ethridge (Eastern Europe). Bingham had first-hand experience of world events, and not since Henry Clay was secretary of state has the commonwealth produced a person of such perception in foreign affairs.

Barry Bingham also believed in responding to readers' grievances. He argued that the public would have more confidence in all forms of journalism if complaints of unfairness and inaccuracy could be voiced. In his keynote address to the 1963 convention of the journalistic society Sigma Delta Chi, he was the first to propose press councils as a means of establishing "a continuing two-way exchange between the journalist and the public." In 1967 his newspapers were the first in the country to create the position of ombudsman. Readers' complaints about news coverage were checked, and if they were justified, appropriate remedial action was taken. Bingham served on the grievance committee of the American Society of Newspaper Editors and kept hammering at the idea in speeches and writings. Believing that a national news council would be more potent, he served on the Twentieth Century Fund's task force that led to the creation of such a body in 1973. Bingham used the occasion of his being awarded the prestigious national medallion of the William Allen White Foundation on 10 February 1973 to present the case for a national news council.

While Barry Bingham was advocating a means of ensuring journalism's fairness and accuracy, he was also helping to protect embattled journalists worldwide through the International Press Institute. As IPI board chair, he addressed the 1966 meeting in New Delhi, concluding:

A vital purpose of the International Press Institute, it seems to me, is to keep the torch of press freedom ever burning. It must always be seen from the dark places of the world, as a light on the horizon that does not fade.

To many of us who conduct our newspapers in the security of freedom, IPI is a pleasant and broadening activity. To journalists in danger and to those in near despair, it is a beacon, a hope, a promise. Such a light must never fail.

After attending an IPI assembly in Hong Kong and visiting Taiwan in May 1970, Bingham flew back to Taiwan in August as one of three IPI delegates going to observe the trial of the Yuyitung brothers. The brothers had been arrested in Manila, where they operated a Chinese newspaper considered subversive by the regime of Ferdinand Marcos, and deported to Taiwan. Because of this display of world public concern, the brothers received lenient sentences. Bingham continued to advance press freedom, especially in the Philippines and in Southeast Asia.

The *IPI Report* in October 1988 recalled that "both Presidents John F. Kennedy and Jimmy Carter offered him diplomatic posts, but Barry rejected the invitations because he wanted to remain in newspapers." Bingham had long advocated that diplomatic appointments should emanate from the career pool and not be political rewards for those who could afford the embassy upkeep. He declined being named ambassador to Great Britain in December 1960 and to France in April 1977.

Although Bingham was a keen and interested observer of politics at all levels, he never aspired to public office. He used his influence to promote the public good and those people he believed would effect positive and useful change. Former Congressman Brooks Hays of Arkansas recalled in his autobiography being invited to the Bingham home in October 1938 for a weekend to discuss the Democratic party's nominee for 1940. The small group assembled found itself opposed on principle to FDR's running for a third term. Hays wrote: "The consensus was that Barry, being closest to the President, should confer with him and let him know how we as his friends felt about the third term. Barry quickly arranged the private conference with him in the

White House, and later gave us in succinct terms the result of their meeting. . . . Barry soon recognized that the President had little interest in what we, his warm friends, thought about his yielding the helm." Bingham's editorial in support of Roosevelt on 26 September 1940 mentioned the newspaper's dislike of a third term.

In 1952 in another editorial, he suggested that both Adlai Stevenson, his old friend, and Dwight Eisenhower were of presidential caliber. He took an active part as cochair of Volunteers for Stevenson in the 1956 campaign.

Barry Bingham was an early advocate of preservation. He was a founder and the first president of Historic Homes Foundation, a trustee of the National Trust for Historic Preservation, and a charter trustee of the Preservation Alliance of Louisville and Jefferson County. He was also interested in the restoration of the Kentucky Shaker community at Pleasant Hill, near Harrodsburg. The Binghams restored the brick tanyard house there and frequently used it as a retreat. Barry Bingham took particular delight in serving on the National Portrait Gallery Commission, and he presented the gallery with the James Reid Lambdin portrait of President Zachary Taylor.

The theater was yet another of Barry Bingham's lasting passions. While at Harvard, he played, among other roles, that of the football hero in *Brown of Harvard* by Foxhall Daingerfield of Kentucky. In a joint performance with Radcliffe College, he met Mary Caperton. After they were married in 1931, the couple appeared in Little Theatre Company productions in the playhouse on the Belknap Campus of the University of Louisville. Barry Bingham took an active interest in the Harvard Theatre Collection, establishing its publication fund. He was also a member of the visiting committee to the Loeb Drama Center, helping to build a solid relationship between Harvard and the American Repertory Theatre.

Bingham was greatly influenced by George Lyman Kittredge, whose lectures on Shakespeare at Harvard are legendary. Years later, he could still recall Kittredge, with his white beard, prancing around as he portrayed the witches of *Macbeth*. "He didn't need to put on costume. He could do it with his voice and appearance." In the spring of 1978 Barry Bingham was asked to deliver the Ramsbotham Lecture at the Folger Shakespeare Library in Washington. His talk, "Why Shakespeare Speaks to Americans Today," was published and widely disseminated. He later served on the Folger's international council. The Mary and Barry Bingham, Sr. Fund both funded and endowed a signature Shakespeare series at Actors Theatre of Louisville.

In November 1986 Bingham played the role of Prospero in a readers' production of *The Tempest* to benefit Bellarmine College and the English-Speaking Union. His long-standing association with the English-Speaking Union culminated in his serving as its national chairman during the Bicentennial, when he had the honor of introducing Queen Elizabeth II at a New York City luncheon on 9 July 1976.

Bingham was thoughtful and courteous because to be so was his nature. He was dignified because he fostered human dignity. In a Jefferson Day speech in Philadephia in 1939, he launched a crusade against the poll tax. He said:

The real opposition to the repeal of poll tax suffrage is lodged in the conviction of a small group of southerners on the upper rungs of the economic ladder, that they are more entitled to rule than the public at large. These people often have the sayings of Thomas Jefferson and the tenets of democracy hot in their mouths, yet they privately fear the dangerous experiment of a government that is really of, by and for the people.

They mistrust the motives of the man in the street, the man looking for a job, the man working another's land. They cannot persuade themselves that these men are created equal to themselves.

In his address to the Southern Conference for Human Welfare in Chattanooga in 1940, he continued his assault with the thesis "Poll tax suffrage is a false friend of southern education."

Bingham's counsel and company were sought because he elicited trust. He was full of joy, ever looking to the future, ever encouraging—especially to young people. In 1939 in Atlanta he chaired the first southern conference on "tomorrow's children" and delivered the keynote address. Writer Kate Stout recalled in *Nantucket Map and Legend:* "I met Barry Bingham in my early teens and was astonished to discover that here was one of those rare people unafraid of taking on a child in conversation as a real human being. My family and his were both members of the Fincastle Beagle Club. For years, thereafter, whenever we both were in the field together on a Sunday, I'd look for an opportunity to listen or join in on his walking conversation" (25 April 1988).

Bingham supported education in a variety of ways. His forebears were educators, and he once said he would have been a teacher if the newspaper business had not been right in his way. "Pedagogic blood runs in my veins as well as printer's ink," he wrote Dean Richard Barber of the University of Louisville in 1972. Besides serving on many boards, including those of the Louisville Collegiate School, the Louisville Country Day School, Pine Mountain Settlement School, and Berea College, he was a director of the Ford Fund for the Advancement of Education. He was also a member of the Rockefeller Panel on Arts in Education, which prepared recommendations for new directions in national policy that were published in an influential report, *Coming to Our Senses.* He served on the University of Louisville's board of overseers for over thirty years and served in a similar capacity for two terms (1942-48 and 1979-85) at Harvard University, where he was also on various committees and advisory boards. He was a strong advocate of the Nieman Foundation for Journalism, which enables young newspaper people to spend a year of enrichment and elective study at Harvard, and with his support many *Courier-Journal* and *Times* employees became Nieman Fellows. He touched many others as well through lectureships, scholarships, and various other encouragements.

The Courier-Journal published a letter from Thomas More on 8 September 1988: "During my tenure as principal of St. Xavier [High School] I grew to appreciate Bingham's personal touch. When I organized a series of lectures for the faculty, Bingham generously offered to send a number of his outstanding writers to address the faculty on a number of current international and national issues. Also, when the National Merit Scholarship program was initiated, Bingham hosted a number of recognition dinners for those high school students in the city and county who had achieved the distinction of becoming National Merit scholars."

For many years Barry Bingham took part in the state nominations of candidates for Rhodes Scholarships, and from 1970 to 1975 he chaired the district committee that selected four of the nation's thirty-two recipients.

To provide topical education and an awareness of community issues for promisingly influential individuals, the Chamber of Commerce in 1978 called upon Barry Bingham, Wilson Wyatt, and Maurice Johnson to foster Leadership Louisville. The program has offered information and interaction for some 575 participants, and since 1988 graduates selected as Bingham Fellows examine thorny community issues and develop innovative solutions.

A year before Barry Bingham died, he told Carmin Pinkstaff, a junior high school interviewer from Henderson, Kentucky: "It's nice to think that I haven't lived so long without having some purpose yet to be served. . . . And there are things I still would love to see done, and I'm going to try to do as many of them as I can while I'm still around. And I have the wonderful support of my wife on all these things. We agree on the things we're trying to accomplish, and we're working together on them."

Former governor Edward T. Breathitt recalled the Binghams in a letter to *The Courier-Journal,* printed on 27 April 1988:

In my lifetime, I know of no two people who have contributed more than Barry Bingham and his wife Mary. They used their resources of money and media holdings to inspire Kentuckians to improve education for our children, provide needed government services and bring cultural enrichment to our people. Their deep concern for our land, streams and rivers resulted in action to protect our environment. They supported those of us who fought for civil rights and help for our needy citizens.

They were always willing, along with other members of the family, to take strong stands for what they believed was in our state's best interests. This resulted in criticism on many occasions, but they have been willing to endure the slings and arrows and were a constant force for good in our state. It is my hope that present and future generations of the Bingham family will continue their family's outstanding service to Louisville and the Common-wealth of Kentucky.

When Professor Wade Hall asked Barry Bingham in 1985 if he minded being called a Louisville booster, he replied with characteristic humor: "Not in the least, but I'd rather be a Louisville slugger."

The first time future Louisville mayor and lieutenant governor Wilson Wyatt met Barry Bingham, they were youths and members of *The Courier-Journal*'s Aloha Club. Wyatt would later take over the newspapers' legal work, and for more than fifty years he was Bingham's trusted friend and adviser. He recalled in a 1987 interview for the University of Kentucky's Oral History Program:

Barry was in the Aloha Club. They had meetings, but not very often. And I remember attending two or three of those, and I remember meeting Barry at one of those meetings for the first time and being impressed with him as both a very nice person and a person who had enormous opportunity. He's always been a very modest, self-effacing person. I was impressed at that time by the fact that there he was, the young son of the owner and publisher of the paper, and yet acting as though he was no different at all from any one of twenty or twenty-five other youngsters that were in the room. It's been a very natural trait, and I think it's one of the reasons that he's one of the most admired and beloved citizens that we have in Louisville.

In his introduction to Barry Bingham's videotaped oral history and comments in 1986 for the NewsLeaders series produced by the Poynter Institute for Media Studies, NBC commentator John Chancellor remarked:

The thing that he seems to care about most is Louisville, his hometown. Louisville is not a large city, but *The Courier-Journal* behaves as though it were. There is more foreign and national news in *The Courier-Journal* than in most papers its size. It's a paper that has cared deeply about its responsibility to its readers and was the first paper in this country to hire an ombudsman who represents the readers to the staff which puts out the paper. Barry Bingham and his wife, Mary, represent the kind of personal concern for their community which can make any newspaper of any size great. You don't have to be big to be good, and *The Courier-Journal* is proof of that.

On 19 November 1983 Mary and Barry Bingham attended another gala opening. The Kentucky Center for the Arts had been sixteen years in the making. Initially, Barry Bingham had chaired a committee to develop design requirements and to recommend an architect for a performing arts center in Louisville, but the project languished. Ten years later, with state support, Bingham was again combing the country for an architect. When the Caudill Rowlett Scott firm of Houston was selected in June 1978, he went on to help Wendell Cherry, chair of the board of directors of the Kentucky Center for the Arts, raise $13.5 million for an endowment fund. Bingham would later draft his recollection of the opening:

We had seen rising before our eyes a shining palace, where only a muddy hole in the ground had existed. Theater, however, only comes to life in performance. And what a glorious performance it was! . . .

In such an array of talent, it was impossible to name favorites. It was the center itself, however, that was the ultimate star of the evening. Metropolitan Opera soprano Jessye Norman said it all when her lustrous voice rang out in a phrase from *Tannhauser:* "Dear precious hall, receive my greeting!"

The audience rose at the end to sing "My Old Kentucky Home" with even more fervor than it is sung on a warm Saturday in May at Churchill Downs. Then they all streamed out to a street lined with young student performers holding candles to light the way to a theater supper and dance at the Convention Center.

The performing arts have flourished in Louisville. They subsist on the hard work and dedication of many people. Then, at moments, that whole tireless effort bursts like golden fireworks in a climax of sheer magic. That is what happened on that unforgettable night.

The organizations that perform in the center have all received Bingham family philanthropy, but Barry Bingham's strongest allegiance was to the Louisville Orchestra. His financial support was instrumental in the conception of the Louisville Civic Arts Symphony Orchestra in 1937. He was a trustee of the Louisville Philharmonic Society, and his typical enthusiasm and far-reaching tentacles brought renowned artists and composers to Louisville. On a 4 October 1977 WUOL radio program, Bingham recalled the beginning of the Louisville Orchestra: "I've always had a great feeling that Louisville has to play to its strengths. We are not the biggest city in the country. We are far from being the richest city in the country. But we have certain things here that have been strong traditionally. I think we have got to build on those things, and hopefully get a better community. One of the things that Louisville has had is a good cultural climate. Out of that I think we were able to create the interest and the support that our orchestra required."

The cause foremost on Bingham's mind, however, was mental health. From the time he escorted Governor Albert B. Chandler through the state mental institutions in 1936 and 1937 and publicized their deplorable conditions in *The Courier-Journal* as well as in the pamphlet *They Can Be Cured*, the plight of the mentally ill engaged his compassionate sympathy. On 2 September 1944, when contemplating his postwar focus, he wrote Mary Bingham: "I can think of no group whose unhappiness so deeply stirs me as those who have some form of mental illness, and the slightest contribution toward relieving their spiritual agony seems to me to offer rich rewards. I believe I must devote a good part of my time to work in this field after the war."

Also in 1944 he made a major contribution that led to the establishment of the Norton Psychiatric Clinic. He helped found the Kentucky Association for Mental Health and served as its first president. At the initial annual meeting of the National Association for Mental Health in Chicago on 30 November 1951, he was elected a director. In a press conference with Dr. William C. Menninger, he warned against wasting money on custodial care when early diagnosis and treatment would ultimately prove more beneficial. At the 1951 meeting of the Louisville Mental Hygiene Clinic (named the Bingham Child Guidance Clinic in 1971), Bingham pointed out that Kentuckians spent much more on chewing gum than on mental hospitals. He chaired the meeting that created the Council for Retarded Children of Jefferson County in 1952 and served on the President's Committee on Mental

Retardation. He later actively supported of the National Alliance for Research on Schizophrenia and Depression.

For six decades Barry Bingham provided incentive and information not only locally but also regionally. As former governor and federal judge Bert T. Combs commented after Barry Bingham died on 15 August 1988: "He has had more to do with the shape of this state than any person I can think of in the past half century. He used his influence for progressive, forward-looking causes." *Courier-Journal* editor David Hawpe said: "That Louisville is a cultural mecca for a community of this size is in large measure directly related to Mr. Bingham's interest and standards." *The Washington Post* commented on 17 August 1988: "Though published in a city of only medium size, *The Courier-Journal* and *Times* were nationally renowned for their courage and quality. The border state papers were early supporters of school desegregation, voices for progress in other forms of civil rights, advocates of the arts, of public education and of aid to the poorer regions of the state and longtime foes of the strip mining that continues to disfigure Kentucky's eastern mountains. The state's politics are earthy; the Binghams' newspapers helped to civilize them."

As Barry Bingham had done so eloquently for others before, Kenneth W. Thompson made notice of his death for *The Century Association Yearbook* (1989). Thompson, a professor of government and foreign affairs at the University of Virginia and a prolific author and editor, had been vice president of the Rockefeller Foundation when Barry Bingham was a foundation trustee (1958-72). He wrote:

Barry Bingham, Sr.'s life was a profile in courage and an experience in tragedy, and that may be why conversation with him and his talented wife, Mary Clifford Caperton of Richmond, often turned to the writings of philosophers and theologians like Reinhold Niebuhr and Paul Tillich. Barry served as a trustee of the Rockefeller Foundation in its golden age with fellow Centurions such as Henry Allen Moe, Robert Lovett, Robert Loeb, Ralph Bunche, Pit Van Dusen, Douglas Dillon, and John D. Rockefeller III. Whatever their contributions—and they were enormous—Barry was the most consistent voice of civil rights and of social reform, including legislation controlling strip mining. However much Barry and Mary did for fellow Kentuckians in charitable undertakings such as their "Crusade for Children," which spread far beyond Louisville, the arts, and the environment, or in uniting Kentucky and Indiana through the Louisville Falls Fountain on the Ohio River, their efforts became public statements to the nation as a whole on urgent social issues.

Joseph Kroh recorded for *Business First* on 22 August 1988 an event witnessed by others on numerous occasions.

Ten years ago, I was standing on the southeast corner of Sixth and Broadway waiting to cross to The Courier-Journal on some piece of business or other, and I saw Barry Bingham, Sr. come out of the building. He headed east up Broadway, looking like a million, natty, erect, brisk, a man with every "t" crossed and "i" dotted. Suddenly, he stopped, looked down, and picked something up. And then he did it again.

I realized in a sort of stunned amazement that he was picking up all the litter by the curb between Sixth and Armory streets. That stooping, from a man who could have hired legions to pick trash from the streets, said in a small way how largely he thought about his block and his city. I really don't think I've ever littered since. I even pick it up sometimes.

Barry Bingham had wanted to be a writer, and yet when his friend and counselor Wilson Wyatt encouraged him near the end of his productive life to write an autobiography, he responded with his usual modesty, "I don't have anything to write about." He had a great deal to write about, and it would have made a compelling chapter in Kentucky history, told in his clear, direct, and precise style. Perhaps he was shading his real reason. Although he enjoyed history and liked to reminisce, his pen was in the present and his thoughts focused on the future. He did not languish in the past; he relished the future—and that was where he wanted to concentrate his remaining efforts. In retirement, however, he seriously contemplated writing a monograph on the career of Louisville's progressive mayor Charles D. Jacob (1837-98), stressing his development of the public parks system.

No fewer than four books have scrutinized the Bingham family since their children's bickering over the running of the family companies became widely circulated. Unable to reach an internal agreement, Barry and Mary Bingham determined that the prudent course was to sell the vast publishing and broadcasting empire. Each book attempts to be both revealing and provocative, often at the expense of accuracy. A more engaging picture was presented by thirty-nine friends in *Remembering Barry Bingham,* privately printed in 1990. Its readers have appreciated the comments of the likes of Arthur Schlesinger, Jr., John Kenneth Galbraith, and Adlai Stevenson, Jr., but they especially treasure the writings of Barry Bingham that were selected for inclusion in the tribute. He was, after all, first and foremost a writer—of prose and poetry, a novel, editorials, articles, speeches, and letters. He had an obsession with language, with words and their meanings.

The late Wendell Cherry, cofounder of Humana, concurred. "I realized that, while the rest of us might have a spectator's appreciation for the arts, Barry Bingham had the heart of a poet. . . . I tell you, a poet is what Barry Bingham was." Although as an adult Bingham did not have the time to indulge his fancy, he was consumed by writing poetry in his youth. His juvenilia were published in *The Courier-Journal,* on the pages of the Aloha Club, and his 1921 poem "The House of Dreams" became the title of Marie Brenner's book about the Bingham family. A collection of his poems written between the ages of nine and seventeen was published by his father in 1923. Other poems written for his father were reproduced in 1990 by Mary Bingham as a keepsake for their grandchildren. Included was his 1984 poem "Lines For A Bequest," which, when published by Ann Landers, brought response from around the country. In 1966 the Binghams presented the University of Louisville with a room set aside for poetry to honor Judge Bingham, and for many years they funded a poet-in-residence at the university.

Barry Bingham spent a lifetime in journalism, cultivating a vision of greatness for *The Courier-Journal.* Reporters and editors were diligent, careful, and considerate because they knew their work would be scrutinized by the writer in the corner office on the third floor. They wanted to meet his standards. Everyone who ever worked in the building at Sixth and Broadway knew that feeling.

Along with most company employees, Mike Kallay preserved his notes from Bingham. The fourteen-year veteran of *The Louisville Times* wrote in the 22 August 1988 issue of *Business First,* which he now publishes:

Over the years, even after I left *The Times* to start this newspaper, Mr. Bingham occasionally wrote me little notes. I saved them.

The first came in August 1967, after I wrote a first-person account about being fleeced in a shell game at the state fair. I was a *Times* intern that summer, and the shell-game story was my first on Page One. The witty note admonished me to be "more cautious" in my selection of "friends" and suggested *Times* Managing Editor Bob Clark "might" reimburse me for my losses—$12. Clark agreed.

Barry Bingham did not wish to cast his own record of considerable accomplishment, although he certainly did want to set straight the published inaccurate interpretations of his family's history. The absence of his autobiography deprives us not only of his immense insight but also of his elegant expression. As former media critic Robert Schulman said in his eulogy for the Louisville Free Public Library Foundation, "He was a lover of words . . . so it was no surprise that for a half-century, Barry Bingham, Sr. probably was the nation's most literate and expressive newspaper publisher.''

Bingham lived in the here and now. "How's the day?" asked his favorite Shakespeare character, Prospero in *The Tempest*. He never prepared for the day when he would have to look back and review. Although he communicated extensively through letters and notes, he did not see much necessity in keeping copies of his correspondence. Others did not agree. His old friend John Lacey Brown would write for *Remembering Barry Bingham*:

Barry Bingham was a rare phenomenon indeed in our epoch when the written word has been largely replaced by typing, by telephoning, and other mechanical forms of communication. He not only answered letters, but he answered personal letters by hand. His letters to me reflect all his enthusiasm for the arts (I often felt that he was essentially an artist), for the beauty of nature, for the amelioration of society, for human contacts. I have preciously preserved them. The last I received, sent from Chatham on the Cape, is dated September 8, 1987, shortly before the onset, I believe, of his fatal illness.

It is to be hoped that the correspondence of Barry Bingham will be collected and published. It will not only be important as a historical document which ranges freely and perceptively over many different areas—communications, politics, the arts, social reform, recollections of persons and places. It will also be a literary work in its own right, resounding with his infectious laughter, luminous with all of his buoyant zest for life. In our time of the anesthetized man, of mounting boredom and indifference, he always communicated to me and to those who knew him that sense of joy, of which e.e. cummings speaks in a poem addressed to his father: "Joy was his son and joy so pure, a heart of star by him could steer."

When oral history interviewer Karen Black asked Bingham in 1986 about writing an autobiography, he responded:

Oh, I don't know, not yet. I've never kept records. Unfortunately, I never kept diaries. I wish I had. I have not kept letters. I haven't kept records of things that would make it easier to attack a project of that kind. I have been urged to try to do it, and I may come around to it. Wilson Wyatt has written a book with a lot of his recollections in it, and he keeps telling me to try to do the same thing, and I may get around to it, but not quite now.

Well, I think maybe I could talk into a tape recorder like we're doing here today, talk about some things, and then maybe get that assembled and try to do some writing around it. But I must say, it would take a tremendous amount of research to go back and check facts on many things. You know, everybody has a tricky memory, and there are so many things that I can remember very distinctly from way, way back, and there are things that happened much more recently that I am not that clear on. I'd have to go back and check my names and dates, and that would get to be quite a chore.

Though oral history is inherently prejudiced, what follows is a balanced record in Barry Bingham's own words. He was not mechanically minded. Tape recorders and word processors baffled him. His tools were long familiar to him—a yellow pad and pencil and a small typewriter set off in a cubbyhole next to his office. But he was also comfortable dictating extemporaneously. He enjoyed the spoken word. As Kristin Linklater, Bingham Professor at the University of Louisville, has said, he could just as well have been an actor. It is rare when these qualities come together, and that is the heart of this book. Presented here are excerpts of oral histories blended with selections from Barry Bingham's written record. Although much of his general correspondence was destroyed, especially that generated prior to his retirement, his Editorial Notebook pieces beginning in 1956 exist, as well as a remarkable collection of letters exchanged with his wife primarily during World War II.

One cannot fully comprehend Barry Bingham without understanding Mary Caperton Bingham. They were absorbed with each other from the day they met, when he was a student at Harvard, she at Radcliffe. Theirs was a meshing of mind and spirit few couples have been privileged to enjoy. It empowered them to persevere during separation and personal tragedy and to endure the wrath and criticism of those who opposed their newspapers' editorial positions. Through times of crisis, they only grew closer together, and they reinforced each other. Some of Mary Bingham's insightful recollections and reflections broaden the perspective of this book.

Barry Bingham never did begin to record his recollections, although he was given a tape recorder, and he put off a proposal by Wade Hall of Bellarmine College to conduct tapings for an oral biography. Over the years, however, he consented to numerous interviews, and at least a dozen were recorded and are known to exist. Many concentrated on his recollections of prominent people whom he had observed closely: Lawrence Wetherby, Thruston Morton, Adlai Stevenson, Albert Chandler, Carl Perkins, and Bert Combs. In an interview done in connection with the University of Louisville's study of *The Courier-Journal,* interviewer Mary D. Bobo obtained an extensive two-part reminiscence of Bingham's life up until his return from World War II. It provides the basis for this book. Also included are excerpts of interviews conducted by Dennis Cusick of *The Louisville Times;* Terry L. Birdwhistell, University of Kentucky; Karen Black, Bellarmine College; William E. Ellis, Eastern Kentucky University; Walter L. Hixson, University of Kentucky; Vincent J. Holt, Jr., University of Louisville; John Luter, Columbia University; Carmin Pinkstaff, for Bonnet Productions, North Junior High School, Henderson County, Kentucky; Wilson W. Wyatt, for Kentucky Educational Television; and the staff of the Poynter Institute of Media studies, St. Petersburg, Florida.

Selected excerpts from Bingham's writing, correspondence, and speeches add to this compilation of oral interviews. The comparison of his verbal and written expression is noteworthy. The written material was selected from his personal papers. Following the sale of the family companies in 1986, Barry Bingham's files were moved from his newspaper office to his residence in Glenview, Kentucky. In 1989 they were transferred to the Bingham Fund offices in the Meidinger Tower, and arrangements were made for their donation to the Filson Club, in accordance with his wish. In 1974 he had presented part of his father's collection to the Filson Club.

By Barry Bingham's own account, his collection is what remains after several cullings. Much was discarded in 1971 when he left the day-to-day operation of the Bingham companies to chair the board of directors. There is very little correspondence in the collection from the period before World War II. A separate collection of correspondence between Barry and Mary Bingham, covering the years 1929-30, 1941-45, 1949, 1950, and 1953, was given to the Arthur and Elizabeth Schlesinger Library on the History of Women in America at Radcliffe College in 1981.

The materials in Barry Bingham's personal collection reflect his interests in journalism and academic life, as well as the cultural enrichment of his native city and state. The major subject areas include the Asia Foundation, the American Society of Newspaper Editors, the International Press Institute, the English-Speaking Union, mental health, the National Portrait Gallery, Berea College, Harvard University, the University of Louisville, Actors Theatre of Louisville, and the Kentucky Center for the Arts.

In arranging these materials for donation to the Filson Club, I made note of oral history and correspondence related to oral history. Fortunately, at the same time, the Kentucky Oral History Commission was preparing an inventory of interviews in repositories throughout the commonwealth. The commission made that comprehensive listing available to me and it greatly enhanced this work. Quite a few of the unrehearsed recorded interviews were not mentioned in the extant correspondence, and without the commission's thorough survey, they would have been overlooked. In preparing this book, I selected those passages that would help illuminate history as well as reveal Barry Bingham the individual. The passages are arranged chronologically by topic (not by date of the interview) and for convenience are collected into arbitrary chapters that follow discernible periods of Bingham's life.

When he wrote for his own newspapers, Barry Bingham expected his work to go through the normal editing process. His oral history has undergone some editing too. Selections have been made to conserve space, and most of the known oral interviews are represented. Also, the interviewer's questions are not included, but they should be clear from the response. In some interviews, however, for clarity part of the question is included in the response and set off by brackets. This technique also provides short explanations. When fuller explanation is needed, it is provided in an endnote.

References to the interviewer, false starts, and other redundant phrasing have been eliminated. Although frequent laughter was recorded, indications of this do not appear. Obvious misstatements of fact have been corrected or noted. Bingham's only colloquial contraction, *'a'tall,'* has been broken into *at all*.

Transcriptions of Barry Bingham's interviews are not easy to punctuate. His comments flow at a fast pace, sometimes very emphatically. Little lingering or voice modulation separates his thoughts. Likewise, in his writing, his initial draft was orderly, clear, and precise, and he did not do much revision or require much editing.

Chapter 1

Childhood

From Interview of Barry Bingham by Karen Black,
Bellarmine College, 21 February 1986

I was born right here in Louisville, Kentucky, on February 10, 1906. It was early on one frosty morning, a very inconvenient time, I expect, for a baby to be born, and I was, I think, a little bit earlier than expected, which meant a lot of rush. Arrangements had to be made at my grandmother's house, where I was born. In those days, most ladies had their babies at home, instead of going to the hospital. So I was born in my grandmother's house, and I think they had to make some pretty fast preparations, and I'm afraid I've been in a rush ever since.

This was my maternal grandmother, my mother's mother.[1] My father's people were from North Carolina. My father only came here in 1896, when he married my mother. I say "only in 1896," because that isn't so very far back in Kentucky tradition. But my mother was a Kentuckian, a Louisville woman, and that's why he came here and settled down here.

My grandmother's house was just a typical Victorian Gothic structure, on the west side of Fourth Street, pretty close to Ormsby, and it had the kind of space in it that houses had in those days.[2] There were quite a few rooms that all opened into each other in the downstairs part of the house, and then you went up into the floor where all the bedrooms were, and then there was a third floor above that, where there were several other rooms, and then on top of all that there was a tower. So the house was, to me, full of interest when I was a small child. I used to love to ramble around in it. And it had lots of space. It had lots of pictures—not only family pictures, but paintings of Cherokee Park by Harvey Joiner, people of that kind.[3] It was a typical house of its period, I guess. There was a big grand piano in the living room which my grandmother used to play. Lots of books. It was, I think, quite a warm and welcoming house, as I remember it.

From Barry Bingham, "The Comet Streamed By in an
Innocent Age," *The Courier-Journal,* 22 May 1960

It was fifty years ago this month that Halley's Comet made itself visible in the heavens.[4] In Louisville and elsewhere the celestial wonder was the occasion for "comet parties," gatherings of families and friends at some suitable point for scanning the skies. Such a party is one of my own earliest memories.

The event began for me in the most impressive way. I was taken up out of bed and carried to the tower room of my grandmother's house. Her house was one of these Victorian Gothic structures so familiar in that day, on Fourth Street near the corner of Ormsby in Louisville, where The Puritan now stands in matronly respectability. Like many such houses, Grandma's had a fanciful tower in one corner emerging from the mansard roof, with long, narrow windows peering out at the top.

This tower was a quite useless piece of architectural decoration, though it had always fascinated me with its air of remote and withdrawn mystery. There were towers in the fairy tales I had heard, such as the one from which Rapunzel let down her conveniently lengthy hair, and another where Sister Ann stood to watch for the tiny cloud of dust that would announce a horseman returning. Grandma's tower served a functional purpose on that one night of the comet, rising as it did above the horse chestnut trees in the front yard, and affording a view of the skies in all directions.

The trip to the tower was an adventure in itself. It involved passing through a large room in the attic which was usually forbidden to children, and which was therefore endowed with a powerful fascination.

This room contained as its central feature a billiard table. It was the sanctum to which the men of the family and their friends retired sometimes in an evening to enjoy their cigars (which it was not "nice" to smoke in the parlor), and to indulge in some mild sport. Down the attic stairs to the room where I lay in bed would come their muffled voices, their knowing laughter, the clean little click of the billiard balls.

The room's only other use was entirely feminine, but it also put the area off limits to children. Here was the place where the lace curtains that hung at the long windows downstairs were put to be stretched on wooden frames after each periodic washing. Peeping in at twilight on an illicit visit to the attic, I had seen these white forms like ghosts standing silently against the walls, and had rushed down the steps with a delicious shiver of fear.

On the great night of the comet, I remember being borne through this sanctum and up the dark, narrow, winding stairs to the tower. In the little circular room at the top were the shadowy figures of the grown-ups, earnestly gazing out of the windows and speaking in strangely hushed voices. The women, picking up their long skirts, were leaning out over the windowsills, while the men behind them were pointing to the sky and offering instructive comments.

It was clear that something terribly exciting was taking place, though I had no idea what it was. My drowsiness dissolved instantly in that air of prickling tension. Then I was held up close to a window, and told to look at a point in the distant sky. Something was there, something fuzzy and golden and in languid motion through the endless darkness of the air. I was told that this was Halley's Comet, and that I was to remember all my life that I had seen it.

It was many years before I understood the meaning of the comet's name. Some neighbors of ours had had a cook named Hallie, whom I had loved with the steady devotion of a little boy who could always count on a cookie and an affectionate pat on the head whenever he strayed into "her kitchen." I was convinced that the celestial marvel had somehow been produced by the same fine hand that brought forth such other golden masterpieces as a corn pudding or a dish of "spoonbread." . . .

The memory of the comet came back to me with surprising sharpness nearly half a century later. Standing on the roof of the Norton Infirmary with a group of silent people, I watched the first Soviet Sputnik cut its course across the heavens.[5] Twilight was falling, and the glow of the strange traveler through space seemed to have a pulse to it, like a heartbeat.

Here was another sight with a peculiar beauty of its own. Like Halley's Comet, it was in a way a symbol of man's increasing knowledge of those boundless fields that lie beyond the earth.

But the comet was a creation of nature, a fragment of an infinite design revealed for a brief period to the eyes of men. Sputnik was man's own creation. Soulless and impersonal as the comet itself, the rocket made a trail of menace in the sky that no thinking observer could fail to perceive. Even a child of our day cannot look at a Russian Sputnik as I looked at Halley's Comet, and go happily back to bed for a night of dreamless sleep.

From Interview of Barry Bingham by Karen Black, Bellarmine College, 21 February 1986

My father and mother didn't actually live there but were there a great deal, and I used to go down there quite frequently to visit my grandmother, after having been born in that house.

People tended to have larger families then than they do now. And then there were all these aunts and uncles and cousins and people who always seemed to be around too. These extended families were so much more prevalent then than they are now. And fortunately, many people had rather large houses to put them up in. And people did have cooks in those days, and sometimes other servants as well, and it made life really pretty pleasant for those of us who could enjoy that sort of thing.

I used to have to go to bed fairly early. In the summer it seemed to me I had to go to bed much too early. But anyway, there were evenings when I was put to bed, and told to go to bed, and I lay awake for a little while, and I'm glad to say that I don't have any bad memories at all of that time. I don't remember any nightmares, or any times when I was afraid, or anything of that sort. I do remember some quite pleasant things that happened. It's a nice thing to wake up during the night, if you're a child, and hear sounds that sound familiar and kind of friendly. It seems to me I could hear those sounds quite frequently. There was the usual hum of conversation from downstairs from the older people who were sitting around talking. That seemed to go on a lot.

Conversation really prevailed in those days. You see, there weren't so many entertainments at that time. People were not listening to television all the time, or anything of that sort, so there was just a lot of talk. A good deal of that talk on summer nights, I remember, took place on the front porch of my grandmother's house, and I could hear this murmur of conversation from down there, and once in a while, I would hear the sound of a musical instrument. My uncle and aunt did also live there, upstairs.[6] Families tended to live together in big houses in those days, you know. And that was not unusual at all. My uncle used to play the mandolin, and I can remember hearing that mandolin, nice little chords coming up to me from below, and people laughing and talking in a nice, quiet way. And not only would I hear the conversation from our own house, but I could hear people coming up and down the street quite frequently—footsteps of people walking up and down. Quite a bit of conversation went on. There was so much life that took place on those old front porches. It was just a different era. And I think people enjoyed it very much. We used to have an old swing on that front porch that people would sit in and swing, and I can hear it now, that creak, that familiar creak, as the swing went back and forth, and it was a nice, cheery sound.

Then there were people who came up and down the street at other times of the day. For instance, if I'd wake up very early in the morning, I'd nearly always hear the milkman come in, and I looked forward to that. That was a nice sound, too. Sometimes if I was awake unusually late, or woke up unusually late, around twelve o'clock at night, I would hear the last streetcar coming along. There was what they called the owl car, which was a late, late car that came back from downtown to the residential neighborhood, which that was, and that was the car that some of the gentlemen took when they came home late at night. And I don't know why they were out quite so late as that, but they were. So I would hear that come along, and I would hear these familiar sounds, and each one of them was very comforting to me, because I just thought, "Well, that's something I know about, those are people I know about, in many cases, and there they are, and there's no reason for me to feel lonely here."

I had an older brother and sister, but they were quite a bit older.[7] My brother was nine years older than I was, and my sister was five years older than I was, so I was much the youngest in the family. She was a little bit too old to be a playmate for me, really. Later on, we became great friends as we grew up together, but in childhood I did not have that kind of companionship with my brother and sister.

There were plenty of children around in the neighborhood. We played the usual things. We skated up and down the sidewalk there; we had some baseball games in the backyard. Girls, much more than boys, used to play jacks in those days. I don't know whether girls play jacks anymore. There was a lot of fun in the neighborhood, just sort of running around together and looking at things and doing things. Also, many of us used to go over to Central Park, which was quite close by, a very convenient playground. I seem to remember snowy winters, and not everybody seems to remember that—maybe they weren't so snowy—but I can remember times when there was snow on the ground, and a bunch of us would go over to Central Park and get on sleds, and we thought we were going down tremendous alps—those little hills in Central Park. But nevertheless, when you're a kid and you're on a sled, it can seem pretty exciting.

My grandmother used to have a day at home once a week when she received friends, and a lot of other people had the same kind of thing. There was a day when—she was Mrs. Miller—Mrs. Miller was going to be at home, and her friends could come by to call. Various other people up and down the street had their days. And there were often just very informal parties for children. We didn't have very many big, fancy parties. But in hot weather there was nearly always lemonade on hand, and cookies, and at other times, in cool weather, there would be something hot to drink if the kids wanted to stop in. There was a great deal of that kind of very informal sort of going back and forth between people's houses. It was just so nice in those days, that nobody was afraid to go out in the street and go up and down by himself or with a few other children. There was just no feeling that anything could go wrong. This is not true anymore, unfortunately, in many neighborhoods. Even in very good neighborhoods it's not true, but that's the way it was then, and nobody ever thought anything about it. It was just the way we lived.

We lived out on the edge of Cherokee Park, and I can remember so often being taken over to Big Rock, or going over to Big Rock with some of my friends. Oh my, we not only used to have swimming when the weather was right, but at other times of the year, maybe in the spring or in the fall, I can remember wading in Beargrass Creek there and trying to catch crawfish and things of that sort. There were always picnics. There were hayrides. There were all those sort of simple pleasures that were a lot of fun for us. I can remember being taken on an interurban streetcar. It was really quite a treat to go out and take a nice little ride, maybe take a little picnic lunch with us on the streetcar. That was an outing. A little later on, when automobiles were more prevalent, on hot nights I can remember sometimes my father would keep us up a little bit late, take us out in the car, and just go for a drive all around town. Maybe we would go to a couple of the parks and drive around until the evening got cooler, and I would nearly always, I think, go to sleep long before we got home. But it was a nice feeling to be with the family, rolling around on wheels, everybody talking quietly, and then by the time we got home I was good and ready for bed. In fact, I think I was usually asleep. But that's the kind of thing we did.

From "Barry Bingham's Louisville, Kentucky,"
The Courier-Journal, 3 May 1976

The movies were special events, eagerly awaited. I early became
addicted to the serials that ran at the neighborhood houses on Saturday afternoons. The plight of the blonde heroine, left dangling
over a cliff or lashed to the top of an express train headed for a tunnel, made it imperative to get back the next week to see if she was
saved. My favorite was *The Diamond from the Sky.* It was a lurid
adventure which forecast some of the thrills of the modern space
films. Special occasions such as birthdays might bring a visit to an
amusement park, White City or Fontaine Ferry. A drive to the top
of Iroquois Park hill, or Jacob's Park as it was then called, was
an expedition.

There was of course no air conditioning in those days. On the hottest summer nights my father would take us riding in his open Rambler
to get a little air. Our route usually took us along what was known as
"New Boulevard," now Eastern Parkway. I was avid for views of the
nighttime city, but I invariably fell sound asleep before we circled
back home.

The world on the edge of Cherokee Park was more open than
Fourth and Ormsby, but it seemed equally secure.[8] Here there really
were hills for coasting. In the summer there was swimming in what I
regarded as a more than adequate pool, a deep place in the Beargrass
Creek at Big Rock. The top of the rock itself was great for picnics.
Shallower stretches of the creek offered fine opportunities for wading,
with snake-doctors skittering across the surface, and the interesting
possibility that a crawfish might nip your toe. The word "pollution"
was unknown to our vocabulary.

Cherokee Park, though spread out, had the character of a neighborhood. When a new house was built, everybody knew who was
moving into it. Douglass Boulevard was the main point of access.
When we moved there, the streetcar line had just been extended
to the "new loop" at Bardstown Road and Douglass. Beyond was
open country.

The park was the scene of a notable display of fireworks on the
Fourth of July. Neighbors used to gather on the slope of our hill to
watch them soar up from the valley below. Roman candles swung up-
ward and burst into stars, pinwheels gyrated madly, firecrackers
roared, and the air was redolent with "punk," the sticks used to light
the fireworks.

Most dreamlike in my memory were the fire balloons, long since outlawed as incendiary devices. They were big colored globes of paper with candles fixed inside, set adrift on the night breezes. They floated slowly above the dark trees, more mysteriously beautiful than all the space vehicles that are commonplace to a modern child.

There were implications of hunger and want, and even of evil, that touched the edges of even a fortunate child's consciousness. Charity was woefully inadequate. It began with Thanksgiving or Christmas baskets to people the family knew as "needy." Adult whisperings conveyed the sense of something ominous about the death of Alma Kellner, a local child who was murdered in a church basement in a crime still unsolved.[9]

The existence of serious trouble in the outside world first came home to me on a night in 1915, when a newsboy came bawling "Extra!" up the street and my father rushed down to buy a paper. It reported the sinking of the *Lusitania* by a German submarine.

World War I became a source of passionate interest to me. My real preoccupation, however, was in keeping a map of the Western Front up to date. I moved colored pins from place to place as the papers reported battles in which distant, shadowy thousands were dying. Things came nearer when soldiers in uniform from Camp Taylor started to throng along Fourth Street. But they always looked eager and cheerful. It wasn't easy for me to associate them with death in some far, muddy place called Flanders.

Were we too sheltered as children in that era? Certainly no television brought us scenes of death on the battlefield, of urban riots, of racial intolerance. We were not bombarded by commercial pitches for snack foods, for gadgets, for toys no child could possibly be happy without.

We were thrown to a much greater degree on our own resources. We, even the lucky ones, were often quite lonely. I can't remember the sensation of boredom when I was a child, but not having anything very interesting to do much of the time was a condition we accepted then without question.

Children today have far more information about their city and their world than we did. That is not to say, however, that they are necessarily better informed. By and large they don't read as much, and don't hear as much or as varied adult conversation.

It is easy to sentimentalize the past. We could not go back to its conditions, and we would no doubt find them much less appealing than we remember them if we did.

If I walk through the streets of Old Louisville on a summer night, however, I am struck by the physical restrictions on people's lives compared to my early days. Doors and windows are closed to protect the air conditioning, and no doubt locked as well. Inside, households are smaller, and include fewer variations of age and temperament.

People almost invariably are looking at TV. The screen is indeed a window on the world, through which a child can view a President addressing a vast audience, a man walking on the moon.

Those are splendid advantages. But does that same child ever look out of the real window at his elbow any more? Does he open it to hear the sounds of ordinary people living around him, somebody singing on a neighbor's front porch, even a moth bumping softly against the screen?

From Interview of Barry Bingham by Karen Black, Bellarmine College, 21 February 1986

I can remember being brought into the parties of grown-ups when I couldn't have been more than about five years old, I guess, because my mother died when I was seven years old, and I can remember being brought in a few times to parties where she and I sang duets together. She had a lovely voice, and she would sing, and then I would join in. We enjoyed doing that together. It was fun. But that was not a real showpiece. It was just something we could do together that she thought was sort of entertaining.

There were other times when I remember being upstairs and hearing a party going on downstairs, and I would hang over the banister, and it always seemed like some wonderful thing was happening below. Maybe it was a very pedestrian kind of party that was going on, but when you're a child, the fact that people are staying up late, and they're talking about things that you don't know about, and all that, it seems very tempting and mysterious. That's the way it always seemed to me.

From Interview of Barry Bingham by William E. Ellis, Eastern Kentucky University, 9 April 1987

My mother died when I was seven years old, so my recollections of her, of course, are only those of a child, but they're very vivid.[10] She was quite a vivid personality—her appearance and her manner. She was an extremely cheerful, humorous, delightful person. I expect I tagged along behind her a lot when I was a child. I remember following her into the garden when she was doing work out there, and I can remember her being in her bedroom sewing or something of that kind, and I would go and sit down by her. And she had a lovely singing voice, and she used to encourage me to do a little singing along with her. I had a kind of little piping voice, a soprano voice, I guess, at that point. And we used to sing duets. Not for company, but just with each other. I have a very warm and rather colorful recollection of her.

And then of course she died in an accident, and I was in the car with her, in fact, was, I think, asleep on her lap, when this thing came on. I had the pretty traumatic experience of being in that wreck without knowing anything about what it really meant and then finding afterward that my mother had died.

My uncle [Dennis Long Miller] was driving. He came to a grade crossing which did not have any gates or warning signals of any kind, and he drove onto the track, and this interurban car came tearing through. I remember hearing my mother cry out, and I waked up and saw the headlight of this approaching car coming toward us. My cousin Franklin Callahan, who was older than I was, and my sister, Henrietta, were also in the car.

It was a terrifying feeling. Then I was unconscious for a while after that and didn't really know what had happened, but came to in a neighboring house where they had taken us in. And it was one of those accidents that nobody will ever know exactly how it happened. My uncle survived, of course, and I think he just felt that he had made a terrible mistake. It was raining slightly. He stopped to clean his glasses, and then got back into the driver's seat and started on, and got across [on] the track before he realized this thing was coming. You'd think there would have been a warning bell or something, but there just wasn't anything there. There was an article which I've seen, of course, long, long since, in one of the local papers, calling it "that death trap at O'Bannon," which was the place it took place, because it was such a dangerous crossing. You couldn't see very far in either direction. The grade crossing was not on the level at all. You went up onto the track and then down on the other side. A bad place. So anyway, that's the unhappy part of it, but I have many happy recollections, I'm glad to say, of my mother.

I remember seeing her dressed to go to parties, and she enjoyed that kind of thing. She enjoyed dressing up in pretty clothes. And of course, I always enjoyed seeing her that way. She always seemed to be in a very cheerful mood. She loved dancing, and after she died, my father went through a rather tragic thing, but I understand so well how he felt about this. They had been at a dance not long before her death, and somebody was taking a home movie. It showed her waltzing on the dance floor in a pretty dress, looking her best. And my father got hold of that film, and he just became obsessed by it almost. He used to rent a little downtown movie theater in the afternoon and just go and sit there and watch that over and over again. Such a melancholy thing, but so understandable, because, for a moment, it was almost as though he had her back, you see. Her death was such a terribly unexpected blow to him. He was not even here. He had to come back from a business trip. She was unconscious for a couple of days and then died.[11]

From Reminiscences of Mary Caperton Bingham, 1984

I like to think of the life the family led in the Cherokee Park house: Judge Bingham, his wife, Eleanor ("Babes"), Robert and Henrietta, and Barry, *and,* very importantly, Lizzie Baker, who was Barry's nurse and whom we inherited and who lived with us in the Big House for many years. She always wore a little white cap, and she used to knock on our bedroom door in the early morning and come in and close the window and make a fire in our coal grate. I can see her dear and generous behind now, as she leaned over the fireplace to light the coals. She was a fixture in Barry's young life, and she must have been a great comfort and a stabilizing factor at the terrible time when Babes was killed in an automobile accident.

Barry's mother was witty, gay of heart, with a wonderful sense of humor. He remembers her riding on a very small bicycle up to the front door of Grandma Miller's summer house in Pewee Valley: "Here I come, meek and lowly, sitting on my ass" (see Matthew 21:5).

I think the Judge never recovered from this terrible loss, even though afterward he married twice. Barry's shock and loss expressed themselves, so Lizzie told me, by a curious habit: he would not touch his heels to the floor for a very long time and would tiptoe about as if not wishing to disturb anyone. At this time he was six years old. He was sent down to Asheville to be with Aunt Sadie.[12] She had loved him very much from his birth, and the love and understanding she gave him at this time must have established the close and deep affection between them that lasted the rest of her life.

I don't know how long he stayed with Zaddie (this was our pet name for this remarkable and delightful woman), but I think he must have been with her a great deal, because his father, almost destroyed by his wife's death, would have had a hard time comforting and succoring his bereft little boy. But at some point Barry returned to Louisville and to Lizzie.

Chapter 2

Education

From Interview of Barry Bingham by William E. Ellis, Eastern Kentucky University, 9 April 1987

I started school at what they called the Patterson-Davenport School out on Douglass Boulevard.[1] My good friend John Davenport's father was the headmaster there. I went to the first and second grade there.

Then after that I went to what was called the Richmond School on Third Street. This was run by a man called James H. Richmond, who was a fine educator.[2] It was a small private school, coeducational, and I was there for quite a number of years. I enjoyed that very much. The old house was the Farnsley house to begin with and was taken over by the Richmond School. That has now been entirely obliterated.

It was in the Old Louisville neighborhood. I had been born just one block away from there in my grandmother's house on Fourth Street. It was in the same block—the 1200 block on Third Street and my grandmother's house the 1200 block on Fourth—so it was kind of a familiar neighborhood. I've always had a special feeling about what they now call Old Louisville. We didn't even call it that then. I thought it was New Louisville. It's now called Old Louisville, and it's a residential neighborhood that has a certain character of its own. So I know both. I was born there, and I went to school there as a child.

From Interview of Barry Bingham by Mary D. Bobo, University of Louisville, 25 June 1982

The Richmond School was a good, solid educational background for anybody who was interested in any kind of career, I think, but maybe it was especially adapted to somebody who wanted to go into writing in some form. The headmaster of the school, Mr. Richmond, was determined that everybody should learn how to write well, and Miss Nannie Lee Frayser, who was the assistant principal, a wonderful teacher, was especially helpful to people who were interested in writing and was always trying to help develop our imagination.[3] She was interested in what we were reading. She used to read aloud to us at recess many times, and it was a delightful experience to hear that lady read good books, and she didn't use anything trashy, I can assure you. So I used to enjoy that. Sometimes while we were having our sandwich at our desks, she would read aloud to us, and I think I maybe got through that some of the feeling of the cadence of prose—the way sentences were structured, when read aloud, so that they sounded right. I now do reading for the blind myself twice a week, and some of the writing that I have to read is obviously not meant to be read aloud. It's very difficult prose. It doesn't flow. So I think that hearing good writing read aloud gives you an extra dimension, because you begin to get the feeling of how the sentences are constructed, and how the thing flows along, and that's what Miss Nannie Lee Frayser was able to give us.

Anyway, this was what I suppose would now be called a classical education—although of course, just in the primary grades. But we got a good background. Everybody, I think, learned how to read and write and how to *like* to read, which is another very important factor. Some people *can* read but don't like to read, and now you get lots of young people, I'm afraid, who don't read for pleasure. They only read what they feel they have to or should read, perhaps. In our day we were encouraged to read for pleasure, and I think almost everybody in my class was interested in reading in that way.

I think my classmates and others that I knew in school in other classes all maintained some interest in literature. Charlie Farnsley was one of them.[4] He was a class below me, but Charlie always was interested. Archie Robertson, who was my classmate, was very much interested in literature and wrote books afterward.[5] Cary Robertson, who was not my classmate but was at the Richmond School too, of course, later became Sunday editor of *The Courier-Journal*.[6] I think perhaps he derived some of his interest from those days at the Richmond School. . . .

A Shakespeare production which my father appeared in as King Menelaus I remember so well. I wrote one of our Editorial Notebook pieces about it some years ago. It was given in an outdoor amphitheater on Mr. Knott's place, which was right next to our place on the edge of Cherokee Park.[7] He had this little theater built down there for this performance, and everybody in the neighborhood was involved in it, one way or the other. Even the kids were all in the chorus, and it

was a very well-prepared production with plenty of rehearsals. And it
fascinated me, because I saw my father appear in armor on the stage
with a helmet with a flowing mane coming out of it. I thought it was
the most magnificent thing I had ever seen. Mrs. Todd, who was a
beautiful woman, played Helen of Troy, and I think it gave me an image of what a magnificent-looking lady on the stage could be, for the
rest of my life.[8] So these experiences, I think, not only fostered my
interest in reading and literature but my lifelong interest in the theater.

From Barry Bingham, "Recalling the Memorable Snows of Yesteryear," *The Courier-Journal,* 5 November 1958

To children, snow is one of the great remaining unsullied adventures
of life.

No snow this season is likely to produce will impress Louisvillians
who lived through the famous winter of 1917-18. We have swung for
years in a cycle of warm winters, wishy-washy with rain. Brief snaps
of very cold weather have been just enough to create confusion. But
the winter of World War I brought to the Ohio Valley two solid months
of ice, snow, sleet, the longest period of severe weather on record.

There were some preliminary warnings as early as November,
when the mornings were unusually nippy. The real business began,
however, on December 8, 1917. That day a blizzard dumped sixteen
inches of snow on Louisville. The Weather Bureau could only advise
anxious questioners that zero temperatures were ahead. By the tenth,
thermometers registered four below.

Traffic was desperately snarled up. Freight trains were running
twelve to twenty-four hours late. Streetcars, on which most people
went to work in those days, kept getting derailed by cakes of ice.
As things got worse, the Louisville Railway Company had to put
1,500 men to work clearing the lines. I can remember the scene
especially along Bardstown Road. There were high drifts on both
sides, and a few automobiles crawled along in the snowy wind like
crippled animals.

The adults of the community worried about dwindling coal supplies. Gas pressure went down to nothing and people had to cook on
coal oil stoves. Heating was a serious problem. There was a shortage
of eggs, butter, poultry and vegetables, as farm wagons were not getting in from the country. Men took hours getting downtown to work,
and had to be prepared for covering the last couple of miles on foot.

For children, the whole period was one of excitement and a break in routine. Schools closed down on December 15, a whole week early for the Christmas holidays. They were shut again for days at a time during January.

Most thrilling of all, the Ohio River froze over from shore to shore. Parents took their children down for the strange experience of walking to Indiana on the ice, and it was even possible to see cars driven across. The busy little ferries that carried war workers to the Jeffersonville Arsenal were immobilized at the shore. An ice gorge moved down the river later on, and the packet boats *City of Louisville* and *City of Cincinnati* were crushed at their moorings.

The weather moderated a little in the week before Christmas, but there was a light snow on Christmas day. By the 29th, another big cold wave had begun. The low point was on January 12, when it was sixteen below zero. On the 15th, snow during the night reached 16.5 inches, a record depth. On the 27th, five hours of continuous sleet put a crust of ice on top of the snow pack. The mercury dipped to zero again on February 4, for the eleventh time that winter. It was not until February 7 that a warm rain began to wash away the now-filthy snowbanks and melt the crusted ice in the streets.

It is doubtful if Louisville children ever had so much fun during a two-month period. Snowmen in the yard remained intact for weeks, and new embellishments could be added on almost any morning. The ramparts of snow forts could be built higher and higher. Unexpected days out of school found downtown children dragging their Flexible Flyers to Central Park for hours of coasting on the modest little hill. The lake in Cherokee Park was alive with skaters, both by day and night. There was a winter carnival atmosphere, for those who didn't worry about food and fuel shortages, and about the sufferings of the poor in unheated houses.

Some adventurous teenagers of the day, obviously without the consent of their parents, indulged in a form of tobogganing that was probably as dangerous as a ride down the Cresta run. They tied a toboggan to the family car with ropes, loaded it up with passengers, and then went spinning along the snowy roads of Cherokee Park. There was plenty of excitement, especially on the curves. There was also plenty of danger if the car should have to make a sudden stop.

The next winter was a hard one in Louisville, too, though in a different way. It was the time of the terrible influenza epidemic. Camp Taylor, still packed with young men, though the war had ended in November, became a center of infection. During the nation-wide epidemic, half as many young men died in hospital cots at the camps as had lost their lives in combat.

But for Louisville youngsters, it was only another break of routine. They realized that their mothers and sisters were going out to Camp Taylor as volunteer nurses, and that their fathers looked worried. They even heard some of the grim reports about the shortage of coffins. But their main impression was that the schools were closed for a considerable period.

The feeble winters of our time offer little in the way of excitement. When snows do come, they quickly melt away in a downpour of dirty rain. Ice forms for a day or two, but melts before the youngsters can remember where they put their skates. Skiing, an unknown sport in these parts during the celebrated blizzard winter, gets a heavy play for a couple of days, and is gone.

From Interview of Barry Bingham by William E. Ellis, Eastern Kentucky University, 24 September 1987

I lived with [my aunt Sadie Bingham Grinnan] a good part of the time. I was, at that time, supposed to have been threatened with tuberculosis, and it was considered wise for me to go to a climate where TB could be well treated, and Asheville was then one of the leading tuberculosis resorts in this country—really, almost like Saranac Lake, in New York. So she lived there. Both of my aunts—my father's sisters—lived there, and my grandfather. So I went down there and spent a good deal of time with her. My father added to her house a floor at the top, with an open bedroom and an open sitting room, and that's where I spent my time. In those days the treatment for TB was almost entirely fresh air. They thought you had to have constant fresh air, day and night, and that's the way they regarded it. But fortunately, in my case, I don't think I was ever really fully developed as a TB victim, but I apparently had a tendency in that direction, and it did do the work, evidently, because I've, fortunately, been very lucky on health ever since. I still want to sleep with the open windows all the time.

From Interview of Barry Bingham by William E. Ellis, Eastern Kentucky University, 9 April 1987

After that I went for a short time to the Bingham School at Asheville, which was my grandfather's school.[9]

From Interview of Barry Bingham by William E. Ellis, Eastern Kentucky University, 17 November 1983

I was there under a little bit of unusual circumstances. I had poor health at that time, and it was considered a good idea for me to go to school in North Carolina, which is a very healthy place. But I lived at my aunt's house right there next to the grounds, but I was not really there completely as a cadet as the other boys were. And after one semester my father thought that maybe it would be better for me to go away to an entirely different environment. So that is when he sent me to school in New England to Middlesex.

From Interview of Barry Bingham by Karen Black, Bellarmine College, 21 February 1986

My grandfather moved the school up to Asheville in western North Carolina in 1891. The school in eastern Carolina [Mebane, Alamance County] had burned down, and rather than try to reconstruct it, he decided to move to what he regarded as a little bit better climate in western Carolina. So I used to spend quite a bit of time with my relatives in Asheville—a delightful place.

My father attended when he was growing up. In fact, he taught there a little while. If I had not gone into newspaper work, which became the natural thing for me to do after my father bought the papers, I might very well have ended up as a teacher too. It's the other profession, I must say, that appealed to me most. I think I would have enjoyed it.

The school closed in 1928, after my grandfather died. There were people who would have liked to buy the name of the school and continue it, because it did have quite a good reputation, particularly all over the South, but the family decided that since there was no Bingham left to work in the school at that time, it would be better to close it out, and it did close.

From Interview of Barry Bingham by Karen Black, Bellarmine College, 21 February 1986

I went to Middlesex School in Concord, Massachusetts. I was fifteen, I believe, when I first went up there. This, I think, was a rather mysterious decision my father made. He decided to send me up there at the spring term that year, and that meant that I went into the school not knowing a human being in that place, and all of the rest of the boys—this was a boys-only school at that time, it's now coeducational—all of the other boys had been there a while and made their friends, and so I was plunged into a rather unfamiliar atmosphere. It was not easy. This was a very New Englandly school, too, in those days, and of course I was considered a boy, really, almost from the Deep South. They thought Kentucky was way, way south, you know. We know better than that. It really was quite amusing. When I went in to be introduced to the headmaster of this school—his secretary, who was a very sharp, birdlike old lady, with eyeglasses, said, "Oh, we're so glad to have you here, little boy. We have another boy here from South America." And she really thought that I was almost a foreigner, I think, because I came from a long way off. So it was not easy. I had bad homesickness troubles for a while at Middlesex, but then, gradually, I began to get used to that.

We studied all the usual things. We took Latin in those days. I wish I had taken Greek, but I did take Latin. And of course, we had math, we had English, we had history, we had geography, which I always loved. They don't really give geography as a separate subject anymore. And we had languages. I had both French and German at different times. That was the kind of thing you were expected to do in those days. Math was always my bugbear, I'm sorry to say. I always had a hard time, particularly algebra. When I got to geometry, it didn't seem quite so bad, because I could memorize a lot, but trying to figure out those algebra problems gave me some bad times, I can tell you.

It was pretty restrictive. We had one long weekend and one short weekend off each term, and that was all. The rest of the time we couldn't leave school. I used to walk quite a long distance into the town of Concord, which was the nearby community, just because I enjoyed walking, even in those days. I still like it. But I would walk down there just to go and have a look, and I sometimes was allowed to go into a soda fountain and have a soda, which was a big treat, and then I would go on back out to the school. I was never very good at games, unfortunately, so I didn't particularly enjoy the games periods at school as much as some of the other boys did. I later on became fond of tennis, but that was not a sport that was much practiced in those days, there.

Unless otherwise specified, all photos are courtesy of Mary Caperton Bingham.

Left: Barry Bingham with his mother, Eleanor Miller Bingham, in 1912.

Below: The residence at 1236 Fourth Street, Louisville, built about 1874 and purchased in 1883 by Barry Bingham's grandparents Samuel Adams Miller and Henrietta Long Miller. Courtesy of James Callahan, San Francisco.

Above: The home of Robert Worth Bingham and Eleanor Miller Bingham, built about 1906-7 overlooking Cherokee Park, Louisville. Courtesy of James Callahan, San Francisco. Below: A party for Jouett Ross Todd, about 1912. Barry Bingham is standing second from right in the front row, wearing a sailor suit.

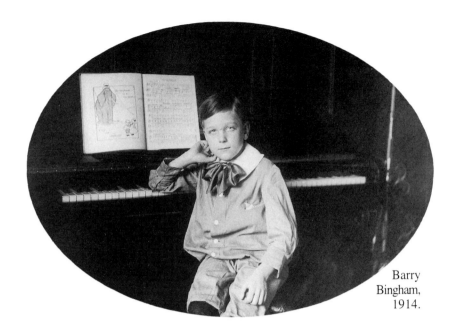

Barry
Bingham,
1914.

Bushy Park, the home of Charles T. Ballard, about 1911. Robert Worth Bingham bought it in 1919 and renamed it Melcombe Bingham. Barry and Mary Bingham moved here in 1942. Caufield and Shook Collection, neg. 6387, University of Louisville Photographic Archives.

Barry Bingham, 1924, as a freshman at Harvard University.

Above: Barry Bingham talking with Eleanor Roosevelt in Louisville, about 1933. Below: Ambassador Robert Worth Bingham (*left front*) and Governor Albert B. Chandler (*right front*) at a special session of the Kentucky General Assembly, 23 February 1936. At rear are Barry and Mary Bingham, Mildred Chandler, and Aleen Bingham. Both courtesy of *The Courier-Journal.*

Barry and Mary Bingham, summer 1934. They were visiting Ambassador Bingham in England for the first time.

Photos by Dorothy Wilding, London.

Right: Barry Bingham examines the Sunday comic section produced by a new four-color press, 12 April 1938. Courtesy of *The Courier-Journal*.

Below: The Binghams enter Calvary Church, Easter 1941. *Left to right:* Barry, Sr., Sallie, Mary, and Worth. Barry, Jr., was at home with mumps.

There was a school called Concord Academy, which was, at that time, all girls. It is now also integrated, boys and girls. But about twice a year we would be taken over to Concord Academy for some affair that was going on there, and there would be, maybe as we got a little bit into the higher grades, there would be a dance, but I can remember very well that some of the girls would dance in their galoshes. They did not take the galoshes off on the dance floor, so you can imagine it was not a very good form of dancing. And of course the boys didn't know how to dance either, but that was about the only mingling that we did. We did have some theatricals at Middlesex, but it was boys only there. They didn't have mixed theatricals, unfortunately. We had a very good singing teacher, a music teacher, and we used to put on Gilbert and Sullivan operettas there, which were pretty good, but they would have been so much better if we could have had girls in the girls' roles and boys in the boys' roles.

Many of the people that I was in Middlesex with went on to Harvard. It was a Harvard prep school, very largely so. Many of my friends when I got to college were those I had known in prep school. We have kept up more or less with each other through the years. There are quite a few of us that are still around, and we still correspond with each other.

From Barry Bingham, "The Nimble Tread of the Feet," *The Courier-Journal*, 23 June 1987

Of the millions of fans worldwide who fondly remember Fred Astaire, I can claim to be one of the earliest. I first encountered that delightful fellow in England in the early 1920s. I was sixteen, he was all of twenty-three.

I was on a summer visit to London with my father, sister and brother. We went to see a musical called *Stop Flirting*. It featured Fred and Adele Astaire, a young American brother and sister.

Their easy, carefree, witty way of performing knocked me for a loop. I went to the show over and over, sometimes timing my arrival to the moment just before one of their big numbers. My special favorite was a celebration of the Charleston, then the new dance rage on both sides of the Atlantic.

"Take a lesson from me," sang a mock-serious Adele. "I'd rather Charleston," Fred responded, suiting explosive action to words. "I'm disappointed in you and your ways," she reproved. His riposte was, "I'm double-jointed, there's no sensation like syncopation."

So much did they fascinate me that I was determined to meet them. I devised a strategy, not quite honest, but based on heartfelt admiration. I sent them a note to the theater, saying I represented *The Courier-Journal* in Louisville, and requesting an interview. Back came a message saying they would receive me backstage in Adele's dressing room after the next night's performance.

Avid to make the impression of a seasoned journalist and man of the world, I decided to rent a set of full evening clothes. It even included a top hat, which I had no idea how to handle. (Fred later gave the world the ultimate lesson in how to wear such attire when he so exuberantly sang, "I'm puttin' on my top hat, tyin' up my white tie, brushin' off my tails.")

On that evening, I entered the dressing room completely out of breath and *savoir faire,* clutching an orchid in my hand for Adele. I'm sure the Astaires penetrated my disguise at a glance. I hadn't even the presence of mind to carry a pad and pretend to take a reporter's notes. I just asked them about the things I wanted to know: their career before the footlights, which started when they were twelve and ten; about their favorite times and places and people. They were wonderfully kind to a boarding-school boy out of his depth. . . .

I last saw Fred at a dinner in 1984, following the Breeder's Cup races at Hollywood Park. He looked old and owlish, but stepped into the room, his young wife Robyn on his arm, displaying the debonair grace that had become his trademark.

When I look up into the sky at night, I am prepared to see a show of light—not a U.F.O. or a rerun of Halley's Comet—Fred Astaire in a theatrical spotlight, dancing on a cloud as he seemed to do all his life.

From Interview of Barry Bingham by Mary D. Bobo, University of Louisville, 25 June 1982

So I stayed there [at Middlesex School] for about two and a half years. I then came back to Louisville for the last year before I went to college, because I had already earned all but one of my college credits, and it didn't seem really sensible for me to go back to boarding school for another whole year to get that one credit. So my father agreed to let me come on back here and have a year at home. I tutored in German that year and did get my final credit in German in order to get into college. I had an interesting time here that year. My sister and I opened a bookstore.

This was 1924. We opened a bookstore called the Wilderness Road bookstore, and we had a wonderful time doing that. It was not very professional, I'm afraid, but we enjoyed ourselves, and it went on for some years after that. Of course, we were not involved in it. Other people took it over, and it continued under other management for quite a few years after that.[10]

It was on Chestnut Street between Fourth and Fifth, and we had a nice little shop there, and we had quite a good collection of books. We tried to get some rare editions even, and then we had, of course, some regular books—the kind of things that you would sell in a bookstore of any kind. We never went in for things that some bookstores always do, that is, greeting cards and lending library, or anything of that kind. We didn't do that. But we enjoyed ourselves. It was an interesting experience to try something commercially during that one year when I was on my own here.

Then after that, in the fall of 1924, I went to Harvard and spent four years there, which were mostly very happy and satisfactory years. It got better and better! I think freshman year at college is rather a terrifying experience. It might have been a little more so for me, because I had not had what you would call the conventional preparation for college. I hadn't gone all the way through high school or boarding school, so that I thought maybe, when I got to college, I would suddenly find that whatever I had been able to do fairly well in my studies wouldn't work out so well at college. I wasn't sure I could even stay in there. But after freshman year began to go by and things weren't too bad, I began to feel better.

I got into a freshman composition course. I could have anticipated this, they said in those days. I could have passed an examination, before I went to Harvard, which would have allowed me to skip that course. It was really almost like a remedial course now. It was for people who had not learned much about writing. Well, fortunately, I did take it, and I got a perfectly fine man that I remember so well to this day named Willard Connely, who was my instructor. And we had a rather large class, but Mr. Connely, again, seemed to take a personal interest in the things I was writing and encouraged me very much, so I was really glad that what would have been a very perfunctory class—just to make up something—turned out to be really an advantage. He really encouraged my writing and I think taught me a good deal about writing that I have been able to use since then.

From Barry Bingham, "Too Good to Last,"
Harvard Alumni Gazette, June 1987

Harvard from 1924 to 1928—those were years I spent at the right place and the right time for me. Memory puts rose-colored spectacles on us all when we gaze back into our youth. In my case, things looked pretty rosy at the time, as soon as I escaped from the qualms of adolescence into what I thought was "real life."

I knew I was lucky to be at Harvard. I had never wanted to go to any other college. I never considered the possibility of dropping out of education to work as a deck hand on a tramp steamer in an effort to solve the riddle of "Who am I?" We were not conscious of such questions or such answers.

So there I was at Harvard. My background had given me no such assurance. Schools I attended in Kentucky rarely sent recruits to Cambridge in those days. My boarding school career at Middlesex, then known as a "Harvard prep school," had been fragmented by health problems and lacked entirely a final year. College Board exams scared the wits out of me, especially math.

That uneasiness lasted even when I squeezed through. Having gotten into Harvard, could I hang on? Then things started working better for me.

Classes proved manageable and increasingly absorbing. Studying at Widener Library furnished a good alternative to working in my room. By senior year it provided the luxury of my own desk high up in the stacks, where I could keep my books and my notes for the honors thesis in English I was writing.[11] (I shall never forget coming out of Widener one icy winter night to find the Aurora Borealis spread like a rippling banner across the sky.)

Lectures were not all of even quality, but some were memorable. It gave me no qualms to listen to a famous professor in a hall seating hundreds of students. We did not expect to "rap" with our teachers in those days, or meet them one-on-one.

You can say that that was the star system in education. The celebrated lecturers were performers in the best sense, putting on a show that might be somewhat theatrical in manner but deeply solid in content. Certain lectures in various courses were recognized as star turns, listed from time to time in the *Crimson*. We slipped into any empty seats to be found at the back and heard them.

Lectures by such luminaries as [Roger] Merriman on history, [George] Edgell on art, [George Lyman] Kittredge on Shakespeare, [Kirsopp] Lake on the Old Testament as literature, [John L.] Lowes on Victorian poetry—such were the high standards of our time. I know I concentrated narrowly on English and related courses of my choice. I might have enjoyed myself less under today's Core Curriculum requirements, but I would have had a broader exposure to learning.

Gore Hall in freshman year, two years in Westmorly, a final year in Massachusetts Hall when seniors inhabited the Yard—all were comfortable and uncrowded. (The house system did not begin until I was out of college.) Our dormitory rooms were cleaned and our beds made by elderly women known as "biddies." They were grandmotherly in their concern for reckless youth, offering words of advice on life's problems while changing the sheets. Ah, Mrs. Ford and Mrs. Holly, where are you now?

The Harvard Dramatic Club was an early focus for me. Small parts led to the role of Grumio as a comic servant in a modern-dress *Taming of the Shrew*. Later I lucked into the title role in *Brown of Harvard*, a revival of old melodrama in which I (preposterously!) played a turtle-necked football hero. [12]

Social life was never lacking. There were debut parties at the Somerset, hilarious dances at Brattle Hall after Dramatic Club performances, with classmate Charlie Henderson rattling out wonderful tunes at the piano. There were hip flasks passed behind the scenes, some holding our own home-made gin, a prohibition concoction with raw alcohol for kick, glycerine for smoothness, juniper drops for flavor.

There was the traditional talk of Radcliffe girls as starchy bluestockings, compared to the dream girls said to inhabit Wellesley and far-off Vassar and Smith. I learned better my sophomore year. I met Mary Caperton '28 in a Radcliffe Idler production of *A School for Princesses*, and quickly saw what a combination of blonde beauty and classically trained brains could be. We did not "go steady" in the later exclusive manner. We were not married until three years after graduation. But from that first meeting we never looked back.

Ours was a college era when the going was too good to last. We never heard the approaching rumble of the '29 market crash, which carried down with it many college dreams of quick success and money. There was far less emphasis on responsibility and social service than I hear among today's Harvard students. We were pretty hedonistic, but I can't say that we didn't have fun.

A grace note on our college era was not sounded until a quarter-century later. We were celebrating our 25th Reunion in high spirits when word reached us that a '28 classmate, Nate Pusey, had just been elected president of Harvard. J. P. Marquand could not have invented such a neat denouement for a novel of Harvard in our time.[13]

From Interview of Mary Caperton Bingham by Samuel W. Thomas, 29 October 1990

I know I was an Anglophile from birth. My grandfather, my mother's father, was an Anglo-Irishman. My grandmother was a mad Anglophile. As a matter of fact, she used to receive Lord Grey's propaganda in World War I and disseminate it, like any kind of spy.[14] So I was always brought up with the idea of liking people of Britain, and we had cousins and aunts and uncles that we were always in touch with. So I had a natural bent toward Britain, and then, of course, the Judge was, too, a convinced Anglophile. I think most people in the South felt that way about England. Maybe, partly, because of Britain's sympathy for the Confederacy. And the fact that when you are brought up in Virginia, you are conscious every day of Jamestown. My grandmother used to take us to Jamestown every spring to make a kind of ritual vow. And Williamsburg, then, I remember, the Duke of Gloucester Street was unpaved. Pigs rooted up and down it.

I was born on North Harrison Street in Richmond, right opposite the statue of the Richmond Light Infantry Blues man. I think it was a good place to be brought up in if you were very poor—wellborn, but terribly poor—because my great-grandfather had established the Richmond German, which became the dance of debutantes. As long as you had some kind of credentials, it didn't much matter whether you had anything else. My poor mother kept on having children, one after the other. She finally had seven children, and then an eighth miscarried, which, fortunately, stopped it. There were six girls. I remember my grandmother used to wring her hands and say, "Who is going to supply the lace-edged petticoats and drawers for these little girls?" She would, she knew.

My grandmother was Sallie Montague Lefroy. Her father was John Henry Montague, my great-grandfather. And that's where the Wallis Warfield [Simpson] connection comes in, because I think it was my great-grandfather's brother who went to Baltimore, and that line came from that.

I think she went to Miss Hattie Daniel's school in Richmond, but probably not until she was a teenager. No woman in her generation had much formal education. I think my grandfather Jeffrey Arthur Lefroy, the Anglo-Irishman, was not very well and then, as was very often the custom, came to Virginia to buy a farm and lead a healthy life. Actually, they were not married, I think, more than about five years before he died of consumption. But my grandmother said to me, they had a tremendously romantic and wonderful marriage, and when they were married, they went on their honeymoon to Europe, and their honeymoon was to start in Italy and follow the strawberry season all the way up to England and Ireland.

My father was Clifford Randolph Caperton. His family were from Monroe County, West Virginia, right over the West Virginia–Virginia border. I think they came over in something like 1790, and there was a big family of Capertons in that county. I used to go and stay with my grandfather and grandmother there. And there were Walnut Grove and Elmwood, and various farms around that had belonged to the family. There was an old senator—I think Allen Taylor Caperton, a U.S. senator, probably the best and most effective person in that branch.[15] My father's mother had been a Stiles, and her brother Major Robert Stiles wrote that book called *Four Years Under Marse Robert*. He was in the Army of Northern Virginia for four years. And he was a lawyer. And my father came to Richmond, the way they did then, to read law with his uncle in his law firm, and then, when he and my mother, Helena Lefroy, fell in love with each other—she was only eighteen—they brashly got married before he had done anything much about becoming a lawyer. So that was one of those early and not very prudent marriages. He never did finish becoming a lawyer. He was a businessman, and not a very successful one, alas. And he tried various things. I really don't remember very much about it. I know at one time he was connected with a big advertising firm. He was the poorest person to be in advertising, because he was very shy and not very outgoing. So I think it was hard on him.

We all went to Miss Virginia Randolph Ellett's School for Girls, and Miss Jennie was an absolutely remarkable person. She was one of those southern spinsters who was a tremendous intellectual. She used to go to Oxford in the summer. She had great friends at Oxford and also at Harvard. Well, the school in English and Latin was wonderful. I never had any American history. We learned all the names of the

Plantagenet kings in order, but we never even read the Gettysburg Address. But it was a good education on that side of the humanities.

Then I went to Radcliffe, which was considered very eccentric. In Richmond nobody ever heard of going to Radcliffe. If you went to college at all, it was safer to go to Bryn Mawr. Miss Jennie had close connections with Bryn Mawr. However, we had at this time in Richmond, as part of the little theater movement, a little theater—very brisk and successful, really. The director of it was Louise Burleigh, a Radcliffe graduate, and she had this children's theater, and I was very stagestruck and used to act in her children's productions. She put on a wonderful production, I remember, of *Gammer Gurton's Needle,* the first English comedy, and we took it all over Virginia, in a little train of cars. And we would play everywhere. And at one point, in culmination of our triumphs, we would play on the steps in front of Cabell Hall at the university. It was a great success.

I must have been about fourteen or fifteen. Then, when I got ready to go to college, Louise Burleigh got interested in my going to Radcliffe. I didn't go and look at Radcliffe. I know I had an interview. I took college boards and applied to Radcliffe, and I got what they called the Distant Work Scholarship, as if I were from Zimbabwe.

Well, I had a terribly happy time in Cambridge. Radcliffe was wonderful then. Of course, we had that curious system that the Harvard professors would give their lecture in the Yard, and then they would walk over to Radcliffe and deliver the same lecture. You'd think it might have taken some of the bloom off it, but it seemed to me perfectly wonderful.

From Reminiscences of Mary Caperton Bingham, 1984

I think no one ever came to Harvard with a more eager and receptive spirit, and indeed, here Barry found a kind of happiness that grew out of the deep satisfaction and excitement of the intellectual stimulus endemic in the Harvard of our day, and the joy of congenial friends and newfound independence.

We met in the spring of our sophomore year in Whitman Hall at Radcliffe, where we were both trying out for a play to be given in Agassiz Theater. I was tremendously drawn to this fair, straight young man with the dazzling blue eyes, and to my joy he found me attractive enough to want to see me again. Thus began our long friendship and a love affair that was full of joy and happiness, sunlight and gaiety. We sometimes took the same courses, and though in that day one never "studied together" as is the custom now (and how could one remember dates and conjugations in such an encounter?), we had the pleasure of sharing Mr. Kittredge's supreme lectures on Shakespeare, Mr. John Livingston Lowes's course in the Romantic poets, Mr. Edgell's brilliant lectures in Fine Arts 1D.

I lived in Bertram Hall, and the mistress of that establishment, Miss Field, was a good and sympathetic friend of mine. So when she thought our good nights on the porch had lasted long enough, she would tap on the front door: "Time to sign in, my dear!" In those days we were allowed to stay out until 10 P.M., writing in the book just exactly where we would be. And weekend absences required a letter from one's parents giving permission.

We graduated in 1928. I had won the Charles Eliot Norton Fellowship to the American School of Classical Studies in Athens that enabled me to study there for the academic year 1928-29. In April of that year my dear sister Sarah Montague Caperton had undergone the death of her fiancé, and she was distracted with grief. It was thought that she might be helped by going abroad for the summer with me, and so we embarked, in July, on one of the small Cunard liners, and traveled up to London to stay with our great-uncle Ted and great-aunt Lilian [Lefroy].

From London, Sarah and I took the *Golden Arrow* to Paris. We stayed there for several weeks, having a frivolous and delightful time, as Barry, Henrietta, Edie [Callahan], and her mother were also there.[16] In September I left for Greece. Barry and Edie and Barry's college roommate, Francis Parks, went with me and established themselves in the Grand Bretagne Hotel while I sadly repaired to the American School, full of thoughts of the wrenching parting that was to come in a few days.[17] It came. I survived only by burying myself in the routine of study and ancient monument visiting that was a remarkable and rewarding part of life at the American School.

Barry went to St. Moritz, where he proposed to write the novel that had been gestating for some time. He found, however, the loneliness of being in a hotel without friends or family not conducive to creation. He left Europe and went to Asheville, where he spent the winter with Zaddie and wrote. The novel was never published, but I think the exercise of forcing himself to sit down every day and write whether he wanted to or not was a healthy one and stood him in good stead later, when he was editor of the editorial page of *The Courier-Journal*.

After that winter he returned to Louisville and worked in several departments of the paper and the radio station. Meanwhile, I came back from Greece and found a job writing publicity at Little, Brown and Company in Boston. I lived back of [Beacon] Hill and shared an apartment with two college friends until the autumn of 1930. Then I went to Paris and spent the winter with the old friends I had made in Athens, Zora and Dorsey Stephens.

When I returned and landed in New York in March 1931, Barry was on the pier, his arms full of daffodils, and we became engaged that evening in the Gypsy Bar speakeasy!

We were married in June in Richmond in a large old-fashioned wedding. All of my sisters, and my old friend Liza Hagen, were bridesmaids, and Barry's groomsmen were his closest friends from college and Louisville.[18]

We went off for a splendid three-month wedding trip in Europe, starting with a North Cape cruise, ending in Venice, where we bought some lovely things for the little Italian house that we were to live in in Glenview.[19]

From Interview of Barry Bingham by William E. Ellis, Eastern Kentucky University, 9 April 1987

English was my major. And I took, of course, various other courses, but I really concentrated heavily on English, which was my principal interest. In those days they didn't have anything like a core program as they have at Harvard now. If I were going there now, I'd be obliged to take more science and more other things that I did not pay much attention to. I just took one science course. I also took language courses, but all those things would be required now. In my case, you could pretty much do as you pleased, so I'm afraid I concentrated really more heavily than I should have on English courses. I liked them and enjoyed them and also got pretty good marks in them, which also helps, I guess. I wish I'd had more history.

I fancied that I might be able to have a career in creative writing. That's what I thought I might be able to do. I was trying to write some poetry, write some short stories, and things of that kind, all through those years.[20] So I was interested in that. I also did a lot of amateur theatrical work, and although I never seriously contemplated a career in that kind of work, I enjoyed it and got lots of fun out of it.

I had an older brother and sister. I had assumed when I was a smaller boy that my brother would be the one who would come into the family business. Later on, it became clear that he was really not interested in doing that. He moved away from Louisville. Then my sister also moved away from Louisville. So as things developed, it came down to the point where I was pretty much the one that logically would come back here. My father wanted me to, though he never put any pressure on me about that at all. He really was willing for me to do what I felt would be most congenial and most rewarding, but I became more and more convinced that probably the thing to do was to go on into the family business. It wasn't exactly the kind of writing that I had in mind, but it was related to it at least—journalism.

I can never remember a time, and I'm sure it never happened, that he sat me down and said, "Now I want you to come back to Louisville and go into the papers." I think it was just a gradual evolution, really, between the two of us. He never put pressure on people anyway. That was not his method. He was a most kind and considerate father in every way. I remember talking to him about what I was going to do right after my graduation, and I did, I think, prevail on him at that time, without much pleading, to let me take a year off before I came back and started to work, because I wanted to write the great American novel.

From Interview of Barry Bingham by Mary D. Bobo, University of Louisville, 25 June 1982

My father did agree to my taking about a year off after I graduated from college to do some traveling and to do some writing, which I then was very eager to get out of my system. I did write a very long, very turgid novel which was never published, and I think it was a great fortune for me now that it was not put in print, because I think it would have been an embarrassment to me in years to come. I just poured everything into it the way young writers tend to do. I overwrote terribly. I wrote very much in the manner of other writers that I admired at that time, and it would not have been a good production. Funnily enough, the novel, which was turned down by publishers in this country, was accepted by a publisher in London. But he wrote me that he would like to take the novel on but would have to ask me to alter the conclusion. He thought that the ending of it was not right. And I was at that idealistic age where I thought, oh no, I could not possibly consider changing what had been my concept of how this book should be written, so I said, "Well, sorry, but I don't think I can do that." And that again was a stroke of luck, because even being published in England, I think, would have created problems for me later on.

Well, it was set in the North Carolina mountains, where I had spent a great deal of time. My Bingham relatives lived down there. It didn't deal with them at all. It was about a country family living nearby there. The principal character in it was a young woman growing up in a cabin there in impoverished circumstances. She had much higher ideas. She was very intelligent, not particularly well educated, but she had ambitions to lead a broader life. And she was frustrated in that. She was illegitimate, and her illegitimacy was a great burden to her. She was tormented sometimes by people in the neighborhood because of that. She was very proud. She wanted to escape from what she regarded as an unfortunate environment and from her disadvantages into some greater, wider realm. That feeling was then frustrated by the fact that she, in turn, fell in love with a young man, and unfortunately, then she bore an illegitimate child. That child was befriended by an older man, who decided to marry the mother and make everything all right in that way. Now much of this story was observed from the viewpoint of a little boy, whose age was about nine or ten. It was not very clearly spelled out. I suppose that little boy was, in some degree, myself, because I was remembering impressions I had from that age and what I was thinking about older people and their lives. The device, I'm sure, didn't work out from a technical standpoint, because the little boy couldn't possibly have known all those things that were going on in the lives of these older people. But he was, in a sense, the focus of the camera in this story, and if I had had a chance to rework that book years later, with a little more experience, I might possibly have made it come into some sort of proper shape. Anyway, it was a long, sprawling novel. It was very literary in the bad sense: it had too many literary allusions in it, and it was not a successful book, but it was a relief to me to be able to sit down and really dog it out, for a period of many months.

I wrote a part of it while I was abroad. I had been traveling, and I stopped off and stayed in Switzerland for a while. I got started on the writing there. I then came back and did some writing in Asheville. I went back down there, since this was the setting of the book, and stayed with my aunt by whom I had been brought up, really. I got a lot of writing done there, so the book sort of broke into two pieces, I guess. It was written at two different times. The literary agent who read it for me said that the second half was infinitely better than the first half, and I think probably that was the fact that I was getting back to the root of the story. It was more immediate and probably had a little more color in it at that point. The rest of it was just entirely a literary effort, I'm afraid. So anyway, I got it out of my system. I cannot say that I was frustrated by being a newspaperman and did not get a chance to write the great American novel. I *wrote* a novel.

From Interview of Barry Bingham by William E. Ellis, Eastern Kentucky University, 9 April 1987

I think I would have been less happy to come back here and go into a regular job, without having had the opportunity to do that. So I think in his wisdom [my father] felt that was the best thing for me to do, and I went ahead and did that, got it all out of my system, and then, when I came back to Louisville, I was only too happy to contemplate staying here. I never felt any rebellion against living in Louisville or working on the papers. I was only eager to see whether I could make myself confident to do it.

Chapter 3

The Family Business

From Interview of Barry Bingham by Mary D. Bobo,
University of Louisville, 25 June 1982

My first contact with the papers was even before my father became owner of *The Courier-Journal* and *Times*. When I was about ten years old I got active in a children's organization called the Aloha Club, which had a special section in *The Courier-Journal* every Sunday. I liked to write in those days, and I liked to do both prose and poetry, and I was very much interested in getting some of my things included in the Aloha Club section. Also, they used to have weekly meetings. The Aloha Club was run by a really re-markable lady, Miss Anna Hopper, and she was known as Aunt Ruth.[1] Aunt Ruth was her pseudonym, and all the kids used to come in there to see Aunt Ruth once a week and sit in her office, and she'd give us cookies and cocoa and talk about things. And she gave out book prizes for people who did something especially notable. She always had a nice book prepared for you. And I really enjoyed that a lot, and that was my first entry into the old Courier-Journal Build-ing. I used to go in there pretty regularly once a week to call on Aunt Ruth and meet with my fellow members. So my feeling about the paper really predated my father's connection with the paper. And then when I was twelve years old he did buy the papers, and I suddenly felt that I was already at home there, because I had been a pretty constant visitor.

So many people were in that club at that time, many of them, I'm sorry to say, long gone now, but Wilson [Wyatt] was one of them. Ruth Wilson Cogshall was one of the important members at that time. She used to draw very well and had her drawings in the paper. And it was a delightful thing. In those days the only thing comparable to it that I knew was called the St. Nicholas Club, and the *St. Nicholas Magazine* was a very popular magazine for children—long out of publication now. But that, of course, was a national thing. This was a local thing, and people all over *The Courier-Journal* circulation area belonged to it and used to send in their little compositions. It was just a delightful experience, and I think it gave many of us the feeling that writing was something that we really could get hold of and that you'd get a little recognition for, which is important to a writer, whether he be a child or an adult.

From Interview of Barry Bingham by William E. Ellis, Eastern Kentucky University, 9 April 1987

It was a rather cavernous kind of big old building, and I never got into many of the offices, but I used to go by a long series of offices and see people hard at work hammering on their typewriters.[2] The city room, which I passed on my way to Aunt Ruth's little office, was always just a beehive of activity in the way that people associate now with newspapers. It isn't really quite the same anymore. In those days there were a lot of people looking just like actors in *The Front Page,* with eyeshades, with things on their arms, you know, to hold up their sleeves, and people that looked as though they were just desperately eager to get out the next edition of the paper—that that was the only important thing in the world. Newspaper work is still just as feverish, I guess, as it ever was, but the atmosphere in a city room these days is not quite as hectic as it was then.

A little bit later, my father took me to meet Mr. Watterson when he was negotiating for the purchase of the papers.[3] Mr. Watterson was, of course, the celebrated editor—and not the owner—of the papers. But my father wanted me to meet him, and it was a historic event for me to meet this great man that I had heard about all my life. He was then a very old gentleman. He was mellow in his old age, but he had a fierce expression on his face, and it was rather terrifying to me as a kid. He had only one eye, you know, and it was a little bit intimidating to see this elderly gentleman with his flowing white hair and his bushy white eyebrows looking at me as though he wondered where I could have come from. But I'm glad to have had a chance to meet him, because he did not live very long after my father bought the papers. So at least I had an opportunity to meet the great editor of the paper.[4]

From Interview of Barry Bingham by Mary D. Bobo,
University of Louisville, 25 June 1982

As I was saying, I was allowed to take a year off at that point—that
was 1929—and I lived part of that time abroad, and I spent a lot of
that year doing this writing—this fiction writing—that I had wanted
to do. Then in January of 1930 I came back to Louisville, and my first
job was with WHAS radio. Those were the days, of course, of radio,
not TV, and I had an interesting experience working at WHAS at that
time. The head of the station at that time was a fine gentleman, named
Credo Harris, who was a great friend of my father's.[5] I believe my
father thought it would be a good idea for me to start out my working
career under the aegis of a fine person of that kind. Mr. Harris was
extremely kind to me and interested in me, so I had about a year's
experience at 'HAS at that point.

From Interview of Barry Bingham by
Terry L. Birdwhistell,
University of Kentucky, 8 February 1980

Mr. Harris was an old personal friend of my father's.[6] He knew that
Mr. Harris had absolutely no technical knowledge at all of this medium, but there weren't very many people in Kentucky who did have.
He decided, I believe, rather than to try to bring a technician in here
at that stage, he would try to get somebody who would have a real
concept of what that station could mean in the way of service. And he
and Mr. Harris talked it over very thoroughly, I'm sure, and he found
that Mr. Harris's ideas corresponded very closely to his as to what a
radio station could be expected to do for a community such as we were
reaching. Mr. Harris was a man of considerable imagination. He had
written several novels, and he had written some plays. He was mainly
a literary man, but he was a man, also, with an inquiring and inquis-
itive mind, and for that reason he was excited about going into a completely new medium and trying to see what could be done with it.

I think I know what my father's motives were in establishing the
station from talking to him, probably in later years. I don't think by
any means he consulted me when he first made the decision. I was still
in high school. However, I know that his main thought, always, was to
increase knowledge and education among Kentucky people. He felt

that there was a great need for more education, not only in the schools but outside the schools. And that there were many people who would never be reached by newspapers. Those were the days of terribly bad roads in Kentucky, and it was really awfully hard to get to people by highways. Trains ran across certain sections of the state, but there were many counties in which there was no railroad. He felt that there must be some other way to reach people in order to give them all kinds of information, as well as artistic creations, and things of that kind. And he decided that radio would be the best way to do it. He tried to combine that with setting up these listening posts in quite remote areas of Kentucky, so that people would have access to radio who couldn't even own a set themselves, but would be able to sit around in a grocery store, or wherever, and listen to radio. And his conception was that this would mean that a lot of people in Kentucky would hear about current events, would know something about the arts, about music, about things of that kind, who would never have any access to it otherwise. That was his motive, very definitely. He never thought of this as a money-making enterprise. Radio was not at that time anything that anybody would have thought of, I think, as a financial investment that was going to produce a lot of returns. He really had this, I believe, quite high-minded view of what it could do for a lot of Kentuckians who needed help, and that was his way of doing it.

Credo Harris and Emmett Graft came in on it after my father decided that he was going to go into this.[7] He wanted them to get the information that would make the station work better. I don't know any specific influence on my father in that way, but he was always a person who liked to keep up with what was going on in the world, and I think he became conscious of the fact that radio was a new instrument for getting through to people. And I don't believe anybody ever said that to him, but I think it was in his mind that he wanted to get to these remote Kentucky areas, and he found that this would be the way to do it. The farmers didn't have any way of getting crop reports and that kind of thing. Information that they really needed in their daily work was just not available to them. It was entertainment pure and simple as far as I was concerned at that point.

To add one word, my father was conscious of the fact that there were radio stations in many other states but none in Kentucky. I think his feeling was that Kentucky probably needed radio more than almost any state in the Union, because of these pockets of isolated populations around the state—that there was just no other way to get to them. Now a state like Kansas or Nebraska, which is just a great big flat prairie almost, in those states it would be much easier to reach them through newspapers, but not in Kentucky.

Well, my first job was with WHAS. I started working for WHAS in January 1930. I was given the title of radio continuity writer. Now nobody these days would even know what that was, I suppose. But for instance, when we had musical programs on—and there used to be a great many recorded music programs—I was given the job of writing out what the announcer would say about each one of these numbers that we played. I had to research music catalogs and music biographies and things of that kind to try to find something a little bit significant to say about that particular composition and who was playing it. And they threw to me a good many of these, I think, rather nice jobs of that kind, to write continuity for shows that they were putting on. It was not an original composition, by any means, but it was something I was interested in, and it fitted in with the kind of thing I had been interested in doing in college.

The station was like a very small beehive. There was a lot of activity in a very small space. We didn't have any queen bee, I'm sorry to say, but we had other aspects of a beehive. It was in the old Fireproof Storage Company building.[8] The quarters were grossly inadequate, even at that time. And of course they were not air conditioned. And it was not an unfamiliar thing to have performers faint while they were on the air in those days. It used to get terribly, terribly hot in there, particularly if you had a choral group coming in to sing. I tell you, it was just awful by the time you got that many people in there. But we had to go on in hot weather and cold weather.

It was fun, because it was such a small staff, and everybody knew everybody else very well. Katie Steel and Dorothy Kirchhubel just knew everybody in the station and would carry messages back and forth to everybody. It was very much of a family type of enterprise at that time. Credo Harris himself was a very fatherly sort of fellow, and he just felt that we were all his children, more or less, and he was going to guide us along the right path.

Emmett Graft was a very serious, very dedicated person, who really loved the engineering side of his job. And he was always ready to stay up all hours of the day and night to be sure that the station stayed on the air. It was almost like the [early] days of the automobile then, when there were an awful lot of flat tires and punctures. There were lots of minor accidents that took place around a radio station in those times. And if there was a big thunderstorm, we never knew whether we were still going to be on the air by the time it stopped raining. But in any case, Emmett Graft was just dedicated to his job and was always on the job. I can remember his being down there at all hours of the day and night to be sure that everything was going right at that station.

[The experimentation] was a combination of Emmett Graft and Credo Harris. Harris was definitely in on that too, because he thought it was exciting to do new and rather unusual, bizarre things, even. I can remember when they did that first broadcast from Mammoth Cave and what a strange idea that seemed to most people. But it was an interesting one, and it was perfectly feasible the way they set it up. They didn't think of it as a public relations gimmick, as you would now think of it. It was just something unusual that they thought radio could do, and they wanted to see if they could do it.

When the station began to go commercial, I think Lee Coulson was the strongest influence in trying to get it on the track commercially. That was where I say he was a good salesman. He was able to sell radio as a medium to a good many advertisers who had never even thought about such a thing. He had a conception of where radio might go in that direction, which indeed it did go, in years to come.

Then we had some star performers that people got fond of. There was a pianist named Jack Turner. Jack Turner, I guess, is long gone now. He's been away from here many, many years. He was a popular piano player who could just drum out nice music, almost endlessly, on the air. He could fill in with lots of music, and he also composed a few songs. And at that time I was writing lyrics for songs, so I did the lyrics for a couple of tunes that he produced.[9] And he used them on the air and would sing them. Jack was not what you would call a glamorous person when you saw him. He had a wooden leg, and he was not a good-looking fellow at all. But on the air he had this dulcet voice, and many women listeners were just determined that they were going to fall in love with Jack Turner. He used to get an awful lot of telephone calls from girls, asking him to meet them after the program was over and that kind of thing, you know. He thought it was funny, fortunately. He didn't lead them on.

But radio in those days was the beginning of these crushes that people got on performers. Since then, of course, I guess it's rock stars that you think of in that connection. In those days somebody who performed on radio was considered almost automatically a sort of glamour person. Personalities were developed in that way, and people got to feel that they knew them, even though they had never met them in their lives. They would write to them and call them up. There was an intimacy about it that nobody had ever experienced before, you see. You didn't get it, of course, by going out to the movies. Here was the first time when you would have an attractive entertainer coming into your room and singing to you, almost that way.

In those days they were doing radio plays. They were quite popular. And I read a role in several plays—not an important role at all, but I was interested in that. I had been doing some dramatics when I was at college, so I did try to do that. I enjoyed that, I must say. There were even a few plays that were written directly for radio by well-known writers, using the medium in an interesting way, knowing that people couldn't see the actors but they could be heard. A rather well-known English novelist and playwright, called Richard Hughes, wrote a play just for radio about some people who were trapped in a coal mine cave-in. And of course, if this had been done on a stage, it would have been done on a black stage—you couldn't see the actors. But he made a very interesting use of these voices, and you heard a crash at the beginning where this slide had come through, and then everybody suddenly realized they were in the dark, and they were trying to discuss how they could possibly get out. And the play ended on a hopeful note, because somebody saw a ray of light coming through where rescuers were coming to them, and then it cut off. We did it. We read it. This is the kind of thing that radio, sometimes, could do very effectively, taking advantage in what were, in a way, its shortcomings, for drama.

It definitely was a commitment of my father's to keep on trying to push forward the frontiers of radio, in a technical way and in the kind of quality of program that he wanted to see put on. He was never satisfied, I think, with what the station was doing, just as he was never really satisfied with what the newspapers did on any given day. He always had a vision that went beyond what we actually were able to do. And I think this was one of the best qualities that he had, really. He was visionary, in the sense that he always could see where you might be able to go if you put your best effort into it. Nobody ever seems to do that day by day. You just have to keep on trying.

My father wanted me to have some experiences in the different branches of our family enterprises, and he wanted me to go on back then and start working on the newspaper as a police reporter, which is what I did next. And I did try to go through various aspects of newspaper work. But he was happy from the beginning, to see me have some broadcasting experience, and when my son Barry started coming along, I went through the same process with him.[10] He did work first for NBC and CBS and then came back here and worked at WHAS. So it's been a great advantage for him, and I think it was to me, to have some background in broadcasting. His was much more extensive than mine.

I would have to say, frankly, that my emphasis would always have been on newspapers. I was ambitious to write in those days, and I wanted to use journalism to carry out my writing thoughts, but I was always conscious of the fact that the two things went well together. I remember saying one time that I thought newspapers and radio were like Damon and Pythias. They really were allies—almost twins. In those days—this may be hard to realize—radio was considered the archenemy of newspapers. By the early thirties there was a great feeling that radio was going to take all the advertising away from us and that we would be on our knees. This came back in a much later form when television began to get really going. But in those days people were scared to death of radio, and many newspapers refused, for instance, to carry [listings of] radio programs, because they said this was helping the enemy. Well, from the very beginning we carried the programs not only for our station but for others as they came along, and we would have done that anyway, even if we had believed they were our mortal enemies. But I always held the theory that if handled properly, newspapers and radio could be friends and allies for the public good.

There was an intense rivalry between the two staffs but a certain amount of understanding and sympathy at the top, I'd say. Radio began to bloom as a larger and larger factor, I think, in those days in the family enterprises. It began to be profitable for the first time in the thirties, but for a long time it really was not a money-earner at all. Then it began to pick up commercially. The newspapers were my first concern, always, but I always tried to keep my eye on what was happening in radio, if from a distance. I did not interfere at all with management over there.

From Interview of Barry Bingham by Mary D. Bobo, University of Louisville, 25 June 1982

Then in 1931 I moved over first to *The Louisville Times,* and I was in the news operation of the *Times.* I was for a while at police court covering crime news, and I really did enjoy the police beat so much that when it was determined that it was time for me to come on back into the office and do some other kinds of work, I really didn't want to leave it. I thought it was just fascinating. I was just young enough and foolish enough to think the most exciting thing in the world was to ride in a police car and go out to the scene of a murder and try to find out what was going on, and talk to the wonderful characters that existed around the police court in those days.

The old pressroom in the police headquarters was one of the most interesting places I've ever been in. It's where the newspapermen did their work, but they also hung out there. And there were many of them that were not really newspapermen but were friends who used to come and sit in there all the time. It was a raffish kind of place, and some of the people that were there were real characters, and I shall never forget.

Some of the actual working newspapermen were not what you'd now consider polished journalists by a long shot. Some of them were people of very limited education who were very good at ferreting out facts and following the scene of a crime, or whatever that might be, and then telephoning in the facts—the details. They were not expected to write those things. They would call in, and somebody on rewrite, then, would take the story. This is very different from the time when reporters are expected to write their own material. And it made a possibility for a kind of person who was a rough diamond but who had a good instinct for journalism to do that kind of work, and to do it quite successfully.

I really enjoyed thoroughly some of those people who were almost what you would call newspaper hoboes who used to hang out down there. I remember there was one of them who apparently slept in that room. At least we could never find out that he slept anywhere else. And he had a dog that he had down there with him, and the dog was always there. And you could go in at any time of the day or night, and that particular old fellow was always there, and his dog was always there wagging his tail. And this was home to them. Whether he had what we now call a pad somewhere else I never knew. Perhaps he did, but I never saw him outside that place. So that was his home, and he ate and drank newspaper work. That's what he loved. It was fun to get to know somebody who was so deeply soaked in the old tradition of newspaper work, and that's what it was. Newspaper work has changed a good deal since then, but that was still a very early era and was one I'm glad to have had a chance to observe.

There was a very fine reporter, called Pinkney Allen, who used to be down there at that time, and a man named Joe Green, who became

a great friend of mine, who was also on *The Louisville Times*. And
these people taught me a great deal about that side of newspaper work
and how you got started in it. Also, Nate Lord's older brother, Fritz
Lord, was on the staff at that time and was just a born newspaperman
of the old school too.[11] These people all gave me a lot of tips about
how to get going on reporting, and they were practical reporters who
knew how to do the job themselves and didn't seem averse to trying to
help somebody also learn the ropes. So I didn't feel as strange getting
into that atmosphere as I might have felt if I hadn't had these friends
who really were trying to help me on it. And I am assured that they
were trying to help me, because they liked helping young reporters. It
wasn't because they were catering to the boss's son or anything of that
kind. They were real friends.

From Reminiscences of Mary Caperton Bingham, 1984

Looking back on our life there at that period it seems wonderfully se-
rene and happy. I was trying to learn how to keep house, talk to
Cordie, our wonderful cook who worked for us for thirty years, and
school James Henry (the Judge's chauffeur's son) in the art of waiting
on table and cleaning silver. I don't think I had any sort of social conscience. I did write occasional book reviews for Miss [J. Rosamond]
Milner, the editor of *The Courier-Journal* Book Page. But then I discovered I was pregnant, and we both became absorbed in planning for
this delicious and frightening new chapter in our lives.

   In April of 1932 Barry developed scarlet fever. Since this disease
can be extremely dangerous for pregnant women and can cause grave
harm to unborn children, I was banished to the Big House, and Zaddie
(who had had scarlet fever) came to be with Barry. I remember how
dear Lizzie was to me when she brought my breakfast tray, and I, very
large and very forlorn, would be cheered up by her reminiscences of
Barry. "Miss Henrietta," she would recall, "was hard to rouse up,"
and so she would say, "Mr. Barry is up and dressed. Time for breakfast!" Aleen, my stepmother-in-law, was as nice to me as she could be
expected to be in view of having to have a bulbous and unhappy
stepdaughter-in-law foisted upon her—just at the time, too, when she
and the Judge were preparing to follow their usual custom of fleeing
Louisville during the Derby.[12] But I remember the heavy sweet lilac
bloom of that spring, when I could cut armfuls and take them to Barry
and Zaddie and talk through the window.

Worth was born on May 7th during the running of the big race.[13] The Judge, rather frantic, had driven me to the hospital, where Dr. Alice Pickett skillfully managed a breach presentation. Barry was well enough for me to come home after a two-week hospital stay. That was the usual thing in those days.

From Interview of Barry Bingham by Mary D. Bobo, University of Louisville, 25 June 1982

About a year and a half later I went on up to the [*Courier-Journal*'s] Washington bureau, which again was a fascinating experience. I was there at the beginning of the first Roosevelt administration, which was one of the great turning points in modern political history, really. There was a sudden change of atmosphere in American politics, and that change was reflected *dramatically* in Washington in those days. It had been a town of depression, a town of failure, a town where people were really almost hopeless about the political future of this country. The Depression had hit *so* hard. The Hoover administration, whether rightly or wrongly, had been blamed for so much that had gone wrong in the country that it really looked as though Washington was a depression place and would stay that way.

Well, all of a sudden, in came Franklin Delano Roosevelt, and he himself, of course, was a born, lifelong optimist. He had that feeling that life was going to get better. I think he had had it since he was a child. It was part of his temperament, and that was a very fortunate thing for this country, in my view, because we needed a leader who could reinspire people, who could make people believe that life *was* going to get better and that the country *was* going to pull itself back together again, and that's what Franklin Roosevelt did contribute at that time. A good deal of it was psychological. It wasn't just the actions of the first hundred days, which have been so much celebrated. The actions themselves, of course, were very worthwhile and forward-looking. It was more the atmosphere that Roosevelt suddenly created in Washington that made such a difference.

Well, I was there as a young reporter, and I was able to observe this, and it was a fascinating beginning for my exposure to national politics. In those days I used to attend the White House press conferences, and there were never more than, I would say, thirty people there. We gathered around the president's desk in the Oval Office, and each reporter was allowed to ask any question he wanted to ask and would nearly always get a direct response, by name, from the president. And the first time I heard him say, "Well, Barry, I think I can tell you that," and responding to me personally was a great thrill—so different from the press conference these days, which is jammed with people and which is largely designed, I must say, now for television coverage. In those days television coverage, of course, did not exist. It was a very different thing. The press conference these days is a good show and sometimes brings out useful material, but I don't think it's anything like as intimate, and it doesn't give as much chance for a real exchange of ideas as the old press conference did in the days when I first observed it. The president, of course, himself was an artist at dealing with the press. His responses were nearly always quite full and free. Maybe not always entirely frank. His responses were usually couched in interesting terms and nearly always touched with a good deal of humor. He had a wonderful sense of humor and a sort of flair for giving a humorous turn to his responses, so that we came out of those conferences in nearly every instance with some good laughs, with a story which we could then go back and write, and with a feeling that we had been a part of the real operation of the United States government at the top. We were close to it. That is a sense that, I'm afraid, nobody in the press could ever have again, because the press has become so huge, the government has become so huge, the whole scene has become such a tremendous, formalized, structured affair now, that it will never again be quite the kind of intimate thing that it was in those early thirties days.

Now an interesting thing happened on that, and I'm going to jump ahead in time a little bit on that. My son Worth went to our Washington bureau, and by a happy chain of circumstances he happened to be there at the time when Jack Kennedy's administration began, which was, again, another change of atmosphere—not just a change of the guard—a change of atmosphere in Washington. All of a sudden what had been stale and tired and rather disappointing became hopeful again. A young president, a president, again, with a very optimistic turn of mind, a president who had a flair for public relations, which I have to say is what it was, who was able to get along well with the press and who was able to give the feeling, again, that the country was on its way. So by an interesting chance both my son and I had a chance to be there just at the time when there was this dramatic turnover in Washington, and I'm awfully glad that he had a chance to observe that too.

I was [working with Ulric Bell in the Washington bureau].[14] Ulric was a fascinating character, a sort of old-fashioned newspaperman, but very progressive, very liberal in his ideas, very much interested in writing his copy as well as it could be written—a good, broad-scale, liberally trained newspaperman. He was a Sunday painter, and he used to go home on Sundays after working feverishly during the week and paint perfectly delightful still lifes or even portraits, and he had that side to his nature, which I found very attractive. He was a good person to work with. He knew everybody in Washington at that point. He had been there quite a long time, and he was one of the leaders in the Washington scene. He was a member of the Gridiron Club and had had various other connections of that sort, so he was able to introduce me to interesting people from the very beginning and able to put me in touch with good news sources.[15]

I remember one of his first introductions that he took me on was a visit to the office of Senator Norris, who was at that time a leading figure, a liberal Republican in Congress, and a most interesting man.[16] And he took me in and introduced me to Senator Norris, and then to my utter astonishment, he withdrew. I thought he was going to sit there with me and we would talk to the senator together, but he said he had another engagement. He went rushing down the hall. This was obviously just to give me a chance to talk to Senator Norris, so I had to polish up a few questions to ask the senator, and I floundered around a lot, I'm afraid. But nevertheless, again, I had an opportunity to sit at the feet, really, of one of the great figures in Congress at that time and talk to him quite openly. He gave me, I guess, at least forty-five minutes. So this was one of my first experiences of interviewing a political figure, and it was a good one. He was one of the best people I could have gone to. Senator Barkley was also in Washington at that time and was beginning to be one of the very important figures in Congress.[17] And I had a very good chance to meet Senator Barkley and talk with him on several occasions. And I met a good many other leading figures in Washington.

From Reminiscences of Mary Caperton Bingham, 1984

The summer of 1932 the Judge worked for Roosevelt's nomination. He lived on the houseboat *Eala* in New York, and we visited him there.[18] It was during the course of one of those visits that Barry and I had an experience that I believe woke us to the real and terrible condition of people in the depths of the Depression. We were young and carefree and frivolous, and we loved to go to the Stork Club to dance. Men in shabby, once-good clothes stood on street corners selling apples, and when we took a taxi late one night back to the *Eala,* a perfectly nice, sensitive-faced, shabby man stood on the running board and put his hand through the window, saying, "Please give me some money. I'm hungry." Up to that time we had been mild Roosevelt supporters, largely because of the Judge's influence upon our thinking. But then, out of our compelling glimpse into the desperation of ordinary people, people like ourselves, we became confirmed, devoted partisans of Roosevelt and the New Deal reforms.

We went with the Judge to the 1932 Democratic Convention in Chicago and were taken up in the excitement and drama of Roosevelt's appearance there, at dawn on the arm of his son James, exuding his special kind of ebullience and confidence.

We spent Christmas that year with the Judge and Aleen at Pineland Plantation, the Judge's beloved shooting place in Georgia.[19] With a pang, we left the infant Worth at the Big House with his old Irish nurse, Ellen. The Judge would be appointed ambassador to the Court of St. James's, and this was one of the last holidays he would have before going to London. This was a happy time for all of us.

I remember riding out in the warm sun, under intense blue skies, the dogs working, the abrupt stop, the pointing, front paw uplifted, tail straight in the air. The Judge was a superb shot. Toward the end of the hunting season he would shoot only cock birds, an accomplishment that was proof of his keen eyesight and his marksmanship. I remember the lunches we would have in the field—quail broiled in the ashes of the fire.

From Interview of Barry Bingham by William E. Ellis, Eastern Kentucky University, 6 January 1978

If you study progressivism in Kentucky, of course, Colonel [Patrick Henry] Callahan would be one of the people you would want to bring in, and an unusual one, because he was an ardent Roman Catholic progressive. Governor [William] Goebel, of course, would be one of our most celebrated figures as a progressive, and probably lost his life as a result of his progressivism. Some people believe that, at least. Urey Woodson called him the first New Dealer, and that strain existed in Kentucky politics long before Franklin Roosevelt came along.[20]

People didn't label it the New Deal, or even necessarily progressivism, but I think we recognize what we mean by that.

Alben Barkley you would certainly mention. I don't think Barkley would have labeled himself, particularly, a progressive, but he certainly was on the progressive side of Kentucky politics, and of national politics. It's hard to think of many others who were well known enough. Now going much further back, I don't know how you would classify, for instance, Henry Watterson, who was, at one time, a great force in Kentucky politics and was very well known nationally. I don't know whether you would call Watterson a progressive or not. Issues change so much that you don't know how to classify people some ways.

His part in the Tilden election [the disputed election of Rutherford B. Hayes as president in 1876] has more or less labeled him that way [a Bourbon], but on other issues, he tended, I think, to be more progressive than some of his contemporaries. But of course, those issues have changed so much since then. Now, for instance, some people think of liberalism, or progressivism, in terms of race relations, and that just didn't exist in Colonel Watterson's day. Nobody was arguing about it that soon after the Civil War.

I never could see Prohibition as a proper liberal–conservative issue, frankly, because some good progressives, such as Colonel Callahan, were ardent Prohibitionists, and vice versa. I think it's one of those issues that more or less cut across those lines. I'm always a little worried, anyway, about putting people into such firm boxes, you know, as liberals, or progressives, or reactionaries, or conservatives. Very few people fit quite so neatly into those niches. Some of them do, but not very many, I think. Many people seem to me to have certain tendencies in one direction and some in the other, and they balance out somewhere in between.

My father was not a Prohibitionist. He just believed in what is now known as law and order, among other things. He also believed that the whiskey trade controlled politics and other aspects of Kentucky life far too much through its influences in the legislature and so forth, and he felt that Louisville was violating the rules of the state in those days by keeping saloons open at all hours and on Sundays and thought no good could come of it. But he himself was never personally a dry. He always enjoyed having a drink and was not for national Prohibition, because he didn't think it would work. And it didn't.

Let me suggest another thought to you, when you are sort of deciding whether people are progressive or conservative. My father was a great supporter of Woodrow Wilson, who of course was considered in his day a leading progressive in many ways. And my father always, I think, identified himself quite closely with Mr. Wilson's administration. He was a lot younger than Wilson, but he believed in the same principles that Wilson did, and eventually my father was a strong supporter of the League of Nations and was very much disheartened when the league was defeated.

He talked a good deal about the bipartisan combine that he felt had much too much power in Kentucky and which, really, in a sense ruled this state, regardless of which party was in power in Frankfort. And he felt that was a bad influence, and he always was out to break that. His registration was always Democratic, but I guess [he] would be known now as a Reform Democrat. That's a phrase I don't think was used in his day, but in New York they speak so often, you know, of the Reform Democrats, who began by being the anti-Tammany people and antibossism people. I think that's about where my father belonged.[21]

Over the long run, I think there have been more reform elements in the Democratic party in Kentucky than there have been in the Republican party here. The Republican party here, over the years, with certain exceptions, has been a very conservative party.

My father was a great friend of Mr. A. T. Hert, who was a big Republican here and was Republican national committeeman from Kentucky at one time. And I think my father felt Mr. Hert was determined to help break up that bipartisan combine, just as he was, and they for a while were working rather closely together—one from the Democratic side, one from the Republican side—in an effort to clear the decks and let the people have something to say about the way they were governed. Then Mr. Hert died at a rather early age, and that was the end of that era. Now, whether you could really correctly call him a progressive, I'm not sure, but he certainly was on the reform side of things.

**From Letter by Barry Bingham to
Michael A. Powell, 9 January 1984**

Thank you for your letter of December 31. I will try to answer your questions as best I can, as I certainly want to help you on your work concerning my father's career.[22]

My father became involved in the Burley Tobacco Cooperative movement as a result of his observation that the extreme fluctuations in tobacco prices were wreaking intolerable hardship on Kentucky farmers.[23] Tobacco was at that time an even more dominant factor in the economy of the state than it is today. He saw the farmers exposed to recurrent crises, and sought advice wherever he could find it on programs that might offer some relief. This search led him to information on farm cooperative movements which had been undertaken in other areas of the country, involving such crops as wheat. He learned of a New York attorney, Aaron Sapiro, who had been active in the legal process of forming such cooperatives, and offered him a retainer to study the Kentucky tobacco problem.[24] They worked closely together to develop plans. At the same time, my father was consulting with Kentuckians who knew the tobacco business and shared his concerns. All, of course, are long since deceased. Some I remember were James S. Stone of Louisville, Guthrie Coke of Auburn, "Pen" Taylor of Winchester, and Ralph Barker of Carrollton. He traveled widely around the state, usually by train in that era of very bad roads, consulting with groups and individuals who could be helpful to the movement.

My father first met Franklin D. Roosevelt in Washington when he was assistant secretary of the navy in World War I. He saw him occasionally when Roosevelt was governor of New York, and they exchanged ideas, especially in the field of conservation, an interest they shared. A social relationship developed with the Roosevelt family, and my father established a particular bond of friendship with Roosevelt's mother, Sara Delano Roosevelt.

My father certainly foresaw the possibility that FDR would be the Democratic candidate for President in 1932, and did all he could through newspaper contacts and other means to advance that prospect. Again, conservation of natural resources was a theme I am sure they discussed as Roosevelt approached the campaign.[25] Father had a personal friendship with Colonel E. M. House, who was a trusted Roosevelt advisor, especially on foreign policy. Father's ideas on such issues as the League of Nations and on the necessity of close ties with the English-speaking nations were extensively discussed with Colonel House. It has been my assumption that House originated the suggestion of offering my father the Court of St. James's appointment, knowing as House did that Roosevelt was already familiar with his ideas and qualifications. . . .

It seems safe to assume that my father's ownership of a leading regional newspaper which gave support to a number of issues important to Roosevelt would also have been a factor in the President's offer. To the best of my knowledge, Father's contribution to the Roosevelt campaign was in the amount of $25,000. This was not one of the larger donations in the time of unlimited campaign contributions, and would not have been seen as suggesting any major obligation on Mr. Roosevelt's part.

From Interview of Barry Bingham by Terry L. Birdwhistell, University of Kentucky, 8 February 1980

[Note: On 15 May 1933 WHAS changed its affiliation to CBS, terminating a five-year association with NBC that Credo Harris had helped to establish for Judge Bingham.] And that is a switch, I have to say, that I have never regretted. We thought about quality programming, and we thought CBS was more interested in broadcast news than any other network, and it has continued to be, I think, pretty outstanding in its handling of news through the years, although there have been ups and downs in all the networks in that way. But I think we did have a feeling that they were more concerned about broadcast news than any of the other networks, and we've stuck with it.

Well, of course we saw [WAVE] as a rival enterprise.[26] There's no question about that. They began taking away business that we had had previously. However, it was my feeling, and my father had exactly the same feeling, that if we were going to have competition here, and certainly there was going to be competition, we were glad that it was in the hands of responsible people who were going to run a good kind of station, because there were beginning to spring up in radio in those days some real fly-by-night stations, some of which were not much dedicated to the public interest, shall we say. And it might have been quite possible that that type of station would have started here and would have given us a lot of competition, commercially, but would not have done anything for the listeners. So we felt that having two rather good-quality stations in the community was going to be a help.

Chapter 4

Transition

From Interview of Barry Bingham by Mary D. Bobo,
University of Louisville, 25 June 1982

My father had talked to me very fully about whether or not he should accept President Roosevelt's appointment to the Court of St. James's. [1] He realized that he was throwing me into the water—pretty deep water—pretty suddenly. I had not had very much experience at that time, as you can realize, and my experience had been pretty specialized. I realized perfectly well in talking to him that he felt he wanted to take that job. He was well qualified for it, goodness knows. He had been in Great Britain a great deal, had friends there. He also had been not a close friend, but a person who had been close to Roosevelt on a good many public issues, and he wanted, I think, to be a part of the first Roosevelt administration, and he was, I think, either the first or one of the very first appointments of Mr. Roosevelt when he took office. So in talking to my father, I realized that he would like to do that. He would certainly have turned it down if I had said, "I just don't think I can take this on, I think it's too much for me, and I don't see how I can do it, and I just don't believe you'd better consider that." Or if I had even exhibited any serious doubts, I think he would have said, "All right, I'll stay here." I didn't want to do that, so I just thought I'd better take my courage in hand and go ahead and do the best I could, and yet I was only twenty-seven years old, you see. It's kind of early to be taking on a responsibility of that size. But of course, there were good people, experienced people, who had been here for years, and I knew some of them well, particularly in the news department. I didn't know many of them in the other departments of the newspaper. But anyway, that was what fate seemed to have in store for me, and I don't regret that that was done.

My father was, of course, available to some degree for consultation at that time, but it had to be either by letter, which had to go by sea. Of course there was no air mail across the ocean at that time, and letters would take *at least* a week going one way and another week coming back, which meant that communication of that kind was slow. There was telephone communication, and my father always assured me that if there was any moment at which I really needed to get hold of him to ask him about something, I must call him. That was, of course, a help, but it was unsatisfactory in one way. Communications on the overseas telephone then had to be only one way. If both people spoke at the same time, it cut off. One person had to speak, say what he had to say, and then say, "Over." Then the other person could speak and then say, "Over." But this made a two-way conversation rather stiff. It wasn't an exchange in the usual sense of sitting down and talking to somebody about something you were interested in. However, there were few occasions when I had to consult him by overseas telephone. In other cases, I wrote him quite fully, of course, about what was going on. He wrote me fully in return. I tried not to bother him with a lot of details of what was happening here, because I knew he was very busy doing a big, and as yet unfamiliar, job to him. So we went along. We did the best we could. And it was frightening, but I felt it was something I absolutely had to do, and I don't regret for a minute that I did just go ahead and plunge in on it.

Western Union Cablegram from Barry Bingham to Robert Worth Bingham, American Embassy, London, 7 October 1934.

UNALTERABLY OPPOSED TO ENTIRE PLAN[.] REGARD IT UTTERLY IM-POSSIBLE IN VIEW YOUR OFFICIAL POSITION[.] FEEL SO STRONGLY WOULD BE UNABLE CONTINUE PRESENT WORK UNDER THOSE CONDITIONS[.][2]

From Letter by Barry Bingham to Robert Worth Bingham, 8 October 1934

I am more relieved than I can say to have your cablegram in regard to the purchase of the Herald-Post.[3] I am pleased and proud that you accepted my opinion as being of value, but I still want to make it clear to you why I was so violently opposed to the plan as outlined to me by Mannie.[4]

The one fundamental objection that I could not put out of my mind was this: It would not be ethical for you, one of the principal appointees of the Roosevelt administration, to own and operate both a Republican and Democratic newspaper at the same time, while you continued to serve as ambassador. This idea of concealed identity of ownership is what stumped me when the plan was first discussed two years ago, but now I regard the objection as a hundred times magnified because of your official position. To me it would be a breach of loyalty and a breach of moral integrity for you to own the Republican Herald-Post, and I simply cannot see it in any other way.

Mannie persists in regarding this objection of mine as nothing more than a personal moral scruple, but I feel it to be a great deal more than that. You have built up two splendid papers in Kentucky in the past fifteen years, through your energy and ability, and particularly through your complete integrity. It is that integrity that I consider the greatest business asset of the Courier and Times since the papers to all intents and purposes are really you. If it should ever become public knowledge that you had operated a Republican paper, under a concealed form of ownership, at the time when you held one of the highest appointive positions under a Democratic administration, I believe it would be absolutely fatal to the welfare of these newspapers.

To get a little further into the details, I felt as you did that under any circumstances it would be a mistake to put Howard Stodghill on the Herald-Post.[5] The set-up which Mannie contemplated was this: Stodghill as business and circulation manager of the H-P, and Jonas as editor.[6] The editorial policy of the paper would be dictated through Stodghill to Jonas, and would emanate from Mannie himself. And there is the rub. Not having seen Mannie since last winter, it will be hard for you to realize how completely disgruntled and resentful he is over the policies of the Roosevelt Administration. I think I can safely say that there is not one policy of the New Deal which he does not condemn and decry, nor does he show the slightest understanding of the purposes that Mr. Roosevelt is trying to achieve. Stodghill, prejudiced by the Child Labor Amendment and the newsboy situation, feels much the same way.

Picture, then, Mannie as director of the policy of the Herald-Post. It would be temperamentally impossible for him to avoid using such an opportunity to crack at various Roosevelt policies, and of course Jonas would be only too ready to take such a stand. Think of the position that would put you in. Mannie says that the paper could be run as a Republican daily without taking any adverse position with reference to the National Administration. That would mean that with the campaign for the 1936 elections already getting under way, the H-P would have to avoid any discussion of Administration policies or else treat them with sympathy. That would cause immediate resentment on the part of the paper's readers, coupled with suspicion that you were behind the scenes holding down on the editorial policy. Furthermore, Mannie says that the H-P would be openly and militantly Republican in local and state politics. That would mean a policy of attack and opposition to Neville Miller, whom you practically put in office yourself with a promise of your support, and it might also entail opposition to [J.C.W.] Beckham or some other decent Democratic nominee for governor.

The fact that your connection with the H-P might never be discovered is to me beside the point, though I am convinced it would leak out just as it has done in the case of WAVE.[7] Whether anybody else ever knew it or not, your dual capacity as owner of a Republican and Democratic paper would be something that you could never put out of your mind, and I know it would never give you any peace. Being as far away, it would be impossible for you to exert direct control over the policies of the H-P and you would never know from day to day what action it might take that would be mortifying and dangerous to you.

I feel that I ought to tell you a little more about Mannie's attitude, not because of any personal feeling of mine against him, but because his conduct is of such importance to you and the papers. He is unfailingly fair and reasonable with me, but with other people he is growing increasingly autocratic and dictatorial to a really serious degree. He handles the advertisers so roughly that he stirs up a constant ferment of resentment, and he has most of the employees here in fear of his harsh manner. Since you went away and he has had to assume increasing responsibility, his natural ambitions have expanded into a lust for power that is disturbing to me, and I feel that the Herald-Post venture is another indication of this motivating influence. Please don't think I tell you this to upset or agitate you, but only because I think I ought to tell you what I feel about such a vital subject. I am on the pleasantest personal terms with Mannie, but I think his nerves, his inability to relax, and his general poor state of health have contributed to a certain state of mind that I regard as not quite normal. He is under constant strain, often without the slightest necessity, and seems preyed upon by what I suppose are genuine fears about the future of the country under its present leadership.

I don't think any action by you could alter this condition now, but I describe it to you so that you can take it into consideration in making decisions which involve him.

Under the circumstances, I think it would be far better, as I cabled you, for you to take entire responsibility for the Herald-Post decision. I have told Mannie that I opposed the plan on fundamental principles and that I had cabled you to that effect, but I don't think he has taken that consideration very seriously. Of course I understand the risk we run of having some stiff competition in this field from a chain or individual owner with large resources, though I do not see why either Hearst or Scripps-Howard would alter their former decisions about coming into this field. Ritter told Mannie in his first telephone conversation that he felt the Herald-Post was of material value only to us, which seems to indicate little prospect of its sale elsewhere. Even if we run into the stiffest kind of competition, however, I would not be willing to buy immunity at the price of your taking a serious risk of your reputation, and that is what I consider the H-P proposition to be. With the Courier and Times in the splendid position they now occupy, I believe we can win out in any fight and make our competition look pretty sad, even though it costs us some time and money to do it.

I hope you won't be worried over anything I have said in this letter. You will be home in two months, and we can discuss it all then. In the meanwhile I'm sure things will go smoothly as they have been doing in general. Advertising is picking up, and the radio station has an absolutely full schedule for the fall and winter, the best business they have had since WHAS was founded. Everything is going splendidly at home, but we do hate to see Henrietta leave this week. I think she has really had a fine, quiet time here with us, and of course Aunt Sadie has loved being here with her. It would have been grand if I could have come over to see you, but under the circumstances I don't see that there is any necessity for either Mannie or me to make the trip. I hope so much that you will see why I have felt so strongly about this situation, and that you will agree with me on the main principles. I am counting the days until you get home.

From Interview of Barry Bingham by Vincent J. Holt, Jr., University of Louisville, 2 April 1975

I would like to go a little into [my father's] background. He was a native of North Carolina who moved to Louisville only after he had married my mother in 1896. So he was not an old Kentuckian. He was a North Carolinian. But he became very much a part of the Louisville community. He started practicing law here when he first came up to Louisville and continued as a lawyer. He was, at one time, mayor of Louisville for a brief period of time. He was county attorney at another time.[8]

In 1918 he saw an opportunity to do what he considered was a valuable public service by buying *The Courier-Journal* and *The Louisville Times*. These papers were for sale. They had belonged, principally, to the Haldeman family of Louisville and had been well-known newspapers. *The Courier-Journal*, especially, was really a famous paper around the whole country, partly because of the great reputation of Henry Watterson, who was the editor.

My father decided that it would be a good move on his part to acquire these papers and to use them for what he felt would be the welfare of the community and of the state. He was very much interested in politics in Kentucky, but not in the sense of wanting to run for office himself. His interest was that of trying to improve the political atmosphere of this state.

In 1918, when he made this purchase, Kentucky politics were in a pretty bad state, I think. There was an old bipartisan ring that was pretty much operating things in Frankfort, and my father felt that this was not in the best interest of the citizens of this state.[9] So he began using the papers as best he could in that connection. . . .

Then the time came in 1933 when Franklin D. Roosevelt, soon after his election, approached my father and asked him if he would take the position of ambassador to the Court of St. James's. And after considerable reflection, he decided that he would accept. He was one of Mr. Roosevelt's first appointees.

So in March '33 he set sail for England.[10] In those days you didn't fly across the ocean. You went by ship. And I saw him leave with many pangs, I must say, because I thought this was an important job for him to take on, but I was then left as the person who was expected to take prime responsibility for these newspapers. I was then twenty-seven years old and not very dry behind the ears in lots of ways, as I now realize. But nevertheless, it was a responsibility that I had to accept, I felt.

So my father then went over as one of the early Roosevelt appointees. He had been enthusiastic about Franklin Roosevelt's candidacy and had supported him for some years when he was still governor of New York, long before he became a national figure, really.

My father was very interested in some of Roosevelt's ideas in politics and was a great supporter of his thoughts in the conservation field. Roosevelt was an early leader in conservation, and he was interested in farm policy and in many other things that my father thought were very important to this country. So he went over feeling that he could represent the Roosevelt administration, as it started out, wholeheartedly. He did not always agree with all of Mr. Roosevelt's policies during the remainder of his life, but in general, he felt that Roosevelt had done great things for this country.

I remember his telling me that at the time of the bank closings, when this country seemed to be in almost desperate straits, that he thought only Roosevelt himself—and with his personal power and his personal prestige and his charm and his experience—could have pulled this country out of that really serious scrape without much more damage to the fabric of our society. We did come out of it. The country did suffer some from it, but we did get through that very bad time, and my father always felt this was Roosevelt's great contribution, really, to the history of this country.

He stayed there until the end of 1937, when he became seriously ill and came back to be examined at Johns Hopkins Hospital in Baltimore and died there in December 1937. That meant that he was in England for about four and one-half years in this post, and these were very interesting—sometimes stormy—years.

There was a naval conference during the earlier part of his service there that was one of the most important things he was involved in. That was at a time when Britain, France, and America were seeking to hold down the Japanese rebuilding program—particularly their naval rebuilding program—and maintain a balance, really, between the Western allies and Japan and Germany on the other side. That was one of the most crucial things that he was involved in.

There was also an international wheat conference at which he served as a top American delegate. These things were in addition to his regular duties as ambassador there. Being an ambassador is always, I suppose, an important job. It depends a good deal, of course, on what the atmosphere is in the country in which you are working.

He had many friends in England. He enjoyed the life there very much, but it was a time when the British were having great troubles of their own. During his time there, for instance, they had the great question of the ex-Prince of Wales who decided that he was going to renounce the throne for the sake of the woman he loved, as he said. And this created what was really a constitutional crisis in England. There was a great question of whether the monarchy itself would be shaken by this very unusual incident, and my father, of course, as an outsider, was only observing this—but observing it very closely and hearing all the discussion and debate that went on about it. Much of that debate was private, between individuals. It didn't even reach the general public in England until a rather late stage in the crisis, but when it did, it was the great, sensational story of the day.

From Letter by Barry Bingham to Norman L. Johnson, 2 January 1982

My father was in London during the Edward-Wallis crisis, and attended the coronation of his shy, sober younger brother.[11] It happens, however, that I saw more of Edward than Father did, in part because of a generation gap.

The key lay in the fact that Wallis was a distant cousin of my wife's. When she heard that we were over to visit my family in the summer of 1934, she invited us to her flat in Bryanston Square for cocktails. I was somewhat startled when she asked me to bite a lump of sugar in two, and then dropped half of it into the Old Fashioned she handed to the Prince. After that we were invited to some of the parties with which the two of them filled their time. It was interesting to have this close-up of a famous if clandestine romance. We were disturbed, however, by the evidence that the Prince had an unerring instinct for the most frivolous and indeed trashy Americans he could find. He plainly felt more at home with them than with his own countrymen.

He was still at that time at least a semblance of the Prince Charming who had so captivated a whole generation. He had a handsome, sensitive face, though his complexion was going brick-red by that time. We saw clear evidence of his over-drinking, especially when he took repeated helpings of the brandy which was passed after dinner.

Then it happened that we were thrown into their orbit once again in 1949, when I went to Paris to head the Marshall Plan mission to France. The couple, of course long since married, was living in a very grand house in the rue de la Faisanderie. Mary had stayed at home until the children were through their year of school, so for several weeks I was living a bachelor life in Paris. Invitations from the Windsors began to come in. I went to one lively party where an expert piano player was thumping out popular tunes, and I was commanded to demonstrate the Charleston, a holdover from my college days. When Mary arrived, we were invited to dinner. Assuming that it would be a large party, we were surprised to find that we were the only guests. Wallis wanted to steer the conversation to American politics. Edward professed interest, but I was reconfirmed in my opinion that he had a short and shallow attention span. A man brought up as he was, to know the world and accept its responsibilities, could only really talk about his game of golf, which was a compulsory daily ritual. Can you imagine an educated man spending every single afternoon on the golf course?

I relate these details because they contribute to the opinion of Edward I formed over two periods of fairly frequent encounters. I found him a fundamentally frivolous person. I have never held that a man has to be solemn in order to be a serious human being. It was not Edward's cocktail-party existence that made me mistrustful, but his apparent inability to engage in anything but the most superficial aspects of life.

I was forced to conclude that he had been perhaps the unwitting beneficiary of a massive public relations campaign by the press in Britain and America. It was true that on one or two occasions he visited a coal mine in Wales, and was quoted as saying something vaguely sympathetic with the plight of the unemployed. On that flimsy structure was built a reputation for understanding and deep concern for the working man. He became the hero of the London Cockneys. Then, when it finally leaked out that his great romance was bitterly opposed by the royal family and by the British establishment, Edward emerged as the champion of the common man against all the forces of leaden tradition.

In my view, this was an inaccurate reading of his character. I believe he was in panic flight from the responsibilities of the crown, from an early age. The pressure grew worse as he came closer to the throne. He had enjoyed the days when he could travel the world as the glamorous Prince of Wales, but dreaded the thought of virtual imprisonment in Buckingham Palace. As to an interest in social reform, I never saw a hint of it.

I am not implying that he was not captivated by Wallis Simpson. She was a tough baby if ever I saw one, who studied to make herself indispensable to a lonely, haunted man. What I believe was that his dependence on her and his aversion to the crown combined to give him an excuse for his abdication. He could attribute the act to his devotion to "the woman I love," a highly popular motive. What it did was to release him from a bondage he dreaded, without the necessity of saying that he just couldn't take such a load of responsibility.

From Interview of Barry Bingham by Vincent J. Holt, Jr., University of Louisville, 2 April 1975

So my father was there to have witnessed that. He was there when the new king came into power—George VI, who was a very gentle and a very fine man. He and my father became quite good friends at that time. And Britain did weather that constitutional crisis, and the monarchy went on, and the country went on in good shape.

However, just over the horizon loomed very serious war storm clouds. And my father was one of the early ones, I felt, who realized the danger and the really imminent threat of war that he believed was coming on if the Allies did not pull themselves together and present a united front. My father was sometimes attacked by some of the press in this country for being what they called a warmonger and an interventionist at a time when sentiment in America was predominantly isolationist.

He was never an isolationist at any time. He had been a strong supporter of the League of Nations and would, in later time, I know, have been a strong supporter of the United Nations when it came into being. In any case, he used what influence he had to try to convince people that there was a serious threat of danger of war, that Hitler's maneuverings were to be taken seriously and not as something of an erratic or bizarre joke, as some people seemed to think they were. He did subject himself to much criticism in this country by people who believed he was going far beyond the bounds of discretion or tact or diplomacy by saying some of the things he did say. But I think the events did prove that he was absolutely right.

The last few months of his time in England—the fall of 1937—began to be shadowed by his increasing illness. He never knew what it was that was causing his illness. It was never diagnosed, in fact, until an autopsy was performed after he died. It turned out to have been Hodgkin's disease, which is a cancer of the lymph glands, and very little was known about it at that time. It was considered, really, just a hopeless disease. They hardly knew how to treat it beyond giving the patient some aspirin to make him more comfortable. So that was the end of his term there. He resigned while in the Hopkins Hospital one week before he died on December 18, 1937.

He was succeeded by Joseph Kennedy, the father of John Kennedy and Robert Kennedy, of the famous family. Mr. Roosevelt appointed Mr. Kennedy to succeed him, and Joe Kennedy went over there shortly after my father's death and took on that job.

Chapter 5

Taking Charge

From Interview of Barry Bingham by
Terry L. Birdwhistell,
University of Kentucky, 8 February 1980

The 1937 flood—it took a disaster, really, to give us the biggest boost we ever got, I suppose, in national publicity. It happened to be the only time when I came back to play, at all, an active part in WHAS.

I was on the air quite a lot during those days, which I had never done before. They were terribly short on personnel. You see, we were trying to stay on the air twenty-four hours a day. We were the only outlet, really, for Louisville, at the time when the whole downtown area was completely flooded, and all of our communications were cut off. We were able to get out only through telephone lines to Nashville by WSM. So the great job was to try to keep on the air constantly, so as to relay emergency calls, which were coming out all the time. And they ran very short on personnel to handle the microphones, so really, for the first and last time, I spent hours on the air relaying these messages that were coming in about a boat was wanted at a certain place—a place you couldn't believe, because it was what you ordinarily think of as high and dry land—at the corner of Fifth and Breckinridge, let's say, something of that kind, which nobody would have ever imagined as being part of the Ohio River, but it was at that time!

And we wouldn't claim any great credit for that, but the amazing part was that no panic took place in this city. I do think the fact that 'HAS was able to keep on the air during all that time was quite an element in that. Also, no epidemic ever took place—no outbreak of disease. There was great concern about that. People were afraid that as the floodwaters receded, we might find ourselves in an even worse situation, with typhoid fever or many other germ-borne diseases. A great deal of time on the air was devoted to putting on public health experts and people who could tell people what they should do—not just about boiling water, but various other things they ought to do.

They were directed to go and get their typhoid shots, constantly, on the air. This was really dinned into people's ears. And not only did 'HAS do that, but they had airplanes flying over the whole city, and the voice would come from the airplane, which is really quite eerie, saying, "You must take your typhoid shots. You must take your typhoid shots." My poor wife was in the hospital having a baby [Sallie] at this time, and I can't tell you how strange it was. All the lights were cut off in the hospital. They had nothing but lanterns. And here was this strange voice coming from the clouds, "Take your typhoid shots." Well, everybody was frightened. It was a good thing we were. And you know, the amazing part is, there was only one life lost during that flood. People couldn't believe there could be such a record.

One other thing came to our assistance, I think, and this is just a curious psychological factor. There's something about stress that makes people come to life more than they ordinarily do. Adrenaline begins to run. I saw exactly the same thing happen in the air-raid shelters in London during World War II. These people were living night after night underground in very unhealthy conditions—no fresh air, people packed into a small space, people sneezing, coughing, and that sort of thing. No epidemics. They never even had a flu epidemic down there. Well, the same kind of thing, in a shorter period of time, happened in Louisville. People were uncommonly healthy. It is really quite strange what happened. And part of that, I do think, was due to the great effort that was made by, for instance, Hugh Leavell, who was the city health officer at that time, who was on the air constantly telling people what to do.[1] And part of it was this strange psychology that makes people do better when they are under pressure.

I lived downtown, because I had gotten my wife into the hospital by the very hardest, when this baby was coming on. We had two children at home, and I got them out and evacuated them. And so I just lived downtown. I had a room at the Seelbach Hotel, which was the nearest place to the office, and I slept for a few hours a night at the Seelbach. The rest of the time I was in the office all of the time. The one thing I could do most readily, I think, was to work on the radio station, because the newspapers were flooded out. We operated up at Shelbyville and then later at Lexington. There seemed to be no particular point in my going up there to try to get out that four-page paper which we were doing, or help get it out. That was well manned. So I just tried to do what I could here at the radio station. We didn't realize, at the time, by the way, that this was attracting anything like so much national attention as it did attract. But then we began getting amazing offers of help from all over the country. People were coming in here from all over the United States to try to bring in equipment, and food and medicines, and anything they thought would be useful.

From Barry Bingham, "Need Theirs Be a Living Death?" *The Courier-Journal*, 4 April 1937

"Abandon all hope, ye who enter here!"[2] The dread inscription that Dante saw above the gates of the Inferno might truthfully be written on the doors of Kentucky's three hospitals for the insane.

"Abandon all hope!" That is the watchword that rang through my mind as I walked through the wards of these three institutions. And yet, is it necessary to condemn men and women to lingering death in these dilapidated buildings simply because some illness has infected their minds? Are all of them hopelessly insane? Are any of these people curable, if they could receive proper treatment?

Modern medical science answers yes, they can be cured, many of them. Experts now declare that as many as half of the people committed to State institutions could be returned to the outside world as normal human beings if their cases were properly studied and treated, particularly in the early stages.

That thought made me look at these unfortunate men, women and children with a new interest. There are over 6,500 of them in our three institutions. They are our fellow Kentuckians, our wards, whose fate has been placed in our hands. How are they faring under our care?

I went to look at Kentucky's hospitals for the insane as a layman who possessed no special knowledge of psychiatry. I write my impressions here with no pretense of an exhaustive study of the subject, which is vast and complex, but only to give the reactions of one person who has spent a day in each of the three institutions, exploring from basement to garret, and who has since studied expert opinion on how the terrible problem is handled in the most progressive states in the Union. I do not intend any criticism of the men and women who work in Kentucky's insane hospitals under the hopeless handicaps of the present system.

Physically, the State has provided itself with three sprawling, old-fashioned plants for the care of the mentally ill. They are: The Eastern State Hospital at Lexington, the Central State Hospital at Lakeland (near Louisville), and the Western State Hospital at Hopkinsville. The

State also maintains an institution for the feeble-minded at Frankfort, where some 750 pitiful creations, mainly children, are crowded into buildings meant to accommodate a maximum of 500, while another 500 have already been committed to the institution but cannot enter because there is no more room. This institution is designed as a training school for handicapped people, however, and it therefore falls into a different category from the three hospitals, whose purpose is supposed to be treatment and cure. . . .

Nothing brings home the horror of our hospital system like a personal visit, but most Kentuckians avoid the institutions and try not to think of their existence. Friends and relatives of inmates hurry in for occasional visits and hurry out again, sick at heart from the sights they have seen.

The visitor passes down long, narrow rooms, with locked doors or iron bars at either end. Against the wall on either side will be a line of chairs, and in each chair a patient. Some sit huddled up, their heads in their hands, the very picture of despair. Some assume grotesque postures, legs and arms twisted in knots, heads wrenched about at the most painful angles. Some patients stare right through the passerby without seeing him. Others reach out with clutching hands and plead to be taken home. Some scowl with demented fury, their eyes burning like live coals with a wild hatred of all life and all humanity. Some poor little figures scurry away like animals and crouch in corners, eyes peeping out from the shadows with the pitiful, helpless terror of woods creatures caught in a trap. . . .

Such conditions cannot be blamed on the doctors and nurses in charge of our hospitals. They have been compelled to do the best they can with antiquated buildings, overcrowded wards, almost complete lack of equipment, and, worst of all, with such inadequate staffs that the merest custodial care is all that can be granted to the unfortunate patients.

Our State hospitals have been well administered at times, badly administered at times. I saw evidences of kindness in all three institutions. I saw floors that were rotting away kept spotlessly clean, and ancient equipment put to the best use it would give. I saw one hospital farm in particular where efficient management was evident. I saw basements filled with vegetables and berries canned on the grounds. I saw a small number of patients happily engaged in occupational therapy, weaving cloth for shirts, making socks, chairs, and I know that there were many other patients who could have benefited from such work if facilities were provided. I saw two doctors trying to attend to the physical well-being of 2,000 people, who are subject to all the same physical maladies as you or I (the minimum standard is supposed to be one doctor for every 150 patients). I saw attendants who obviously had no training for psychiatric work, but who were trying by gentleness and kindness to quiet the jangled nerves of forty or fifty human beings who had landed behind institutional walls through no fault of their own. I saw exhibitions of bravery on the part of young attendants assigned to night duty, alone, on wards filled with violent patients.

I did not see any evidence of modern facilities for treatment, such as hydrotherapy, which soothes shattered nerves and restores the calm of reason. I did not see anything like adequate facilities for occupational therapy, so valuable in the treatment of nervous disorders. I did not see doctors and attendants with the time to concentrate on individual problems or to do anything, in fact, except to maintain some semblance of order and cleanliness in the institution. Worst of all, I saw little evidence of people getting well and preparing to leave the institution for normal life, as one sees in every hospital for the physically sick. Yet the present national yearly average in mental hospitals is 40 percent recovered and improved, and the best institutions have records as high as 60 percent.

Our institutions are no longer "hospitals" for the treatment and cure of mental ailments. They are big, dingy custodial barns where the mentally ill can herd together with a roof over their heads until they die. Some people get well and leave the places (there are forms of mental illness that clear up in time even without treatment), but it is significant that over 25 percent of the admissions to our institutions are readmissions, if the number found to be not insane at all are excluded.

It will not do to shoulder off all the blame for these conditions on the "political appointees" who man our institutions, hopelessly incompetent as some of these appointees have been. The fault lies with the people of Kentucky, who are allowing their unfortunate wards to rot behind dark walls while they ride by in the sunshine on new highways and talk of "progress" in Kentucky.

From Interview of Barry Bingham by Mary D. Bobo, University of Louisville, 25 June 1982

My father had assured me that he did not feel it necessary for me to follow exactly in the pattern that he had observed, and I tried to make

my son Barry understand *exactly* the same thing. A newspaper is a
growing organism. It cannot stay exactly one way. It cannot remain
static, or it's gonna die. So my father said, "Go ahead and think about
what you want to do with the papers, and don't feel that you are bound
by the things that I have done." . . .

In some way, I began to develop a feeling of what I thought the
papers ought to be, and there were some individuals on the staff at that
time that I thought were not in sympathy with the way I wanted the
newspapers to go. I had to move slowly on this because I did not want
to jump too far beyond what my father had seen as the role of the
newspapers, and yet I felt that I had to move in the direction I believed
was right, and do it deliberately but do it quite definitely. Now that
meant making some changes on the staff. There were some staff members who had worked with my father and who were associates of his
that I thought did not have the vision of the future that I believed we
had to have for these papers.

So it gradually came to the point where these people went on to
other jobs, and I then was desperately eager to bring in somebody of
the type that I thought would give me the forward-looking, firm management that I needed here. My own experience was still too limited
for me to undertake to do the whole thing myself. I realized that. So
I began to look around in the field to find somebody with a very sound
newspaper background, who had what I would generally call liberal
instincts and impulses, who was a kind of person that I could be thoroughly congenial with. And in this sort of close relationship that Mark
Ethridge and I established, there is a kind of chemistry which is very
important. You've got to be able to get along together, not just because
you agree on everything, but because you seem to have a kind of natural affinity, and I think Mark and I did have that. Well, I was determined to find such an individual if such a one existed.

I looked around as widely as I could through newspaper organizations and through contacts in the press to see if I couldn't find the
right person. And I began to hear a lot about Mark Ethridge, who was
at that time with the Richmond newspapers. Fortunately, I had a sister-
in-law living in Richmond at that time who had become a great friend
of Mark Ethridge and his wife, Willie, and I asked her what her impression had been, and she said, "Oh, they're just the most wonderful
people, and you've got to come here and meet them. I'll give a little
dinner party, and you must come, and we'll all get together." So that's
exactly what happened. And that was the first time I had a chance to
meet Mark and his wife, and we kind of took to each other, I think,

from the beginning. So I thought, well, after pondering that very thoroughly, I decided this was the man I wanted. From all I'd heard of him—I'd gotten various reports from various directions about him—and *everything* was so favorable, and then I had this personal contact with him, which was exactly all I could have hoped for it to be.

So I then took it up with my father and said, "This is the man I would like very much to bring into the papers, and I want very much for you to have a chance to meet him so you can make your judgment on that." Well, that was in the summer of 1934 [spring of 1936], and at that time my father was coming home on a leave from his job, and he had the chance then to meet Mark, and his opinion of him was equally as high as mine. So he said, "Let's go ahead and make a proposal to Mr. Ethridge." We got Mark to come here at that point, and my father and I sat down with him, and the proposition was made. Mark accepted, and from then on, Mark was an important part of these papers and of my own life.[3]

From Interview of Barry Bingham by William E. Ellis, Eastern Kentucky University, 8 December 1983

There was a rumor at the time that Mr. Roosevelt had suggested Mark Ethridge to my father. This was the other way around. When my father heard that I was seriously interested in Ethridge, he was seeing the president on some other business and just casually said, "Do you happen to know about a newspaperman in Richmond by the name of Mark Ethridge?" And Roosevelt said, "Oh, I hear fine things about him and think he's a very good newspaperman and the kind who is sympathetic with what we're trying to do." So that confirmed my father's opinion, but the opinion came before the advice from the president.

From Interview of Barry Bingham by Mary D. Bobo, University of Louisville, 25 June 1982

He and I, together, recruited a few people, but in general, there were people who came toward us who wanted to work on these papers, and we were able to recruit, I think, some first-class people of that kind. On the editorial page, which was always a great interest of mine, the editor at that time was Mr. Harrison Robertson, a splendid man, a man who had been very close to Henry Watterson but who was also rather close to Mr. Watterson in age.[4] At the time when I came into responsibility for the paper, he was exactly fifty years older than I was, and this was quite a gap—more than a generation gap. He was such a fine person. I wanted to keep Mr. Robertson on the staff if it were possible to do so, and yet I felt that some of his ideas about editorial matters were just not going to be, in the long run, congenial with mine and that we'd have to make a change. I tried hard to persuade him to retire—he was already well past retirement age—and do a history of the paper. He would have been wonderfully qualified to do it: he had been with *The Courier-Journal* for so many years. But he was one of those people, I suppose, they now call workaholics. He would not stay a day away from the editorial page of the *Courier*. He would not take a vacation. He would not consider taking a year off, which I had urged him to do and try to do the history of the paper. So I decided, really, almost the time had come when I would have to see if I couldn't find some other way of dealing with that problem. But at that point, quite fortuitously, Mr. Robertson suddenly died of a heart attack, so I was then in a position to try to start over again with the editorial page staff. I was able to keep some of the people, but I was able to bring in some other people at that point and form the editorial page in the direction that I thought was necessary.

I always felt that the editorial page was in many ways the heart of the newspaper. I was always interested in the news operation, goodness knows, but I did feel that the editorial page function was especially important and especially vital in a one-newspaper-ownership town, which this became soon after I got back into the newspaper. I think the responsibility of an editorial page editor, or whoever is running the editorial page, is tremendous in a community which has only the one ownership voice. I always felt that it was the obligation of a single ownership of this kind to keep the news as fair and clean as possible but to keep the editorial page vigorous, to express vigorous views as well as you're able to express them, not to be too timid about it, not to try to reflect what many people seem to believe ought to be the way an editorial page should be run, not to try to reflect majority feeling or opinion in the community.

I've had many people say, "Why don't you just gauge the editorial page on what you think people in Louisville or in your readership area want?" Well, I can't see that that would be an honorable thing to do, to begin with, because you're then just trying to be a pale reflection of opinion, rather than somebody who's helping to form opinion in what you think is the right direction. Beyond that, how in the world would you operate an editorial page of that kind? You'd have to have an opinion poll taken once a week, I think, of your readers to find out what it was they really *did* want. You'd get a great variation of opinion among them. But suppose it came out one week that the majority believed in a certain issue, or took a certain position on an issue, and you hastily adapted your editorial policy to conform to that. Two or three weeks later that opinion might change. We've seen these extraordinary shifts in the Gallup Poll, and other opinion polls, as to national politics. Sometimes overnight, almost, ten or fifteen percentage points change on an issue, so I *dread* to think what it would be like if you were trying to run an editorial page on the basis of what majority opinion was at the moment you were writing that editorial. You'd have to rewrite an awful lot of editorials, and in the long run, I think, in trying to satisfy everybody, you would satisfy nobody.

One thing I had to realize early in thinking about developing an editorial page of the kind of vigor that I wanted was that it would never be satisfactory to many of our readers. Thus the old saying You can't please all of the people all of the time. I sometimes have almost thought you can't please *any* of the people *any* of the time! But the fact is that if you're going to have a bold editorial page, you've got to put forth strong opinions on important issues, and you've got to make them as fair as you can. But they *are* opinions. That is what they are. That's what the editorial page is: it's a place where opinion should be found. So in trying to cater to so many different views, I was very much aware of the fact that in the old days there were newspapers to represent almost every point of view. There were at one time seven newspapers in the city of Louisville, when it was less than half the size that it is now. That meant that almost every reader could find a newspaper with an editorial slant—and I do say "slant" in that case—that was similar to his. There were not only Republican papers and Democratic papers, but there were factional papers within the parties, and that made it much easier. When you've got the only game in town, it isn't possible to do that. So I thought the only thing to do was to go ahead and try to express as strong views and as vigorous views and as fair views as we could, knowing that that would create a very serious dissension among many readers.

Now we had two ways of dealing with that dissension. One was to be available at all times for people to come and express their dissatisfaction to us. That is one of the virtues, I believe, of local ownership. It is known by everybody who is the responsible person at a newspaper if it's locally owned. If it's a chain ownership, the person who is at the head is somebody who has been hired for that job. In a town where there is a kind of local ownership, at least people know whom to blame, perhaps to praise once in a while. So the other device we always used was to have a very open "Letters to the Editor" column. People have always found it hard to believe that we really do publish at least part, and usually most, of every letter we receive, unless it is libelous or obscene or something, which, obviously, could not be allowed by the lawyers. We publish things that are so diametrically opposed to our own editorial views that people notice it, but they still, in a funny way, don't quite believe it. They think that somehow or other we're just letting this one through to show that we're on the square. The fact is that we publish many letters that are diametrically opposed to our own views, but I think that's a very healthy thing. I think it's a necessary safety valve in a community such as this.

We also publish, and have published, on the op-ed page, columns which are distinctly different from our own point of view, again giving readers the feeling that they have access to other opinions rather than the ones that we are expressing. I hope that this has been able to give people a little bit more satisfaction in their attitude toward the page, even though they don't agree with a great deal that they read on it. I have some friends who say, "You know, when I pick up your newspaper I really like to read it, but I just skip over the editorial page 'cause I know I'm going to disagree with it." Well, that's all right. That's everybody's privilege. Anybody can read whatever he wants to in a newspaper and can put aside what he doesn't want to read, and that's perfectly satisfactory to me. Of course, I'm always glad if people read the editorial page; I'm glad if they have vigorous responses to it, whether pro or con; and I'm particularly glad if they express those responses and allow us to publish them. I think it's very helpful. It gives us some guidance as to what people are thinking in the community, and though we don't have to be guided by it, necessarily, it's always wise to know that. It's always helpful to know it.

All right. Then you come down to questions of possible disagreements within the editorial page staff itself. Well, to begin with, an editorial page staff is assembled in a very special way. When you're hiring people on a news staff, you would never *think* of considering what their political registration might be or what their political outlook might be. They are hired because they are good newsmen or -women. When you're picking an editorial page staff, I think for your own satisfaction as well as for their comfort, you're going to pick people who are more or less like-minded on the major issues. Otherwise, I think you would have people who were writing editorials on subjects that they did not agree with. This, I think, is a kind of penal servitude that I would not want to see people in. I know newspapers in which this happens. In our newspaper, I thought the best thing in the long run was to have a group of people who were not altogether, of course, similar-minded but who had similar approaches to the main issues of the day.

One of those issues which is of recurrent importance, of course, is the issue of race relations. And I guess that is the one issue on which our papers have taken the hardest beating from many of our critics in the community. They feel that we have been overly soft on that issue, that we have actually given favor to the minority groups, and that we have been unfair to the majority. I don't see it that way, but that has been a strong conviction of mine that we must take the kind of position we've taken on racial issues, particularly on civil rights. That issue never became, in any way, a matter of difference among our editorial writers. I never detected any feeling except that we must go along the lines that we had been pursuing on that. And this went through all the times when the race issue was extremely hot in Louisville—the busing episode and all of that.

As to other issues, there were lively discussions. I used to hold five editorial conferences a week. Every morning, here in this room, we would all sit around. I usually came in with a list of subjects that I had noted out of the papers, not only ours but other papers, that were things that I thought we might discuss because they looked like likely editorial topics. I then welcomed *complete* participation by the other editorial writers, not only questions of whether they disagreed but questions of which would be the most effective way to present that if we were going to have an editorial on it, how should we approach it, what would be the way that you would write this that you think readers would best respond to. And then in other cases there were minor disagreements on matters of tactics, usually, and I always listened to those. In many cases I was influenced by them and would change what the editorial approach was going to be on that particular editorial. In other cases where I thought there was an issue of such importance that really there had to be a final, decisive voice, I had to take the responsibility for that. Now where there was a question of an editorial on which there was not general agreement on a point of any real substance, if that editorial was going to be run, I wrote it myself. I never wanted to ask somebody else to write an editorial with which he didn't thoroughly agree. I think that's unfair and uncomfortable and just not good journalistic practice. So in many cases I found myself responsible for writing an editorial which was on a touchy subject, because they were usually the touchy ones, and trying to do the best I could, in view of the other views that had been expressed, to do a decent job on it. This, I think, is the responsibility of the one who is the owner and who is the one who has the final responsibility for the editorial page policy.

There were other disagreements, which were of a jovial kind. We used to have a lot of fun in the editorial conferences. There was a lot of joking back and forth, and it was not altogether a serious, heavy thing by any means. We had a couple of members of the staff, one, Jim Hutto, on the *Times* staff, who had the most wonderful sense of humor and could *always* get a laugh out of almost any editorial discussion that we had.[5] So we often left this room in gales of laughter, even though we had been having some very serious discussion. We talked freely about these things. There was not a set time for these conferences, so that if there was a lot to be discussed and if people had a lot of ideas they wanted to bring out, we could go on for an hour. We could even go on longer. We had no telephone in the room. I never had a phone in this room because I didn't want us to be interrupted by telephone calls. If somebody had to be called out for an emergency, that would happen, but that happened maybe once a year or something of that kind. But otherwise we were free to sit in here and talk. And some people used to think there was some mystery about having a group of people who were talking about these things, and who were they? Well, my answer to that was "You know who they are because their names are all carried on the masthead." We started that practice. I think we were one of the first newspapers that did that: to publish the names of all the editorial writers on the masthead every day.

Now recurrently, there were demands that the editorials be signed, because it was said the anonymity of the editorial page was an evil, wicked thing and that we were hiding behind somebody. There were even bills introduced in Frankfort to *force* all newspapers to have their editorials signed. Well, that would be utter nonsense and I think certainly would have been thrown out by the courts. But in addition to that, I didn't see any occasion for that. My feeling was that when an editorial appeared on our page, it was *the* voice of the *newspaper,* not of an individual, and that's the way I think it should be. Otherwise, what you would have would be a succession of maybe four or five columns, signed columns, each day by the individuals who are signing them, and that isn't really the same thing. That really is not an editorial voice. That's a lot of opinions being expressed by a group of people, and that would be, perhaps, quite readable, but it wouldn't have the same meaning at all that an editorial page expressing the view of that editorial staff would have.

Now one other thing about that. I did worry a little bit about the anonymity of editorial writing, not that I think there was anything unfair about it. But it bothered me that editorial writers were so cloaked in anonymity that readers very seldom had a chance to get to know them or to recognize what they wrote as their work. So I started something called the Editorial Notebook—we mentioned this a while ago—which was a feature that ran occasionally.[6] We didn't have a regular schedule for it, but each editorial writer was encouraged to write something for that column under his own name on *any* subject he chose and taking any position he chose on it. This, I thought, was a chance to do two things: one, to give editorial writers a chance to ride their hobbies and do things under their own name, which is sometimes very satisfactory to see your name connected with something you've written. It was an opportunity also, I thought, for readers to get to know these editorial writers a little bit better and perhaps when they read an unsigned editorial to think, "That must have been John Ed Pearce's work," or "That must have been Russell Briney's work," or whoever it was. I thought it made the page a little more personal. The impersonality of editorial pages has always worried me a little bit. Well, this was one device. It had some interesting results. We got some attractive little essays written for the Editorial Notebook. We published a collection of them under the title *Leaves from the Editorial Notebook*, in which each writer had several things reproduced.[7] And I think it served a certain purpose.

Not all the editorial writers really wanted to write that way. Some wanted to do it much more than others. Rather noticeably, John Ed Pearce was more interested in writing that kind of thing than any of the other editorial writers. And of course John Ed has developed into a very excellent, now nationally recognized feature writer. And I think a lot of the background for that feature writing really began with his writing for the Editorial Notebook. It's been interesting how that developed. So anyway, he always had a chance to write whenever he wanted to, on whatever subject he pleased, and he began exploiting the kind of thing he's done so well afterward: family reminiscences, light, humorous things, rather philosophical contemplations of autumn and that kind of thing. And he wrote them well from the beginning,

and he's gone on and developed that technique, I think, very effectively in his writing for the *Sunday Magazine*.[8]

From Letter by Barry Bingham, Paris, France, to Mark Ethridge, 26 August 1949

Fundamentally, my feeling goes back to Father's conviction that the
editorial direction of a newspaper has to be concentrated to the utmost
degree, along with the attendant responsibility. You and I think so
much alike on all vital matters of policy that a two-way sharing of this
responsibility is, I think, an added source of strength for the papers
with no danger of division. But I feel positive that the editorial policy
function cannot be split into any more segments, regardless of individual ability, knowledge and judgment. So let's get that point nailed
down at the beginning, in order to avoid future misunderstanding and
friction. . . .

I am less concerned about editorials lagging several days behind
the news, though that is sometimes a definite handicap, than I am in
the lack of thorough research that makes some of our editorials a good
deal less than authoritative. At our worst, we sometimes fall between
two stools on the page—we do not provide quick editorial coverage
hot on the heels of the news, and we fail to achieve the full and
thoughtful treatment that should come with a more leisurely pace. As
I have so often said to our editorial writers, I consider our unusually
large staff, research facilities, and system of full consultation on policy as providing an opportunity for really distinguished editorial coverage. There is no excuse in such an organization for the slapdash,
ill-considered, inaccurate editorials we often see on pages where the
writers work under terrible pressure. At the same time, there is certainly no excuse to use our method as an opportunity for slow, lazy,
uncoordinated work. If our large staff is worth anything, it should be
in the chance it gives us to produce the most thorough and thoughtful
editorial page in America.

I very much agree with the idea of giving assignments to each editorial writer *outside* his usual field of interest. You will remember that
last year I urged the staff members in a memorandum to choose at
least one local field of activity apiece and become really expert in it.
I also urged each writer to have an editorial project on the fire at all
times, the sort of project that required some continuing research, and
which may produce an editorial, a series of editorials, or several

signed pieces for the op ed page. The end of the summer is a stale and unprofitable time. But with the beginning of fall and the end of the vacation season, I think we have a right to ask the editorial writers to attack their jobs with renewed vigor and imagination.

By the way, has Tarleton ever taken his vacation?[9] If not, will you kindly take a stick and beat him out of the building, not to return until *all* his vacation time is expended. I'm not insisting on this for anything but selfish reasons. We must have his full freshness and energy on the page, and we can't get it without his taking a reasonable amount of vacation time.

I like the more frequent use of pictures in the editorial columns, though several times they have looked too low on the page to give the best effect. I know how tricky and incalculable make-up can be, but I think it might be a good idea to get Louis Dey to dummy several pages with the art shifted around from place to place, so as to see how it can be most effectively used.[10] It will not always be possible to run an illustrated editorial in the spot where it would contribute most to the appearance of the page as a whole, but we might as well know what place or places give the best effect, and run the art there whenever possible.

From Interview of Barry Bingham by William E. Ellis, Eastern Kentucky University, 8 December 1983

General Haly had known about Lisle Baker, and had seen him in operation in the bank there in Frankfort, and had thought this was an unusually capable, fine young man and that somehow or other he would fit in with the *Courier-Journal* and *Times.* So eventually he presented that idea to my father and to me, and Mr. Baker came in and was with us until his retirement—all those many years.[11]

I really attribute that quite largely to General Haly's advice in the beginning. I felt it was an unusual quality, that he was always trying to develop young people who would do something in the future that he would be able to live to see himself. He used to come and see my father quite frequently and sit down and talk with him about things, and they had a very confidential relationship. I think they understood each other perfectly, and my father realized that he was a man without ambition: he didn't want anything for himself. He used to live over here at the Brown Hotel, in one room, and had a very simple kind of life, but he kept his eye on everybody that came through that lobby. He knew everything that was going on. He had an amazing kind of network of information about everything that was happening in Kentucky. He enjoyed it so much. It really was his sport—his pastime.

From Reminiscences of Mary Caperton Bingham, 1984

The Judge had a friend and adviser who, in time, became a very important part of our education in Kentucky politics and affairs. This was General Percy Haly, a man unlike any other I have ever met, completely without self-interest, with a passion for the public good, a deep understanding of what motivates men in public life, and a shrewd ability to gauge them. He and the Judge used to have breakfast with us now and then, and I wish we could have recorded their wise and sometimes biting exchanges.

From Interview of Barry Bingham by William E. Ellis, Eastern Kentucky University, 8 December 1983

[Percy Haly] was a remarkable old fellow. I say old, because he was already pretty old by the time I first got to know him. He was a man who was fascinated with politics but never in the world wanted to run for office. He never wanted to have any power of his own, but he was always interested in trying to promote what he considered good politics in Kentucky and particularly in trying to develop young political talent. He had a great eye for that. He would get his eye on some young person coming along: it had to be a young man then, because women had very little authority. When he saw a young man start developing anywhere, he would start taking an interest in that person. He would talk to him and try to put him in touch with people who he thought would be helpful to him. And through this—not on the political line at all, but through this in a different way—we really inherited Lisle Baker.

General Haly came and was downtown during the flood and was trying to help operate things during those very bad days. He caught pneumonia and died. He was a supporter of Neville Miller, who was at that time mayor of Louisville. I think partly because of that, General Haly just wanted so much to see the city administration do everything possible to make matters better during that colossal disaster of the flood of '37. At that time, you know, none of us knew if the town would really recover from it. It looked almost like a knockout blow, because so much of the city was underwater. It looked like it might almost break the spirit of this community. Fortunately, I think it had quite the opposite effect. I think Louisville came back after the flood in rather a remarkable way. Disasters sometimes have that effect, but unfortunately, when you're undergoing them, you don't know that it's going to come out that way.

I know [Haly] brought [Albert B.] Chandler to my father's attention. Now whether or not he actually introduced them to each other physically I don't know, but it could well have been. He was one of the people who was a strong supporter of Happy Chandler when Chandler first came along, because General Haly thought, "Here's a very vigorous, attractive young fellow who's going to go far in politics." During his first administration, I think General Haly was very happy with the way Chandler was handling things. Later on, less so.

From Letter by Barry Bingham to Robert Worth Bingham, 3 October 1935

As I told you on the telephone, the political situation is developing beautifully, and it looks like Chandler is increasing his majority every day.[12] Of course there will be a lot of Republican money in the State to defeat him, but he showed in the primary that he could overcome the handicap of bucking organized money, and it looks like he will be able to do it again in November.

Last week he called me and asked for an interview, just a few days before he made his opening speech at Lawrenceburg. I told him to come on by the office, and we had a talk for nearly two hours. I must say that I was pleased and impressed with everything he said, and particularly with his attitude. He gave the Courier-Journal credit for putting him across, but not in a slavishly flattering way as some of the politicians would have done. He then went on to outline to me the plans he had for the conduct of his office after he gets elected, and it seemed to me that he had an excellent programme with the practical knowledge of Frankfort politics that it will need to put it over. I had planned to question him about various points of policy, but he anticipated me in every instance by telling me exactly what he proposed to do and how he wanted to accomplish it. For instance, he says he is determined to secure state-wide registration, a reorganization of the state government on the lines laid down by the Efficiency

Commission, an entire revisal of our tax system in accordance with recommendations to be made by a committee headed by Governor Beckham, an honest racing commission, a reform of our state institutions with complete rebuilding of the penitentiary at some new site where there will be room for the prisoners to work out of doors and under humane conditions, a reorganization of the Road Department with an engineering expert in charge, and a number of other important changes. [13]

He impressed me as really meaning to do these things, and not as just holding them out as bait for support in the campaign. He went on to say that he expected to have the advice of three people in the formation of all his policies, and that he hoped to act in all cases on the unanimous recommendation of these three, who are Beckham, Dan Talbott, and General Haly. He has a most ingratiating way of presenting his case, and I can see why he has been such a success as a stump speaker. Howard Henderson says that never in his experience has he seen such a campaigner. [14] He is not only tireless, but he works his audiences up to such a point of enthusiasm that they hang around for hours after his speech is over just to have the opportunity to shake hands with him. . . .

I may be more enthusiastic about Happy after talking to him than I will be a couple of months after he gets into office, and of course he may still be too easily led, but I do believe we have a chance of decent government through him and that he will try his best to make a good Governor. As long as he remains under the influence of Beckham and the General, we surely have nothing to fear, and it will be difficult for the other crowd to win him away after these two have shown him how to win and have put him across against such odds. He may be too much imbued with the Frankfort political spirit, but it seems to me that his knowledge of the State Government and the men who go to make it up will stand him in good stead when he is trying to do his job.

From Interview of Barry Bingham by Walter L. Hixson, University of Kentucky, 10 March 1981

I was at that time [1938] publisher of the newspapers, and our editorial page had been pretty vigorously in support of Roosevelt in most of his policies, particularly during the early part of his administration, which this still was. [15] My father was Roosevelt's first diplomatic appointment and had been a friend of his, so I naturally had a good deal of interest in it.

My interest in seeing how the campaign train worked out was great. I always enjoyed riding, I must say, on the old-time campaign trains, because you could talk to all of the other newspaper people who were going along and get their impressions. There was quite a load on there, and they traveled with the president—not in huge numbers as they do now, but there were plenty of them there. Talking to the Washington correspondents is always kind of rewarding. You get to hear a lot of things, as well as seeing it firsthand—how the stars behaved in public. Because although they were making set speeches that they had made many times before and would make again, there was always a chance that there would be something different that time or that some intervention from the crowd might make a difference.

I was [sitting] pretty close [to the president. He was] very upbeat, the way he so often was. I think the man, who had, as we so well know, a very severe physical handicap, enjoyed, tremendously, being able to get out of the White House and meet a lot of people and see a lot of people. He responded to crowds more enthusiastically than any man I have ever seen. They just seemed to renew his spirit. The minute he would get out and see a big crowd in front of him and start talking to them, you could just see his adrenaline flow. It was interesting.

I heard the speech [in Covington] at firsthand. I cannot say that I personally saw [the car incident]. I heard it recounted by others who said they did see it, but I was not really a witness to that particular moment. It's become a part of the mythology of Kentucky politics, I think.[16] Whether it did happen or not, most people think it did. We'll never know. It's just a small item, but it was a kind of indication of what people thought Chandler was doing—that he was just pushing right in front there, getting as close to Roosevelt as he possibly could. You see, he had a difficult problem there to try to make it appear that he was closer to Roosevelt than Barkley was, and Barkley was in a better position, perhaps, to capitalize on the president's popularity than Chandler was. So he had to overcome that handicap, and I must say, Happy went at it hammer and tongs.

We did [endorse Barkley for U.S. senator]. Of course, I was at that time running the editorial policies of the newspaper. I thought we had a pretty obvious choice. [Chandler's] first term as governor was a good term. No doubt about that. But we were strongly in support of the main outlines of the Roosevelt administration, and it seemed to us that Barkley more clearly represented what we

were interested in nationally than Chandler did and was more experienced in the national scene than Chandler, who really did not have
national exposure at that time.

We were New Deal supporters in the main, and Barkley seemed
to be a pretty effective symbol of the New Deal. The editorial decision was not made, really, against Chandler. It was for Barkley. We
thought Barkley had a better grip on the issues that we thought were
important. But we were not doing this because we were dissatisfied
with Chandler's record as governor. I do think his first term was a
good one.

It seemed unwise at that particular point [for Chandler to enter
that race], but I think he just wanted to move ahead. You'd think he
could have waited a little longer. He was still a young man at that
time. But he just wanted to keep moving, and I think he may have
thought somehow or other he could overcome Barkley, who was a
slower-moving candidate. [Barkley] didn't have quite as glamorous an
approach to the public as Happy did.

[Chandler] used what has been in other races sometimes an effective issue—that [Barkley] had sort of forgotten Kentucky and was so
interested only in the national scene. Sometimes that works. It didn't
work in this case. Barkley had such a strong Kentucky flavor to him,
with all of his wonderful old stories. That was an earlier day, and he
did talk at great length. Sometimes we'd think he had come to the end
of the speech, and he'd just get cranked up and go right on. And in the
days before television there was no reason for politicians not to do
that. And particularly in small county-seat rallies, this was the big
form of entertainment—to go to a political rally and hear somebody
speak. He would talk for two hours or two hours and a half, and people
just seemed to love it. We had two remarkable entertainers, really, in
that race.

[It] really is untrue [that my father encouraged Chandler to make
that race].[17] It isn't true. Now maybe Happy misunderstood that,
somehow or other. It just couldn't have been. In the first place, my
father was out of the state. He was in England during those years.
He did come back very briefly two or three times, but he wouldn't
have been in a position to make any such declaration to Happy,
and he was a pretty strong supporter of Alben Barkley and, certainly,
of Roosevelt. So it would have been most unlikely that he would
have ever made such a declaration, even if he had felt that way. I'm
quite certain that he did not feel that way. I don't think Happy has
purposely misrepresented that case, but somehow or other, I think

he had a misunderstanding there and felt that he had some comment from my father that would have indicated that, but it just couldn't have been.

My father knew perfectly well what the editorial policies were that I was pursuing and was well aware of the endorsement of Barkley that we made and certainly did not indicate that he wanted to defeat Barkley. I had talked it over with my father. There was a lot of talk about it for a long while that this was going to be a confrontation between these two big Kentucky politicians. And some people believed that Happy would make the race. Some didn't. But it did get discussed a good deal. If I'm not mistaken, Howard Henderson, who was then our Frankfort correspondent, had speculated on this in some of his columns. I think there were people who understood what our position was in this race and were not puzzled by it, to say the least. A lot of reporters from other parts of the country came in here to cover the race. There was an unusual amount of coverage. It was seen as one of the most interesting races of that year.

I understood [Chandler] told people at one time that he was born with a caul over his head and that that meant he was a child of destiny. So for that reason, you can see that he thought it was just time for him to move on up. He didn't want to waste any more time on it.

I don't know how much direct encouragement he had [from southern conservatives]. I think Chandler was pretty aware of the fact that there were some Democrats that were getting very restless with the more liberal aspects of the New Deal and that they might be glad to see it go into reverse. There was a strong feeling among more conservative people in this country to that effect. This included some of the Republicans, who had been in support of Roosevelt at the beginning of his term, because they were so desperate and thought we needed a strong president to save the economy of the country. Some of them, who had been ardent, lifelong Republicans, were supporting him then. Later on they sort of wanted to get away from that and were beginning to move gradually away from Roosevelt. And I think by 1938 there was a good deal of feeling that they better move in a different direction.

I think [Roosevelt] had a great deal of support here, and not entirely because of the WPA. That was made such an issue—that all these WPA workers came in here and helped to tilt the election in Barkley's favor. But there was just general support. Now we didn't, in those days, use the kind of Gallup polling that people do nowadays, so there is no evidence that his popularity would show on a Gallup index.

I think there were no holds barred, on either side. Now in those days there wasn't a tremendous influx of money into these campaigns, because we just weren't doing it that way then. Nowadays there would probably have been a huge fund-raising effort on both sides, but that didn't, thank goodness, exist then. I think we've gone much too far in that direction in modern times. But all the resources that both sides had were brought to play without anything being overlooked. I think [the outcome of the election] was pretty much preordained by the mood of the Kentucky people at that point and the hold that Barkley still had on people in this state.

Did you talk to Chandler about the famous poison pitcher episode?[18] Did he have anything to say about that? If you put it into a TV script, you would say, "Oh, that just couldn't be"—too wild. There was, of course, just a great deal of laughing about it. It just seemed like a last desperate ploy of a candidate who thought he was going to lose and he had to find some way to get out. It's very hard to know, because Happy admitted himself that he had been having some sort of stomach disorders, digestive troubles. I remember that he did make those statements. Well, I'm sure it was reported in the paper and at that time was not denied at all. Now later on he may have decided that it wasn't so. But Happy was always pretty great at saying he was misquoted if something didn't come out exactly the way he would have liked for it to. And I think it was quite possible that Chandler had been having some troubles of that sort, although he had always been considered the iron man of the campaign trail. Then he ended up having some troubles, and Barkley went right through. But I would say that both of them were about as rugged as any campaigners I have ever encountered during my life.

Barry Bingham, on leave from the navy, with sons Barry, Jr. (*left*), and Worth, 30 May 1941. Courtesy of *The Courier-Journal*.

Lieutenant Commander Barry Bingham is congratulated by Admiral Harold Stark on being awarded the Bronze Star Medal in September 1944.

Sixth and Broadway, headquarters of *The Courier-Journal,* 1948. Caufield and Shook Collection, neg. 234296, University of Louisville Photographic Archives.

An editorial conference, 6 August 1948. *Left to right:* Barry Bingham; George Burt, editorial writer for *The Louisville Times;* Vance Armentrout, editorial writer for *The Courier-Journal;* Robert York, Pulitzer Prize-winning cartoonist for the *Times;* executive Lisle Baker; publisher Mark Ethridge; Grover Page, *The Courier-Journal*'s cartoonist; A. Brown Ransdell, Indiana correspondent; Tom Wallace, editor of the *Times*'s editorial page; John Ed Pearce and Tarleton Collier, both editorial writers for *The Courier-Journal;* and (*standing*) Neil Dalton, managing editor of *The Courier-Journal.* Courtesy of *The Courier-Journal.*

Christmas dinner in Paris, 1949, during Barry Bingham's tenure as head of the Economic Cooperation Administration for France. *Clockwise from left:* Mary, Jonathan, Worth, Sallie, Barry, Sr., Barry, Jr., and Eleanor.

Barry Bingham receives a flower from a worker at the inauguration of the Passy hydroelectric plant in the French Alps, 4 February 1950.

Above: Barry and Mary Bingham say good-bye to Adlai Stevenson at Louisville's Standiford Field, 27 September 1952, following his campaign appearance. Below: Lisle Baker, Mark Ethridge, and Barry Bingham, May 1959. Both courtesy of *The Courier-Journal.*

Above: Barry Bingham in his office, 12 February 1969. Courtesy of *The Courier-Journal.*

Left: Barry, Sr., talking with Barry, Jr., 28 May 1971, as the thirty-seven-year-old son takes over as editor and publisher. Photo by James N. Keen, courtesy of *The Courier-Journal.*

Above: Barry Bingham conversing with Queen Elizabeth II at an English-Speaking Union luncheon in New York, 9 July 1976. Below: Mary and Barry Bingham at the dedication of the Bingham Humanities Building at the University of Louisville, 5 November 1979.

Barry Bingham as Prospero in Shakespeare's *The Tempest,* pointing to fellow readers Leon Driskell and George McWhorter, 14 November 1986.

Mary and Barry Bingham at the Geranium Ball, Louisville, 1986. Photo by Charles Traub.

Editorial cartoonist Hugh Haynie's tribute to Barry Bingham in *The Courier-Journal,* 16 August 1988. Courtesy of *The Courier-Journal.*

Chapter 6

World War II

From Interview of Barry Bingham by Mary D. Bobo, University of Louisville, 5 July 1982

Well, you're taking me back a long time, but to an era that was pretty important in my life, I think, going back to 1941. I had felt for quite a while that America was going to get into World War II, and I had felt also that America ought to get into World War II, as I began to learn more and more about what had been happening in Europe.[1] We began to get these disclosures about what the Germans were doing— what the Nazis were doing—and the stories of the concentration camps and things of that kind were beginning to leak out. And it seemed to me that it was essential that the United States should line up on the side of the Allies against this terrible tyranny that Hitler had organized in Germany, appealing to all the worst elements of human nature there. So in view of that feeling that I had, I believed that I myself ought to go ahead and volunteer for military service of some form. I was not awfully young to be doing that kind of thing, even then, but it seemed to me that I'd better go ahead and get in as early as I could and see what I could do to help. I did volunteer for naval service, and I was enrolled in the navy in April 1941. My commission dated from then.

Barry Bingham, "Shall We Go to War?" in *Defense for America*, edited by William Allen White

I am well within the age for active service, if this country should soon become involved in war.[2] I am 34 years old. I have a wife and three children, and I have today a deeply satisfying personal life.

These things I tell at the beginning, because they are bound to affect my thinking on the problem of American aid to the Allies. I can imagine few people in our country who could face this question with complete objectivity, and I certainly make no pretense to any such Jovian rationality. I have a vital personal stake in maintaining the kind of peaceful world in which I have grown up and lived a happy life. I want my children to live in such a world. Those are fundamentals that lie for me beneath the surface of a world conflict of ideologies.

I am not insensible to the emotional appeal of the Allied cause, but it is not that appeal that speaks clearly to me today. In England I have felt that atavistic pull that must affect all Americans of British heritage when they see all about them the monuments of their own racial history. I have walked the solitary English countryside and the lovingly tended fields of France, and they have given me their sense of ancient beauty and security. I have known friendship and kindness in those countries, but today I can feel only sadness for the destruction of a village I have known in Dorset or a line of hills in Picardy. It is the hills of Kentucky and the villages of Maine and California that concern me now.

With my physical body, I do not want to fight on any battlefield, yet I do not believe I have more of physical cowardice than the average man. With my mind, I know that there are things I would fight and die for, and I know too that I could call on some immemorial strain of toughness and endurance that lies in the human race to carry me physically through such trials as I might have to face.

Let's dismiss at once any discussion of sending American troops to Europe. That is simply not a practical consideration at the moment, for we have no troops ready for the purpose even if we had the will to send them. Why butt our heads against the stone wall of an academic argument till we can see nothing but stars? We need to keep our vision clear for the immediate and practical problem before us.

That problem is this: should we try to save the Allies with every possible assistance short of war? I believe we should, and I believe we must on grounds of enlightened self-interest.

My decision does not rest on a conviction that we Americans are divinely appointed to preserve democracy in foreign lands. I regard it as our duty to save ourselves, but it cannot be enough to save merely our hides. We must make our fight to protect our heritage of freedom. Who among us would value what the Declaration of Independence calls our "inalienable right" to life if it were not accompanied by the right to liberty? Under a world order dominated by Adolf Hitler, the best we could hope for in America would be to substitute a desperate pursuit of security in place of the pursuit of happiness.

Some Americans of my age and younger have concluded that nothing is worth their fighting for. I am convinced this is a very small group. Such tragic nihilism is old age in youth, death in the midst of life. A far greater group of younger Americans believe that nothing is worth their fighting for except the protection of our own country. With them I heartily agree. I can only quarrel with some of them on their definition of protection. American safety may be far more easily protected along a heavily fortified battle line in France than along our own unguarded Mexican border.

Our thinking is much confused today by conflicting opinions on what Hitler might do to us if he conquers Western Europe. The possibility of physical invasion of the United States cannot be anything more than conjecture, based on the whim of a man whose mind does not follow rational patterns. There seems to be general agreement in the United States, however, that we must arm ourselves as thoroughly and as swiftly as possible against any potential threat of invasion. To that policy we are already committed, but we have not faced the full implications of an isolated position in the world.

When we move along to consider the economic consequences of a totalitarian victory, we enter a realm that can be charted with some degree of precision. We know the nature of Hitler's economic theories from his written and spoken statements. It is not difficult to bring the position of the United States into focus in the kind of economic world that the victorious dictators would establish.

In the first place, it is entirely inconceivable that the magnified German state and its vassals would buy anything from the United States that could be obtained from within their own economic orbit, or would permit conquered countries to buy from us. It would be only logical for Germany and Italy to appropriate our South American markets, while Japan, greatly strengthened by a totalitarian victory in Europe, would virtually cut us off from Asia. We would inevitably face the loss of most of our foreign trade. All right, perhaps we could let it go since it constitutes but 9 percent of our total business. We must admit, however, that that 9 percent makes the difference between a relatively high standard of living in this country and a standard roughly equal to that of the Balkan nations.

Furthermore, the 9 percent of our trade that flows into foreign channels is not equally distributed among industries or among sections of our country. I live in an agricultural state and an agricultural region.

I know that an average of 37 percent of our tobacco has been sold in foreign markets. Tobacco is Kentucky's big cash crop. I know furthermore that 38 percent of American cotton, which is unhappily the staff of life in the South, has been sold abroad.

Pull these markets out from under the South, and you have several hundred thousand farmers left without visible means of support. Subsistence farming would be their only salvation, but most of them lack all knowledge of how to support themselves by such a method. In addition, a great proportion of them live on worn-out farms that could only furnish a subsistence standard by the most intelligent program of cultivation.

A gigantic effort to re-educate the American farm population would seem to furnish the only answer if we must live in isolation. The sole alternative would be starvation for those who could not readily readjust, and America would not accept that solution. The program of education, of course, would have to be accompanied by a system of planned economy for agriculture that could allow for no deviation from a rigid pattern. There could be no talk of letting the farmers vote on quota restrictions. Such democratic methods would have to be discarded in a situation that required careless, wasteful, extravagant America to conserve her natural resources for the first time in her history.

Along with a strict regimentation of our agricultural life would have to come a corresponding straitjacket for our industrial economy. Free competition would be forced to bow to the necessity for obtaining maximum efficiency from our industrial production.

Our program would have to be one of total defense, to guard against the threat of total war. We would have to provide ourselves with a two-ocean navy and a huge modern mechanized army, since we could count on no ally to co-operate with us on either wing of defense. At the same time, the government would have to make itself financially responsible for millions of citizens stranded by the sudden reversal in our economic system. Taxation would reach new heights hitherto undreamed of in the United States.

American prestige would undergo a swift decline in a world dominated by Hitler and Mussolini. That might be harder for our people to bear than any amount of financial sacrifice. We have accustomed ourselves to the luxury of passing moral judgments on the rest of the world, but we would suddenly be confronted by a totalitarian world that had passed a moral judgment on us and found us, as a "decadent democracy," hopelessly wanting.

If the British lose the war and are deprived of their navy, the United States will have to make up its mind to abandon the Monroe Doctrine, much as that will wound our national pride. It will be a difficult enough problem under such circumstances for us to defend our own territorial borders. Obviously it would be madness for us to set out alone to defend two whole continents.

Some of the changes forced upon us by a totalitarian triumph might have some social justification, curiously enough, if they could only be carried out gradually and without compulsion. The American farmer needs to be won away from slavery to the cash crop, but none of us ever thought to see the job done by harsh regimentation. A more even distribution of wealth is desired by many of us who view ourselves as liberals, but money poured into armaments impoverishes the rich without benefiting the poor. By contrast, the expenditure of millions by the WPA for the building of schools, roads, bridges and other constructive projects would cease to seem an extravagance to many of our people.

The United States as an isolated nation would have to give up many of its luxuries. It would be compelled to lower its standard of living, and by that I do not mean that the man with two Rolls-Royces would be obliged to get along with one. Every American citizen from the richest to the poorest would have to pay dearly for the cost of our defense, and no man could be certain that, after the billions were spent, we might not find that we have been unable to buy protection with all our wealth.

There are luxuries still dearer to the hearts of Americans, however, that would have to be sacrificed. We have regarded our constitutional liberties, our free speech, our free press, our free assemblage, as matters of course, but in reality they are the greatest luxuries ever enjoyed by civilized men. Under a program of rigorous national defense, these liberties would have to be sharply curtailed, lest they breed obstruction and disunion. We have already seen the hysteria that can be produced by the mere phrase "fifth column."

I have said that I share with many other younger Americans the conviction that only the preservation of our country as a democratic nation is worth the sacrifice of American lives. All of us who grew up after the World War have been inoculated against propaganda. We are wary of slogans and suspicious of high-sounding phrases. A speaker who abjured us to fight "a war to save democracy" would risk a volley of boos from most audiences of young Americans. The only war we would willingly fight would be a war to save America, and we might be fortunate enough, God willing. to win that war without laying down our lives on the battlefield, if Britain and France can get enough help from us to escape destruction.

That would be the easiest way out of America's present dilemma, and a way that we could take with honor. Even such a course, however, would entail some genuine sacrifice on our part, the expenditure of very large sums of money, and the use of wisdom and self-restraint in the difficult period of readjustment that must follow any conclusion of the war. These problems, however, are as nothing compared to the problem of leading our country along the narrow ledge of isolation on the verge of a totalitarian world. It would not be easy for us to see money withheld from schools to be spent for ships, to see revenues for hospitals cut to build guns, to see military security placed above social security in the scale of national importance.

I have the strongest faith in the American people, and I believe that if they were sufficiently aroused they would stand equal to any trial that fate might devise. I cannot but wonder, however, whether we could weld this sprawling democratic nation into a unified whole in time to face the full test of isolation. I am not thinking of traitors in the conventional sense of the word when I envision the possibility of Americans who would give under the strain of such a new order of life, people who might be willing to compromise with Nazism by a sacrifice of our liberties to save our skins, or who might choose to take the desperate gamble of Communism in the hope that any change might save us from going down in the ruins of democracy.

I have spoken of the losses in a material sense that face the United States if the Allies meet defeat, but it is the spiritual losses that may come to us that I fear even more. We could surrender ourselves to the Nazi ideology tomorrow and save ourselves from the physical threat of destruction. Perhaps we could even work out some compromise with the dictators that would leave us some shreds of material well-being. But what the dictators would not and could not leave us is our democracy.

We have been fortunate on these shores, more fortunate than any nation in history. God has granted the American people a supreme opportunity to try a new way of life that pledges every man justice and equality. We have never employed this great gift with half the strength and devotion of which we are capable, but we cherish it as the heart of the American tradition.

Whatever may be the moral issues of the present war, we know we stand no chance of losing our democracy if France and Britain win, and we know that the abolition of democracy is the sworn intent of Germany and Italy. For myself, for my children and for my country I pray that American help may yet make possible an Allied victory.

From Interview of Barry Bingham by Mary D. Bobo, University of Louisville, 5 July 1982

In May 1941 I was ordered to Great Lakes, a naval training station there up near Chicago. So I went on up there, not knowing, of course, how long I might be away, but I felt that this was something I should do and should prepare myself for as best I could. So off I went to Great Lakes. Before I left, as you can well understand, I had talked this thing over pretty thoroughly with my principal associates in the papers, primarily with Mark Ethridge and Lisle Baker, explaining to them that I felt it necessary for me to go ahead and take this step and that this meant I was going to have to throw a lot more responsibility on them during my absence, the absence being for a completely undetermined length of time. I didn't realize then, I must say, that I'd be gone nearly four and a half years, but I knew it wasn't going to be a short thing. So off I went to Great Lakes and found myself up there at this naval training station. I was given a commission as a lieutenant, junior grade, and I started in, working at this station there doing public relations duty, because that's what they immediately assigned me to, knowing that I'd been in newspaper work for many years. And I stayed there for about three months, and then I was transferred to the public relations office of the U.S. Navy in Washington and moved on down there. By that time it looked as though I might be there for a while, so I moved my wife and family there, and we got a house out in Georgetown and settled ourselves in for what appeared to be maybe a pretty good stay in the capital.

We were not then wearing uniforms when we were off duty, because the United States was still not in the war; and when we went out in the city of Washington, I never wore a naval uniform because we were told not to do that. They didn't want it to appear that Washington was becoming an armed camp with a lot of people in uniform there, when we still were not in the war. Of course, that all ended in December with the attack on Pearl Harbor.

Of course, everybody remembers where he was, I guess, on Pearl Harbor Day. My wife's sister had gotten married in Richmond the day before, and we were down there for that event and were going to drive back to Washington that day. And we were having a family lunch party at the Commonwealth Club in Richmond, and the head-waiter, who was a very, very courtly gentleman, came into the room and said: "Ladies and gentlemen, I must inform you that the Japanese have attacked the American fleet at Pearl Harbor." Well, of course, this was almost unbelievable, but we then realized that it was true. We immediately began listening to radios and found repeated reports coming in—each one, it seemed, worse than the last one—about the damage that had been inflicted, and horrible confusion at Pearl Harbor, and nobody knowing exactly how this had happened or what it might be followed by. Nobody knew whether this was going to lead quickly to a Japanese invasion. In any case, that was, of course, the breaking point. I got back to Washington just as quickly as I could and reported in to the navy department that evening. This was a Sunday. And from then on I was regularly in uniform and a part of the operation there. Not long after that in early 1942—January '42—it was decided that I should go over to England on a mission concerned with civilian defense. They wanted to get as much information as possible about the British system of civilian defense, which had already been very well organized and was operating with considerable efficiency. And American authorities thought we needed a lot of information about exactly how they had done that job. Now civilian defense there, of course, was under great pressure because London had already been under enemy attack. They were digging people out of the ruins of buildings. They were rescuing people under the most dreadful circumstances. Many hundreds of thousands of people were spending the night in underground shelters and that sort of thing.

I went over there to take a look at it and to send back some reports, and I stayed there from January until about early April and sent back a number of reports on what I was able to observe. I was made an honorary member of a shelter team at one point, and I used to go down to that same shelter quite often and sit around and talk to these people. Some of them, of course, had wonderful personal stories to tell, but at the same time I was trying to learn all I could about the techniques they were following, and I observed some amazing actions on the part of these people. There's just recently been a series on television called "Danger UXB," about that era in London when unexploded bombs landed. And they knew where they were, but they had to cordon off that whole part of London so as to keep people from going in there until the demolition experts could come in and defuse them. I saw some of those activities myself, and they were thrilling, in a way, because you knew the danger these people were running in doing it, in any case.

I was there until early April of 1942, and then I came back to Washington, back in the navy department, and stayed there until August of that year, when for the second time my superiors decided that I should be sent over to England, this time on a regular naval mission, to be attached to the naval headquarters in Grosvenor Square.

From Letter by Barry Bingham to Mark Ethridge, 22 March 1943

I was delighted to get your letter of February 16, which arrived this week. Mails have been slow, but I think we ought to start getting a faster service within the next few weeks. As always after hearing from you, I suddenly felt much closer to home and much more in touch with the things that are happening in Louisville.

I have been thinking pretty constantly about the governorship, and I certainly subscribe to your analysis, as given to [Governor] Keen [Johnson], of the importance of the race in the national sense. Kentucky has swung away from the Democratic party in other critical periods, and it looks now as if we were in for just that kind of political storm. It would be a real service to the administration if we could produce a candidate so strong that the evident trend would be reversed, and we all know that just that kind of thing can happen if the right man runs for office, with the full publicity that we can help him to get.

The possibility of Wilson [Wyatt]'s running, of course, appeals to me more than anything I can think of. I believe he would be doing a very great service not only to the state but to the President and the people who think as we do in national affairs, if he would take on this task right now. The effects on Kentucky life for many years to come would be most salutary, and it would seem inevitable that Wilson would be in a position after his term in Frankfort to move on to Washington, as Barkley cannot live forever. I can fully appreciate all the reasons that make Wilson hesitate, but I hope to hell the trick will be turned and that he will come out. A campaign against such a stuffed owl as [Simeon] Willis would be a grand thing to watch. I am glad you laid the cards on the table with Keen, as I think we are sometimes too maidenly modest altogether about political affairs in Kentucky, which after all are of deep concern to us as citizens.

If Wilson runs, of course our problem is solved. We can support him with even greater ease than we supported him for mayor, because now we have his public record, as well as his character and integrity, to point to. If he does not run, however, I think we may be up against a very difficult problem. Ben Kilgore has written me asking openly for the support of the papers, which he did not do in the first instance. I will naturally not make the slightest commitment to him, as I cannot be sufficiently in touch with the situation at home. I was favorably impressed with his platform, as announced in the C-J of March 4, and I feel that we could support him in the primary with a good conscience if Wilson were out of the race, and I believe we should probably do so. The thing that worries me is that if there develops a three-cornered race between Kilgore, Lyter Donaldson and Rodes Myers, I am afraid the first two will split the more decent and independent vote, and that Rodes will capture all the rest, including much of the state organization support, which is likely to run out on Donaldson, I believe, if it looks as if he is a loser. With Rodes the nominee, we would have to make a sour choice between him and Willis, and I fail to see how we could support either of them on their records. That would put us back in the old, dreaded "plague on both your houses" position, and I hope to hell we will not have to be backed into that corner. I am much too far away from it all to analyze the possible ways in which this contretemps can be avoided, but I know you must be giving it a lot of thought. If our support of Kilgore might swing the pendulum enough to give him the nomination, I think we ought to get out strongly for him and see what we can do. Would there be any possibility of Keen's accepting him as a candidate in order to head off Myers? I suppose that is too much to hope for, unless Keen can be convinced that Donaldson really has not a prayer and that his presence in the race would only assure the nomination to Rodes, the defection of the C-J from the party standard, and the probable election of Willis in the fall.

All these considerations would vanish in a moment, of course, if Wilson should be in the race. But I am trying to think ahead on the basis of his not doing it, as I very much fear B.E.W. [Board of Economic Welfare] will give him such important work to do that he will get heavily involved and committed to them, and it may be impossible for him to put himself in the frame of mind to make a political race when the other job is at hand. I hope this won't happen, but it looks awfully likely to me.[3] . . .

The offer from Smith Davis in regard to Parade is a most amazing one, and I should think quite without precedent in the newspaper business, but I think you took exactly the right stand on it.[4] We might have made a good deal of money on the proposition, but after all we are not looking right now for a chance to make a lot of extra income, most of which would go at once into taxes. I think it is far sounder policy to build always toward the greater strength of the papers as papers, rather than as financial assets. The flavor and character of the Courier is essentially our greatest asset, and the thing we need to cherish with the greatest care, I think. The magazine is a part of the Courier as we want it to be, a sound, deeply indigenous regional paper, and I would hate to see it sacrificed for the possible profits of Parade, which would do nothing for the paper in any other way. I am glad to know of the various ways in which you have met the newsprint cut, and again you have obviously taken the course that would do the least injury to the character of the papers, regardless of the short-term financial considerations. We may be pretty starry-eyed about the role we want the papers to play, but I think the whole record of the enterprise since you came into it has proved that this is the best business policy in the long run, as well as the only policy in which either you or I could find any real satisfaction.

From Interview of Barry Bingham by Mary D. Bobo, University of Louisville, 5 July 1982

So I left my wife and family. My wife moved back to Louisville. We had to give up the house that we had gotten in Washington, and she came back here with the children. And again we had no idea how long our separation might be then. So I went on back to England and arrived there on the most beautiful moonlight night I've ever seen in my life, absolutely clear, and a friend of mine took me in an open car all around the city of London that night to show me the devastation that had occurred in the months previously. I remember seeing St. Paul's Cathedral with nothing but ruins all around it, everything brilliantly illuminated by this moonlight. In those days a brilliant moonlight night was considered a matter of danger rather than beauty. They called it a bomber's moon. They could see their target so clearly. That night there were no further attacks, but I had a chance to see what had been happening to London in the months since I had been there. So I was then put into the naval headquarters in Grosvenor Square, where so many Americans were, and I stayed there until January of 1945, in other words, for about two and a half years.

During the latter part of that time, I had one diversion. I was temporarily put off into another section called Logistical Plans. This was a group that was doing a lot of the planning for the Normandy invasion, and I was sent down to the West Country in England to some bases where they were doing specific amphibious training, getting ready for the naval invasion. This was fascinating duty, I must say, and I found myself in some of the most delightful small towns in the west of England that you could imagine. Oddly enough, I was first sent to a place called Appledore in west Devon. Appledore was a perfectly charming little village, but right next to it was the town of Barnstaple, from whence one of my early ancestors had sailed to come to America. My father had been down there during his days in London to unveil a memorial. So I felt myself somewhat at home because I knew that my ancestors had been in that very part of the world, and I found it a most appealing place.

Well, there I was stationed for a while, and I moved from one of these seaport towns to another, going around the coast where we were doing this amphibious training. And we had a Russian party down there at one time. I never shall forget it. Some Russians were sent down there to observe our landing preparations. Part of this, I think, was an idea of convincing them that we really were getting ready for opening a second front in Europe. The Russians were very dubious about that. I had these Russians on my hands, and they spoke very, very little English, but I found that they did speak a little English— one of them, at least, that I was standing next to. While we were standing there looking out over the beach, suddenly a dud shell fell right between us, missed us, didn't hurt either one of us. But this man, who previously had not spoken a word of English, turned to me with a great big smile in which some flashing metal teeth showed and said, "A very unexpected present." All of a sudden it was like hearing a child speak who never had said a word. It was a pretty unpleasant present, too, I must say.

So I spent some months down there, going from one of these communities to another and trying to help out on these amphibious planning exercises that were going on there. And then I got sent back to London, and then we were really getting into the final stages of preparing for the Normandy landings. So I was back in London during the early stages of 1944, when the whole of England was really an armed camp. The whole country was so much involved with preparations for this great joint operation that was to take place, and yet the whole thing was done under such secrecy. There were not even any signposts on roads in England. Everything was kept absolutely quiet. There were thousands of troops massing on the south coast ready for the invasion attempt, but nobody was allowed to talk about that. I have a strange angle on it because my job, of course, really most of the time had been to help with coverage, and at that time coverage of what was happening became virtually impossible. The many, many dozens, even hundreds, of American newspapermen over there were pretty much waiting impatiently for the big moment to come.

And we had an amusing episode in that case. It was decided there should be a diversionary movement of the correspondents down to the south coast, giving the impression to Germans who undoubtedly were monitoring what was happening that the invasion was about to take place at that moment. So I had to summon all the naval correspondents—there were about a hundred of them—to my office and tell them that they must prepare to go the next morning down to the West Country, under sealed orders. Nobody was to say where they were going and all that. This word was rather purposely leaked in the bar of the Savoy Hotel, which was a place where many American correspondents used to hang out, and we knew perfectly well that somehow or other the word would get back that this was taking place. So we got all these fellows together, and I felt somewhat embarrassed about fooling them, but I had to do that. And they had their gear with them, and they had their typewriters, and they had said good-bye to their girlfriends and others. And off they went to the West Country to get ready for the big operation. When they got down there, they were told that this was a diversion, that this was not going to take place at that moment. We called this Operation Mock Turtle at that time. But the men themselves, after their first disappointment that they weren't getting into the big story of their lives, found it delightful, because they were all put up at a perfectly charming house in the West Country that belonged to the author of *Rebecca,* Daphne du Maurier—a lovely place. I had to stay in London, unfortunately, and couldn't be with them, because I was trying to keep this thing in order. But they stayed down there for two or three days, and then they came straggling back to London and thought, "Oh, gee, this isn't going to happen now. The whole thing is probably a fake."

Two weeks later the word really came through that the operation *was* going to take place, and we'd better get all these people down there and get them ready for coverage. And this time when I summoned them, they were pretty dubious about whether I was really telling them the truth and said, "Oh, well, I hope we're going to a nice house again, and I hope there'll be plenty of booze there," and that kind of thing. But this time it was for keeps.[5] So I got them down to their points of departure, mostly in Portsmouth and in that area of England, and then I *hastened* back to London myself to be there when the curtain really rose. And there came that great, breathless moment when the Normandy invasion, for which we had waited *so* long, was beginning to take place—beautiful, clear morning in London. As I waked up that morning very early, I could just hear drone and drone and drone of planes overhead. An *incredible* number of planes were passing over. And it must have been pretty obvious to everybody in the street that something big was happening, but there had been so many exercises and things of that kind that it was hard to tell that this was the real thing. But I did know it was the real thing. And I realized that this was going to be one of the great events of modern history that was taking place right there, and under my eyes, as it were.

I stayed in London when the Normandy invasion took place, because I had to then be sure that the copy that was sent back and the photographs sent back by all these correspondents would get handled quickly, get through censorship, get sent out, and get back to their destinations back in this country. This was a fascinating and somewhat complicated process, and for three or four days I've never been quite so busy in my life. I was trying so hard to keep everything going and to keep it moving, and it was not an easy thing to do, but thank goodness, it did all go through quite well. We had with us many famous correspondents. The most famous, I suppose, of all was Ernest Hemingway, who had come in there just not very long before the invasion and who had run into a static water tank one night and had his whole head bound up. He had an enormous bandage, and he looked like some sort of bandit. But there he was, ready to go over to France and ready to go on his big story, as was everybody else.

I had had to assign these various people to whatever naval vessel they were going to be crossing over the English Channel in, and one of my great friends has accused me of, in a sense, putting him on an ammunition ship. It really wasn't true. I didn't put him on an ammunition ship because that would have been the worst target, the worst place, I must say, for anybody to be—but this gentleman has always joked with me about it since then. We tried to put them wherever they could best be fitted in, and only a few could go on any one vessel. And of course, they all wanted to be in at the very beginning of it. They wanted to see the big thing and have the big excitement. And they had plenty of excitement before they got through, I must say.

For a few days nobody knew for sure, of course, whether the landing attempt was going to be just an attempt and would be thrown back into the sea or whether they would really get ashore and be able to stay ashore. And then gradually we began getting reports that the troops were moving further inland: they were moving up toward the Cotentin peninsula, and that was one of the objectives. The area around the landing beaches became secured after *dreadful* fighting and a great many casualties, and it began to appear that the landing was going to work.

I must just mention one thing about this: part of the success of the landing was undoubtedly due to the element of surprise. The Germans knew that we were going to try to put a force ashore somewhere, but they did *not* know where or when, and this was a marvelous asset to the invading forces. The Germans believed that we would have to land—make our major landing, certainly—at one of the main existing ports, so they thought we would have to confine ourselves to two or three of the major ports on the English Channel there, and they did all their preparations involved with those big ports, trying to put plenty of troops nearby and all of their equipment and everything of that kind. The beauty of it was, partly by the inspiration of Mr. Winston Churchill, a plan was worked out to put an artificial harbor off the coast of Normandy. They took across the channel some great big ships and sank them offshore in shallow water and then built an artificial harbor off of this beach—the Normandy beachhead—and they were able to bring in troops and supplies through that artificial harbor. Now the Germans never suspected this, although some of the elements of this, when they were brought across the Channel, were as tall as eight-story buildings. But for some reason German reconnaissance, if it saw these things, didn't have any idea what they were, couldn't understand that this was going to be a major landing port for the American forces and the British forces, and so the element of surprise prevailed for several days, really, long enough to throw them off their balance at the beginning of the operation. They then hastily brought more troops in, of course, to the points where we had landed, but by then there was the possibility that we could stay ashore and keep these troops supplied and move on into the inland, and that's the way it happened.

About ten days after this I finally found my chance to get over to Normandy, which I had been wanting very much to do, but I felt by then I could turn over the things I had been doing in London to some very able assistants in my office there. So I was sent over to Cherbourg, which was a port that by that time the Allies were very eager to obtain. It would give us a much better place for landing supplies, and so forth, but Cherbourg was strongly held, and the country behind it [was also] strongly held by German troops. I was put aboard a cruiser, the *Tuscaloosa*, and the *Tuscaloosa* went in for a tremendous attack on the batteries at Cherbourg, and these big guns were booming for a couple of hours, and [this was] a fascinating experience for me because I had never been that much involved with actual military operations in all of my work over there. But in any case, the shelling took place. The German defenses were very much weakened. At the same time American army troops began to move up the peninsula from the south, and in a short time the port of Cherbourg fell to the Allied forces. And very shortly after that I was put ashore on a landing craft and was able to move into Cherbourg myself, along with three or four other officers.

And there we spent the most amazing week. We lived in an almost ruined house that had been deserted, of course, by its occupants. There was no roof on it, but fortunately the weather was not too bad. And there were walls, and we had a little stove in there on which we could do some cooking. We had nothing to cook except C rations, but we managed to cook up C rations. We had no water, because the water supply had been completely cut off and was still not back in shape during those early days. So I must say, we had to use cognac to brush our teeth. There was no other liquid that was available, and cognac was a great product, of course, of Normandy, so we were able to get this delicious cognac. I never, however, want to brush my teeth with it again. I was there for about a week while we were setting up facilities for American correspondents to get their dispatches out of Cherbourg in that region. And then the war began to move again further south and into the main part of France, and I eventually went back to London.

I then was in London most of the time until early September, when Paris was secured, and I was able to go over to Paris and spend a little time setting up a naval headquarters for correspondents there. And I lived in a hotel in Paris and had a most interesting time. I was one of the early naval officers to appear on the streets of Paris. There were plenty of GIs by that time, plenty of army people, but a naval uniform was still something of a curiosity. So I still had a few people throwing their arms around me and offering to buy me a drink at the bar, and that kind of thing—just a lovely experience, I must say. The French were so happy to be liberated and so grateful to us. Anybody they saw with an Allied uniform on they just wanted to express their joy to. I got a little of that, although not, of course, what they had when they first came in there.

From Letter by Barry Bingham, London, England, to Mary Caperton Bingham, 2 September 1944

My dearest,

I feel as though I can hardly wait long enough to get your letter giving the details of your interview [with President Roosevelt] in Washington.[6] I saw in one of the bulletins that reaches us here that [Henry] Wallace was a guest for lunch that same day, and I wonder if you and Mark [Ethridge] stayed on for that event in the bosom of the family. Bad as the handling of that deal in Chicago smells, I feel it is a good sign that your letter and Mark's got just this sort of serious and conscientious reception. Both of the letters were models of the kind of attitude we need to take, I think, when we do strongly disapprove of some action on the part of That Man. It was so clearly brought out that there could be no question of support of the ticket in November that there could have been no misunderstanding which could have led to this interview. The whole approach which you both took, too, must have been completely disarming to the people addressed, who could not fail to appreciate the liberal sentiments leading to your declaration of distress over this particular incident. Lord how I wish the liberals in the country in general could chastise their leadership in such a spirit, instead of flying into a waspish rage and bringing charges of such exaggerated corruption and betrayal.

It fascinates me to speculate on how the principle figure in this drama will meet your representations in person. I was a little disturbed by the phrase in Mrs. R.'s letter in which she spoke of your having observed the workings of the party in recent years, with the implication that the answer to your questions lay there. Mark's point I thought particularly true, and particularly designed to strike home with the recipient of his letter—the argument that the conduct of the war had cut that one [President Roosevelt] off from contact with the people, and that therefore he had been given a distorted impression of the public mood by the group of service brass hats and Long Island fat cats who now surround the throne. I know that dart will strike home, and will rankle. It is a thought that must have entered his mind before, in the watches of the night, but I doubt if any of his other supporters or friends had voiced it. I do hope, darling, that there will not be a display of personal charm unaccompanied by serious effort to face up to this situation, when you have your interview. I'm sure you will omit no detail of the whole affair in writing me, but I couldn't resist cabling you to emphasize my hunger for every scrap of information.

My own plans have gone into one of those periods of inanition which afflict all people in service jobs, I suppose. My visit to the haunts of Lady Bidolph [Biddulph], though still on the books for the future, does not seem to take any more definite shape, and the time element is so very vague as to cause me a certain amount of restless uneasiness. It now seems assured that Vic Blakeslee will assume permanent duty as P.R.O. [public relations officer] with that command, which is what I had hoped for. He is the nicest person in the world to work with, and we should be able to establish a very close liaison between his office and mine, which would be a great advantage. I could easily get the organization started along with him, and then come back here, with the understanding that I could furnish what further personnel might be needed. The wonderful war news moves so damned fast that all plans of this kind are apt to go stale every few days, and I don't feel too sure about this one, but we'll just have to wait and see.

In the meanwhile, I have a steady stream of visitors who have been in Paris and are now back, with their tongues hanging out of their mouths from excitement. Paul Gallico, who was in my office for a long time yesterday telling me about what he saw, emphasized the point that Ernie Pyle and others have made, that no human being will ever be able to write an adequate story of those first days in Paris. The pressure of emotion was so great, apparently, that the whole scene had a dream-like, allegorical quality which defies description. Everybody agrees on a few homely details, such as the amazingly good clothes worn by the women, including silk stockings and really good shoes; the shortage of food, which necessitates placing all restaurants and cafes out of bounds for service men except for drinks; the rapid return of the Ritz Bar to its old atmosphere; the almost complete lack of motor transport, which has led to the use of all sorts of fantastic devices on bicycle wheels; and the fabulous appearance of some of the shop windows, notably Cartier's, which is said to be loaded with the sort of jewelry that made people's eyes goggle even in peace time. Perfume is attainable in large quantities, and at reasonable prices. Every other luxury, practically, can be had, but some of the normal and average things are hard to obtain. One of the navy censors, who drew lots with army censors and ended up by being one of the first dozen officers to get into Paris, writes me that he went outside the regulations and had a lunch at one of the Rond Point restaurants, consisting of a huge omelet of a fluffiness that we can so well remember, fresh green peas, a beautiful salad, quantities of fresh fruit, and a good deal of wine. This meal for two people cost him $16.00, but since he did not specify the amount of wine he and his companion guzzled, it is hard to tell how heavily he paid for the food. God knows that sort of lunch would be worth anything you could manage to pay for it. He spoke feelingly of the real olive oil in the salad dressing.

I'm sure you will have seen the wonderful, exciting newsreels of the entry into Paris and the attempt on de Gaulle's life. I took time out after lunch yesterday and went to see all this at a newsreel theater. The drama of all those people milling through the streets in such obvious and voluble joy, only to be raked by machine gun fire and forced to throw themselves on the ground in wriggling heaps, is beyond anything that could ever have been staged. The austerity, and even sourness, of de Gaulle's expression in all the many shots of him struck me very forcibly. I couldn't quite decide whether this was his idea of a proper pose for the great, serious, sacrificial leader in his hour of triumph, or whether his nature is such that he simply could not summon an expression of pleasure even under such extreme provocation. It was not endearing to see how perfunctory and mechanical his salutes to the public were, as he rode along through all those madly cheering throngs. Each salute was made in precisely the same way, in the same tempo, and with not the slightest change of expression on the face. What an unattractive figure he is, whatever his virtues may be!

Darling, I have the outline and the long letter from Spaff.[7] I am deeply impressed with this project, and with its potentialities for good in Louisville and the state. I am much convinced by the thesis that this sort of specialized mental therapy should properly take place in a division of a general hospital, with obvious advantages from the training point of view. In addition, I believe the inclusion of a clinic for mental disorders within the walls of a hospital such as the Norton is a step in the direction of breaking down the old horror of insanity, and placing it in its proper perspective in relation to other physical disorders.

I would write to Lisle [Baker] about the financial arrangements, but I want to discuss them with you first, and get you to take the whole matter up with him. If you don't agree with the conclusions I have reached, you must let me know, darling, as I think this is a matter for the most serious consideration. As you know so well, I have wanted ever since Father's death to establish some really important and constructive piece of work as a memorial to him, and I have thought almost from the beginning that I would like it to take the form of an endowment for some institution to help the mentally ill. I would hate for any money I could put into this memorial to go simply for bricks and mortar. I would like the money to be spent in some way which would ensure a new development in education along specialized lines, and I believe there is a very great opportunity for education in the rapidly expanding field of mental therapy. The whole subject of mental illness has undergone what seems to me an amazing development just in the last few years, and I feel we are on the edge of one of those quick forward leaps that science sometimes takes, after generations of maddeningly slow progress.

In view of all this, I would like to put as much as possible into this project. In fact, I would like to be able to undertake the whole sum that is required, as set forth in Spaff's outline. Of course this decision would have to be weighed against several vital factors. I don't know whether Lisle would feel that I could obligate myself, or the papers, to such a large expenditure of money over a period of the next two or three years, but I would like for him to give it some thought. This is one instance in which I would be willing to borrow from the bank, if there seems a reasonable assurance that the loan could be repaid over a period of years without risk of involving the papers. There will always be considerable demands for contributions to this and that charity, of course, but I certainly would like to make one big contribution to something really exciting and constructive like this, as a proper tribute to Father's memory.

The other consideration which I think we should weigh very carefully is the possible effect of such a gift, if it should be possible to make it. Would it be a handicap to the future of the work, do you think, if it became too much a one-family show? In other words, would the future of the project be damaged by having the original initiative limited in this way, instead of being spread over a larger number of people? I don't know what the chances of raising this amount of money would be in Louisville under present conditions, but I suppose there would be a good incentive in our pledging a certain proportion of the sum as a starter, contingent on other contributions to make up the needed total. Would Jane and George [Norton], for instance, be interested in this type of work, do you think, and would they take a greater interest in it in the future if they were involved in the original donation?[8] I can't imagine that any individual or family is going to be able to make large contributions to such endeavors from now on, except in very rare instances, and I feel that most people who can afford to give liberally are already tied up with other interests which would make a stronger appeal to them when they want to lay out some money. The Nortons have such strong Baptist connections, for instance, that they are certainly obligated to support the enterprises of that church. We are involved in enough enterprises ourselves, heaven knows, but I think it might be more useful for us to concentrate what we can do in one limited field. I would only be satisfied if the money were spent in Kentucky, and if it gave some promise of bettering conditions in a general way in the state. I think such an improvement might be possible if we could help raise the level of psychiatric training in the state through this project, and at the same time provide the means for expert experimentation in this very fluid field of medicine.

I wrote you last year about how Andy Duncan had decided what he wanted to devote his time to when he got out of the navy, while he sat on the deck of his LCI in the Mediterranean.[9] I have heard of other Americans who have followed the same line of thought, and in my few tranquil moments I have certainly given the subject my most earnest consideration. These things I would never want to say to anybody but you, but you know so well how I feel. The absolutely amazing happiness that has been given us, beyond all reasonable hope or expectation, must surely convey some opportunity for helping other people. I can think of no group whose unhappiness so deeply stirs me as those who have some form of mental illness, and the slightest contribution toward relieving their spiritual agony seems to me to offer rich rewards. I believe I must devote a good part of my time to work in this field after the war. What contribution I can make must be of an unprofessional nature, of course, but there may be a certain value in the interest of a layman who could try to interpret the work of professional experts to other laymen. I don't know how an opportunity for work along this line may develop, but I must find some way to make myself useful. The Norton Infirmary project is directly in line with my feeling on this subject. We might be able to provide an opportunity there for advanced work, under thoroughly sympathetic lay auspices, if we did take a strong lead in providing the initial sum of money. It will never be easy to carry on such work under conditions that will encourage experimentation in new methods of treatment, unless a small and very sympathetic board of laymen can be found to act as a governing body. I don't believe we have progressed to the point where such work could possibly be done in a public institution, at least not in our part of the country. A private institution seems to offer the best chance, if other conditions are correct. I would hate to think that the work done in such an institution would be without effect on the public care of mental illness, and there is the great opportunity, I believe, for leadership.

Would you think this all over, my darling, and investigate several salient points? You might talk to Lisle very tentatively about the amount of contribution which he thinks I could obligate myself to make, explaining to him that I want to make this a major piece of work, beyond anything else we might be interested in supporting. Further, you might talk to Spaff, tell him how we both feel about the proposal (if your feelings are close to mine), and explore the further aspects of this matter with him. I would want to know how free a hand would be given to this work by the board of the hospital. I would certainly like to know if the Norton board would really welcome the addition of such a project to the hospital, and whether they would be willing to look on it as a laboratory for advanced experimentation. It would be terrible to get into the middle of such an undertaking and find that we were ham-strung by some governing body which would disapprove of new methods and be fearful of trial and error. I also want very much to know what you think would be the effect of our taking what might appear to be a dominant part in the project. I do see a potential danger there, if others who could afford to support the work should be lulled into inaction by the feeling that this was one enterprise that had been taken off their consciences by somebody else. Let me know all you think about it, dearest, and later I will write to Lisle on the financial considerations, after you have opened the discussion with him.[10]

I'm so glad you sent me the really impressive display of Weldon's story on the Texas from the C-J.[11] You were perfectly right in assuming that this was an account of the same action I saw from the Tuscaloosa, though Weldon was in the bombardment group on the other side of the operation. We got word on the bridge of the Tuscaloosa that the Texas had been hit, and that there were casualties, and I was naturally very worried about Weldon until I saw him in port the next day, as lackadaisical as ever, and only betraying a slight attack of nerves by smoking even more continuously than ever. He was directly next to three of the men who were killed on the bridge, but was only knocked to his knees, and not scratched. His story was held up for weeks by censorship because of its description of damage to the ship, and was only released when that had been rectified. Other papers used it with a proper date-line and somebody on our desk must have had the bright idea of slugging it June 6 (delayed). We are expecting him back absolutely any day, and I think he will be back in Washington very shortly thereafter. I'll get him to call you. He has been having a hell of an interesting time, but his ship did not get into as much action this time.

Last Thursday I had an amusing theatrical evening, starting with the opening of the Old Vic production of Peer Gynt. I went with Sybil [Sibyl] Colefax, who is an inveterate first nighter. She is very pleased by the effect of Woollcott's letters to her in his collection, by the way, and I did think they presented her in an unusually favorable light.[12] This was the first opening in many weeks, and also the beginning of a new repertory company under Old Vic management, so all the theater people turned out en masse. We had seats in the second row, just as I like it, and were wedged in next to Rex Harrison and his wife, with Prof. [John Maynard] Keynes and his wife, who used to be the Russian ballerina Lydia Lopokova on the other side. . . .

Afterward I took Sybil to the Savoy Grill for supper, along with Jamie Hamilton, Norris Houghton, and a good actor called Michael Redgrave, who is a friend of Norris's.[13] The whole place was a buzz of theatrical conversation, and Noël [Coward] circulated from table to table, looking more than ever like a paper doll, with his high-cut shoulders and that amazing thinness through the body. Still later we went to a party at Adrianne Allen's, where Coward was again holding forth, and a good many other people. Alan Campbell was there, and I am delighted to find that he is going to be in town from now on. . . .

We have had parts of several days recently that were just like early fall in New England, cool and clear, with that wonderful freshness in the air. It never lasts more than a few hours, but it is so lovely, and makes me feel suddenly more brisk and energetic. The leaves have already begun to fall in quantities in the parks, and there is a smell and atmosphere of autumn in the air. It is depressing to think that this will not lead to a fine spell of Indian Summer weather, but only to a gradual lessening of sunlight, the onrush of the blackout, and the inevitable autumn rains and fogs. I hope you will find the Berkshires as wonderful as they should be when you take the dear boys up to their school, though the full, strange melancholy of that season at the height of its beauty might make it even harder for you to bear leaving them. I will write to Barry soon, so that a letter will be there on his birthday, and cable him as well.

I am enclosing an article from the Daily Sketch to show you the sort of comment that is being aroused by Happy Chandler's statements. He is rapidly becoming one of the leading thorns in the side of the British. This particular attempt to counter his charges I consider about as unfortunate as possible, as it assumes that horrible huffy attitude in which no fault on the part of the British Empire can be admitted. It is getting so that every statement Happy makes is quoted by the papers here. I don't quite see what this type of publicity can do for him at home, but then I have never been clear as to the exact current goal of his and Mildred's ambitions.

This is a rainy Saturday afternoon, and I have the office duty until ten tonight. I had planned that I would spend the latter part of the afternoon in an unbroken spate of writing to you, but the telephone has been ringing pretty continuously, and there have been manifold interruptions. I keep feeling that the work of this office is going into a decline, and indeed it is nothing like it was before D-day, but it has a way of continuing with a stream of minor details and an occasional assignment of some importance.

I have brought *A Bell for Adano* to the office with me, and I am going to read it this evening.[14] Did you read it? I have been wanting to see what it does to Patton, and I finally found somebody who had a copy to lend me. You have never told me how Jane's book fared with the reviewers, and whether it has sold well.[15] I do hope it has had a success. I had a call yesterday from a man who used to work at Fight for Freedom, and who has recently arrived here. He reports that John Mason [Brown] is on the last stretch of his book, and expects to be finished by the end of this month. I gather he may go out to the Pacific with his admiral after that. The other piece of news from this same source is that Ulric and Dorothy [Bell], who are installed in New York, have named their daughter Ulrica, which seems to me to approximate the gypsy curse. Sebastian [Herbert Sebastian Agar] has been put to bed for two weeks, with his blood pressure so low that he is threatened with a thrombosis. He really looks ghastly, and every movement seems to require a superhuman effort. He was scheduled to go home, as I wrote you, but his boss does not want him to go for policy reasons. He is recuperating in the country now, with his usual companion, who I am afraid will not grant him complete rest.

And so I must stop, my own darling. The immediate future is very cloudy indeed from our own personal standpoint, but I still have hopes for a decisive change before the end of the year. These hopes are not based on any definite piece of information, but I feel somehow that we won't be asked to go through another whole winter apart. Oh darling I do so want to be with you, at this moment, and in every moment of my life.

From Interview of Barry Bingham by
Terry L. Birdwhistell,
University of Kentucky, 8 February 1980

At that point we were going to have to spend a great deal of money putting up this building, and we did not have large reserves on hand. We felt that we had to go and borrow a large sum of money and pay a good deal of interest on it. It seemed to me, and I took advice, of course, from others at that time—it seemed to all of us, that probably it would be better for us to divest ourselves of our broadcasting station and try to put all of our resources into the newspapers to be sure that we were going to be able to continue with those on the level that we had always tried to operate on. At that time that was a sizable debt—it wouldn't seem like so much now, but it was a very large debt for those days—in proportion to the kind of earnings that we were able to make. So we made, fundamentally, a decision that we would consider a sale if we could get the proper kind of offer.

We did have at least three bona fide offers, and our decision was that probably Crosley would be the best one for us to sell to, not because they were offering more money, as a matter of fact, but we felt that they knew this part of the country.[19] They were interested in Kentucky, among other things. They had operated in Kentucky a good deal, and [we felt] that they would run a very high-class operation here, as they had done in Cincinnati. So we decided that was the thing to do. Well, in the long run, that, apparently, was a decision not acceptable in Washington, because [Crosley's Cincinnati operation was] too close to us, and it was felt that this would be too much concentration of broadcasting power in this area. And therefore, they did not allow the sale. When that was turned down, we then decided that we would just stay in the business and try to go on with it. That's what we did. We were turned down by the FCC, and that's the reason we're in broadcasting today.[20]

Remarks by Barry Bingham, Aired on WHAS-TV,
27 March 1950

It is good to be able to say hello to our friends in Kentuckiana, even though in this indirect manner. Naturally I am quite disappointed that I cannot be in Louisville tonight. But by the time this film is televised on WHAS-TV, I shall be back in Paris at my duties as head of the Economic Cooperation Administration for France.

It is certainly typical of the tempo and nature of our times that I shall be in Paris on the night that you of Kentuckiana see this film made several weeks ago in Washington, where I had testified before Congress on ECA.

Tonight's debut of WHAS-TV is a tremendous expansion of our broadcasting activities. Certainly it was not foreseen back in 1922 when my father, Judge Robert Worth Bingham, put the *Courier-Journal* and *Louisville Times* into radio with the establishment of WHAS. What had started out as a modest radio-telephone service twenty-eight years ago now embraces a fifty-thousand-watt, clear-channel station heard by millions, an FM station, and a myriad of shortwave broadcasting stations. And finally, we have the miracle of television.[21]

The small group headed by Mr. Credo Harris, who gave Kentucky its first radio voice in 1922, has as its counterpart today a staff of almost 150 persons handling our broadcasting operations. The modest technical facilities and studio and office quarters of those days have grown into a plan as modern and efficient, we like to think, as any of its kind in the country.

Despite this fabulous change and growth, we have tried to adhere to a basic principle set down by my father. He wanted WHAS to serve and be a vital part of the progress and well-being of this community. This philosophy has guided us throughout the twenty-eight-year history of WHAS. And it continues to guide us as we go into television.

TV is a new medium with new techniques, and we make no pretense of having mastered all of them. But we have assembled a capable and enthusiastic staff, and I feel sure that the energy, ingenuity, and skill of these men and women will see us well through this first period of initiation.

Many of the people whose voices have been familiar to you through WHAS broadcasts will now come into your homes via the screen of your TV receiver.

Just as we have done on WHAS, we will do considerable local programming on our television station. We want WHAS-TV to reflect and serve the interests of the people of Louisville and its environs. On this first night of telecasting, I am happy to dedicate WHAS-TV to that end. May it serve Kentuckiana well.[22]

Barry Bingham, *Problems of Germany*

[After the war, Barry Bingham twice inspected occupation conditions in Germany for the secretary of the army.]

Rain on the ruins is still the outward symbol of Germany this winter.[23] When the rain drifts into snow, the outlines of bomb craters and jangled masonry soften, and the light of a candle in the basement window of a wrecked tenement can gleam almost cozily. But mostly it is a country of winter rain, bedraggled, dispirited, and infinitely sorry for itself.

About 66,000,000 people have been living in Germany since the end of the war without any real government, a situation without parallel in history. The government of four powers designed to operate from Berlin never really functioned at all. The Soviets never meant it to work and never allowed it to work.

I came back to Germany after a lapse of just over a year, from October 1946 to November 1947. The visual impression is almost more depressing than before. Rubble in the big cities has been picked up and stacked in neat piles, but it is an order that looks worse than chaos. The appearance of Berlin today is that of an organized shambles.

My strongest impression this year was of a new sharpness in all the issues. A year ago we were still hoping for quadripartite agreement, still hesitating even to pool the technical functions of the American and British Zones for fear of closing out Soviet cooperation. This year the two zones are almost completely merged. Bizonia is in many respects a new nation, with its capital at Frankfurt. Soon it will expand and become Trizonia, if the French yield to necessity and throw in their lot with ours. Thus will arise a Western Germany of 48,000,000 people, an Eastern Germany of 18,000,000, divided by the River Elbe and the Iron Curtain. . . .

What about the German people this winter? The strongest change I saw was the shift in their outward attitude toward Americans. A year ago they were still telling us largely what we wanted to hear, emphasizing their "democratic traditions," their wish to cooperate with American authority. Now they are setting up such a gaggle of complaints, criticisms and self-justifications as never smote human ears before. . . .

These people are a race of political illiterates. We have tried to erect a full structure of democracy among them in two years, when it would be remarkable to build a firm foundation in twenty. It is an ivory tower democracy, and its cornerstone is a textbook. The Germans half-heartedly built such an edifice of their own in Weimar days, and it crumbled at a blast of Hitler's horn. Now that the real test is at hand and we must establish a viable state west of the Elbe, we will need to take back some of the power we dealt out too quickly. The Germans can only use power properly if we hand it to them slowly, carefully, in accord with a long-range design.

Chapter 7

Chief of Mission

From Interview of Barry Bingham by Mary D. Bobo,
University of Louisville, 5 July 1982

By 1949 another opportunity arose that I really thought I should take
advantage of. The Marshall Plan by that time had gotten started. It had
been announced, as you may remember, at a Harvard commencement
exercise. I wasn't there, but I had read about that and was *fascinated*
with the purpose and efficient organization of the Marshall Plan, and
I wanted *very much* to be a part of it. I thought this, next to the war
itself, was the most dramatic and interesting thing that the United
States would be involved in during my lifetime. And indeed, it did
prove to be so. So I went up to Washington, and I was interviewed by
various people, particularly by Paul Hoffman, who, along with Averell Harriman, was the cochairman of the Marshall Plan operation, and
they said they would like for me to take an overseas assignment.[1] I
said I would be glad to do so for one year only. I didn't think I should
be away from the papers for more than a year, but I thought I would
give a year to it. To my surprise, it turned out they wanted me to go
as Marshall Plan minister to France. I didn't know it was going to be
France. I thought it would be some much smaller, less important country, but France is a country, of course, I had always had been interested in and had visited as a tourist, but not otherwise.

So I found myself going over by ship and in June 1949 taking
over for a year as the head of this Marshall Plan office in France.
Now there was one thing that caused a little confusion. There was a
main Marshall Plan office for the *whole* operation in Paris, presided
over by Averell Harriman. Paul Hoffman was back in Washington
presiding over the whole operation on this end. I was in an office
which dealt only with France. Now when you say "only with France,"
even so, it was a pretty large operation. The year I was there we expended one billion dollars in American credits for the restoration of
France, after the terrible war damage that that country had suffered.

And it was all done with the close collaboration of the French authorities, particularly a wonderful man named Jean Monnet, who had himself devised something called the Monnet Plan or the Plan Monnet for the restitution of France after the war, even before there was any possibility that American funds would be available. He was trying to find a way to bring back France to a situation of prosperity in the European world, and when the American Marshall Plan was adopted, we were able to take over almost the whole aspect of Mr. Monnet's plan for the work we were to do in France. That didn't mean, of course, that we simply turned it over to the French. We were working in close collaboration with the French in every possible way. The railroads in France had been largely destroyed by attacks during the war; the ports and harbors were in absolute shambles. So it was almost impossible to bring anything into France at that time. The French needed desperately to import a lot of goods in order to get their economy moving again.

The Marshall Plan was able to do many constructive things. Ports and harbors, I think perhaps the most dramatic, we did restore with Marshall Plan funds. The railroad system of France we restored with Marshall Plan funds. We also were able to build some additional dams on some of the rivers of France, and we were able to increase the electrical capacity of France by 50 percent, which was a tremendous contribution to the economic recovery of that country. We weren't able to do very much about housing, and this was a problem, because many French people wanted the first priority to go to restoring housing. They were in desperate need of good housing, but it was determined, and I think wisely so, that if the money went into housing, that is not productive. That is simply something that helps the people to live better. But what we needed to do was to get the factories started again, get the ports and harbors opened again, get the railroads operating, get the country back on its feet industrially and economically, and then improvements of housing could come along in its natural train.

So that's the way it was organized, and I did have one very interesting year there in that office. The French I had known previously, as I say, more as a tourist, and I had always enjoyed my times in France. I found a very different aspect of the French from what I had expected: terribly hard-working, terribly serious, terribly eager to put their country back on its feet; not at all the kind of image of the fond-of-dancing-and-light-wines French that we always have heard about traditionally. I was working with some of the most serious-minded and some of the best organized brains that I've ever encountered during my time in France. So I stayed there for one year, from June 1949 to June 1950.[2]

My wife and children came over, and we had that one year in France, which was a wonderful experience for them. Unfortunately, I was so busy most of the time that I didn't get very much time to spend with them, but it was something that I think they will remember all their lives. The children went to school, two in Switzerland and the rest in France, and had a most interesting time there. By June 1950 my time had run out—my year that I had agreed to spend—and I thought it was time for me to turn back and come on back to my own job here in Louisville. So with some reluctance I did leave the job in France. It was passed on to a very able successor, Harry Labouisse.[3] I came back to my own job here and took up the reins once more in close collaboration with my close associates here. And I was back in newspaper work, and that's where I stayed from then on until the time of my retirement.

Barry Bingham, "One Who Directed Aid Program Is Sad That People of U.S. Weren't Fully Aware," *The Courier-Journal*, 31 May 1987

It has been forty years since the Marshall Plan was first proposed under the shade of the elms in the Harvard Yard on a June commencement day.

To me, it is sad that the American people at large still do not comprehend what they accomplished in that unique mission. They have missed the surge of pride that was their just due. Nobody denied it to them. Essentially, they denied it to themselves.

Four decades later, it is interesting to inquire what caused that single failure in a gigantic success story. The failure lay in the inability to show the American public how and why they managed to save Western Europe, and by extension the free world, from the ruins of World War II.

It may be helpful to point out what the Marshall Plan was not, in order to clear the air of some old misconceptions.

It was not simply what Winston Churchill called it, with his superb gift for hyperbole: "The most unsordid act in history." It was not an act of charity, a demonstration of compassion such as the Hoover Plan for feeding starving European children after World War I. Most accurately, it was an example of enlightened self-interest by the American people, one that only they could have exercised at that moment in history.

It was not simply designed to thwart the thrust of Communism westward. [George C.] Marshall said it best himself: "It is logical that the United States should do whatever it is able to do to assist in the return of economic health in the world, without which there can be no political stability and no assured peace. Our policy is directed not against any country or doctrine, but against hunger, poverty, desperation and chaos."

The Soviet Union was not excluded from the European Recovery Program, which emerged from Marshall's proposal. The Soviet Union was offered a chance to join its own resources to the massive general effort. Its leaders refused. There may well have been secret sighs of regret in the Kremlin as the evidence of success emerged.

The Marshall Plan did not promise safe and certain recovery. It harnessed American skills and resources to a program never before tried or even imagined. It ran its planned course in four years, at a cost of some $12 billion. It operated on that budget without a single scandal, without even one recorded instance of corruption. Amazingly, it worked.

The plan did not involve shipping vast stacks of American dollars abroad for greedy Europeans to squander. No cash was given or received. The Marshall Plan opened a line of dollar credits for 17 recipient countries. Up to 90 cents of every dollar was spent in America, to buy the products of our fields and factories.

I take France as an example, since I spent a year there, from June 1949 to June 1950, as the Marshall Plan's Chief of Mission to that country. Everything I write about France applies to the other recipient countries as well. I use my own personal experience to indicate the results of the billion dollars in Marshall Plan credits we spent in that year, in daily coordination with our French associates.

Those results began with massive purchases of agricultural supplies, to enable the French to restore farm production and feed their own people. The effort extended to the full restoration of French ports and harbors, whose installations were 70 percent destroyed by Allied bombers as we shouldered the grim task of assaulting Hitler's "Fortress Europe."

Also included was the reconstruction of France's railway system, blasted to ruins by war's end. It entailed such achievements as a doubling of the electrical capacity of France, largely by building huge dams on swift-flowing French rivers.

In all of this, no French citizen received a free gift of a single dollar's value. The farmer paid in francs for an American tractor he could not buy in his own country (since the Germans had converted French tractor plants into producers of tanks), and for which the farmer could not pay us in dollars because his country was broke for dollar credits. The factory manager who required machinery to put his plant back into production went through the same process. Every transaction had to be screened by a joint French-American panel, which was instructed to determine whether it would contribute to national recovery.

The francs the French farmer or industrialist paid for his essential purchases went straight into the Counterpart Fund. No brilliant economist ever claimed or received credit for this dazzling innovation. The Counterpart apparently sprang from the collective brains of a group of anonymous technicians in Washington. Its effect was to double the force of every American dollar invested in the Marshall Plan.

Funds that remained from these major investments in recovery were put to use in another innovative program, the Fulbright Fellowships, which have financed two generations of Americans studying in foreign institutions.

The Marshall Plan did not establish a pattern that could be duplicated to help every country or region in need of economic assistance. Its example is often invoked as the solution to problems besetting Third World nations fighting for economic survival. The Marshall Plan worked in Europe because it relied on a solid economic infrastructive, served by skilled technicians. In France, it was built on a plan of recovery devised in 1946 by a brilliant and sophisticated French economist, Jean Monnet. We applied our system of dollar credits to the home-grown Monnet Plan, producing results of near-miracle proportions.

The Marshall Plan was not designed to induce gratitude from the recipients. The purpose of the exercise was not to demonstrate our generosity, but to achieve recovery, for the mutual benefit of all concerned.

I never expected or wanted to see French people dancing in the streets to celebrate Marshall Plan victories. They cast no flowers at our feet as they did when American armies broke through into Normandy villages and crashed on to the streets of a liberated Paris. The French are not temperamentally disposed to easy displays of gratitude. Yet in my time in Paris, our office was receiving an average of 4,000 letters a week from plain French citizens, giving full credit to America. The message over and over was: "You have saved France."

The dedication of a dam in the lower reaches of the French Alps, financed by Marshall Plan Counterpart funds, stands out in my memory of those exciting times. A tablet was unveiled which still stands at that picturesque spot. The French inscription reads:

"The Bimont Dam, whose waters will bring fertility and richness to 50 communities of the Rhone and Var Valleys, has been built with the help of the Ministry of Agriculture and thanks to the generous aid of European Recovery funds furnished by the United States of America."

That was only one instance among hundreds I could cite from personal involvement. It was enough to make my heart swell. I wish Americans in the millions could have shared with me that moment of deep satisfaction. I wish even now that they could feel the warm glow generated by an American intervention that had no precedent in the annals of history.

From Letter by Barry Bingham to Joseph Bryan III, 11 January 1974

Thanks for your letter of January 8. I am interested to hear that you are doing a book on the Windsors, and I look forward to reading it.[4]

I welcome the opportunity you have given me to expose the complete falsity of a rumor which has reached you about the [1951] visit of the Windsors [Edward and Wallis] to the Kentucky Derby. This story, in more or less the way in which you have related it, has apparently become a part of the local mythology. A number of friends over the years since the event have taken the trouble to inquire whether such a strange happening could ever have occurred, and of course, I always provided them with the correct version.

The facts are as follows: My wife and I first heard about the prospective visit of the Windsors from Wathen Knebelkamp, who was at that time president of Churchill Downs. I believe it is correct that the president of the C&O Railroad had invited them to Louisville, but we had no direct contact with him. Knebelkamp was eager to see that the Windsors were suitably entertained during their visit, and suggested that we might like to invite them for some luncheon or dinner during their stay.

We were eager to cooperate. We had known both of them pleasantly in London during the 1930s when we made occasional visits to my father during his term as ambassador (1933-1937). This was, of course, before they were married, but we used to see them together at various parties, and we were invited to a couple of occasions at Wallis's flat. You may remember that she is a distant cousin of Mary's. We had been entertained by them several times in Paris, when I was there as Marshall Plan administrator in 1949-50. We were, therefore, happy to offer them a little return hospitality.

They accepted our invitation, but there was no question whatever of a guest list. We had several house guests of our own that included Adlai Stevenson, Helen Kirkpatrick, Paul Hoffman and his wife, and Mike Cowles and his then current wife, Fleur.[5] We added a few other guests and organized a dinner party. No suggestion was made about guests arriving after them or leaving before them. We took them on to a dance at the River Valley Club after our dinner. We had a table for our party, but the rest of the people present were the regular members of the club and their guests.

The most absurd part of the whole rumor is that the Windsors sent us a large bill for coming to our house. Nothing could be more completely unfounded. They were our guests on exactly the same terms on which we had been theirs in London and Paris. Wallis wrote Mary a nice letter afterward, and we received an autographed copy of the Duke's autobiography.

That was the full extent of the story. As you will see, the whole thing has been misrepresented in the most preposterous way.

Chapter 8

With Adlai Stevenson

From Interview of Barry Bingham by John Luter,
Columbia University, 21 August 1969

I first got to know [Adlai Stevenson] in Washington at a time when I was on duty as a reserve naval officer and he was in the navy department at that time.[1] I was there in late '41 and early '42, having gone in the navy in the spring of '41. I was first stationed at Great Lakes and then transferred to Washington. While I was there I ran into Adlai, and we began a sort of personal friendship, which continued then for the rest of his life, I'm glad to say. Our families were friends. I had sons very near the same age as his sons, so we began seeing each other on that kind of basis. We were both living out in Georgetown at that time. Then we shared a country cottage up the canal in Washington, which is a place we often went for weekends. His wife and children often came out there, and we took ours out there, and we saw each other in that way very informally.

I was overseas for three and a half years after that, so I didn't see him anymore. Then I began to see him again as a personal friend when I came back to Louisville, and he was back in Chicago by that time, and we often exchanged visits, and that's the kind of thing that went on then for a good many years afterwards.

I had thought that the Senate might be the most appropriate forum for him, but then of course when he decided to run for governor I was very anxious to see him elected in that office and was very much interested in the record he made there, and I followed it rather closely and occasionally wrote editorials about what he was doing as governor. I thought it was not only worthwhile for the people of Illinois, but I thought he might provide a kind of benchmark of how an important state could be run, which indeed he did in many ways.

I suppose I began seriously to think of [Stevenson's being a nominee for president] in the winter of 1951-52. This was the time when he began to be increasingly mentioned for the job but at the same time seemed to be extremely loath to consider himself a candidate.[2]

Then in early '52—I believe in March—he came through Louisville and changed planes when he was en route to talk to Mr. Truman. Mr. Truman had asked him to come for the second time and discuss the idea of his being a candidate, and Adlai was running away from it just as hard as he could but nevertheless felt that he of course must go and discuss it fully with the president. At that point I had a long and rather interesting discussion with him at the airport about his candidacy.

He asked my advice, I'm afraid not really wanting it when it came out the way it did. I think he would have liked to have personal friends say, "Oh, no, don't really do this because it will ruin your life, and you ought to go on being governor, and you ought not to fool with national politics." I was sorry to say that I had to say almost immediately to him: "You're not going to like what I'm going to say to you, but I do feel that probably you are marked for going into national politics and going right to the top in it, and I think you just must not fight against it. I can realize so well how there are personal factors that make you reluctant to get into it. I can understand those things very well. But I just think the country needs the kind of leadership that you can give. You have shown what you can do in a large and important state, and I feel that you cannot escape the responsibility for trying to show these same principles on a national scale."

So he went on to his interview with the president, and from then I think it was only the natural next step that he eventually decided that he would have to become a candidate.

I really was not very active in the '52 campaign. I was at the Democratic convention, as I had been doing for many years, covering it for the paper, and saw a good deal of Adlai during the convention, during that turmoil that was taking place there. And of course, I was there when he made that remarkable speech of greeting to the convention and set the place on fire, and then I was also present when he made the acceptance speech, which was a remarkable document. I was sitting in the press box at that time, and the advance copy of his text hit us just a few minutes before he began to speak, and I ran over it quickly, and I really drew my breath in quickly, because I felt that this was a most unusual statement for anybody in public life to make, and I began urging all my friends who were sitting around to take a look at it quickly.

Then he came on and made the speech, and of course, it was even more effective in the way he delivered it. And this was sort of a landmark, I think, in American politics in my era. From then on I knew he was going to put on a most unusual and most challenging, stimulating kind of campaign. There wasn't any particular place for me in that campaign. I had already made plans to go abroad with my family for a little while that summer. I did go.

When I came back I did go up several times to Springfield and spoke to him and others who were working with him, but I had no formal position in that campaign. I wish so much I'd had [one] now, because the '52 campaign was a classic, of course. The '56 campaign, in which I was involved, was intensely interesting, but it was in many ways a rerun, and it was not as dramatic, anything like, as the '52 was.

He asked me just after the nomination if I had any suggestions for campaign manager, and we discussed several possibilities. He later on came back and asked me if I didn't think Wilson Wyatt would be a good choice.[3] His name had been suggested to him from others, not from me. Wilson happens to be a very close personal friend of mine. I immediately then discussed Wilson with him and told him how very good I thought he was and what an excellent choice it would be, and then he proceeded from then on. I don't mean he was checking with me before he decided to do it, but I think he wanted to get a personal impression from a man he knew was close to Wilson. And of course, it was entirely affirmative.

One of them that was mentioned was another Kentuckian, Earle Clements, and this may seem strange, because later on Clements was not the type of person who was involved with the Stevenson type of politics in the Democratic party. But Clements at that time was a very capable political organizer.[4] He had shown real ability in organization here in Kentucky in his political career, and he was a person that might have lent a sort of professional touch to the campaign, which Stevenson seemed to think he probably needed.

Now Wilson Wyatt was to me a much better choice, because he was not only adept in the ways of politics, but he was more sympathetic as an individual to Stevenson and his ideas. There may have been others who were specifically discussed, but as I recall, it was more a question of discussing the kinds of people that he thought he needed and then trying to fit some individuals into that pattern.

[After the 1952 election] Stevenson and I were both invited to serve as speakers on a program in Alton, Illinois. It was the dedication of a memorial to Elijah Parish Lovejoy, that wonderfully named hero of journalism, and while we were there I spoke briefly.

Remarks by Barry Bingham,
Alton, Illinois, 9 November 1952

We are here today to celebrate the memory of Elijah Lovejoy.[5] We know him as the first man who died a martyr to the principle of a free press in America.

We shall do him little honor, however, if we merely repeat the facts of his history. What he would want us to do today, I believe, is to examine his motives and try to apply them to our own lives. What was Lovejoy's conception of freedom of the press? Why was he willing to die for such a principle?

It is clear that Lovejoy did not regard this freedom as merely the personal possession of the man who owns a printing press. That is a mistake too frequently made today. The American Bill of Rights does not guarantee a special privilege to the few hundred of us Americans who are so fortunate as to own a newspaper. A free press is a guarantee granted to all the millions of the American people. This is no such thing as the divine right of kings. It is a near-divine right, but it belongs to the masses of citizens in a democracy.

If press freedom is a right given to all Americans, it is something more to the man who owns a newspaper. To him it is a solemn obligation. He enjoys a special power. With it comes a special responsibility.

There are two sides to the medal that fate places in the hands of a newspaper owner. One side is the obligation to present the events of the day in his news columns without staining them with the color of his own opinions. The other is the obligation to express his own views on his editorial page with all the clarity and vigor he can command.

We all vow allegiance to the principle of press freedom. There are many of us in the newspaper business, however, who fail in one or the other of the major obligations it entails.

Some of us who own newspapers fail by not expressing our opinions editorially, for fear of offending some segment of our readers. That is a failure caused by lack of courage. Some others of us fail by not keeping our news columns free of bias. That is a failure caused by lack of conscience. The spirit of Elijah Lovejoy would condemn failure in either of those duties.

Lovejoy accepted both of the obligations of a free press with the deepest seriousness. He was convinced that slavery was an evil practice. He could not content himself with speaking against it, as any other citizen might have done. Since he controlled a newspaper, he felt an obligation to write against slavery with all the power of his pen, and to publish his words for everybody to read. He could have kept quiet and printed the news. Nobody in the community would have condemned him. He would not have died at the hands of a furious mob. But he would not have lived true to his conviction of what freedom of the press demanded of him. "I can die at my post," he said, "but I cannot desert it."

Few people are required to die for their faith in press freedom; but it is not easy for the owners of the newspapers to live for that belief in all its moral responsibility.

The expression of vigorous opinion on an editorial page does bring angry reactions from many readers, yet I am sure readers have more respect for a paper that says what it thinks than for a paper that merely panders to public opinion. The editorial page is not supposed to be a pacifier for babies or a dose of soothing syrup. It has an obligation to lead. Readers can follow or not as they choose.

Completely unbiased treatment of news is difficult to achieve. Every piece of news is handled by one or more human beings, each with his own personal opinions. The average daily newspaper carries some 5,000 statements of fact, any one of which can be distorted either by human error or by human prejudice.

In defense of my own calling, I must note how hard it is to make readers believe in the impartiality of a newspaper. It is possible for an editor to take two exactly equal stories, one dealing with a Republican candidate and the other with a Democratic candidate, and place them in exactly equal positions on the same page of a newspaper. Violent Republicans will swear that their candidate's story was shorter and less prominent, while violent Democrats will insist that their man got inferior treatment. Political partisanship brings on a kind of blindness.

Newspapers must always welcome criticism, however, for it sharpens our sense of responsibility. Many Americans have questioned the fairness of the American press in its handling of the news during this campaign year. We cannot dismiss those public doubts as ignorant or misguided.

I would like to see the American press make an exhaustive study of its own performance during the political campaign, to determine whether Stevenson newspapers slanted their news coverage toward Stevenson and Eisenhower newspapers toward Eisenhower. We have all heard those charges. If the press failed in that way, it would be far better for us to expose the failure ourselves, and try to avoid it for the future, than for the public to expose it and leave the press to a huffy defense of its virtue. Newspaper people are trained observers. It should not be impossible to get a group of journalists or journalism professors to make such a study without fear or favor.

I am not afraid of a one-party press in the United States for the reason that 75 percent of the editorial pages endorsed one candidate for President. What else can the owners of papers do but speak their political convictions? They are living up to one side of their special obligation in doing so. But what of the other side? There, I believe, lies the only real danger: it is that the opinions of more and more newspaper owners may seep over from their editorial pages into their news columns.

We must remember that the mob can destroy the press of an Elijah Lovejoy, and can even take his life, but it cannot destroy the principle of a free press. The only way that freedom could be destroyed in this country is by the press itself.

If those of us who hold the responsibility for the newspapers of America should fail in our mission, if we should make our readers turn away from us in disgust and disillusionment, we would lose our press freedom one day. We would deserve to lose it. And it would not be just our loss. It would be a great and tragic loss to the whole American people. It would be a loss which democracy could hardly survive.

From Interview of Barry Bingham by John Luter, Columbia University, 21 August 1969

Stevenson made a very good speech on this program, and he asked me to drive back in the car with him, going back to Chicago, so we had a chance to sit and talk as you really only do driving in a car.

I was asking him what his plans were, what did he expect to do now that the campaign was out of the way? did he have any plans for travel? and so forth. He began to discuss this projected trip to the Far East which he had in mind, or really around the world, because of course it included Europe too, but the Far East was the principal objective in his thinking. And as we discussed it alone, he said, "Why don't you come along with me?" and I said, "Sure."

So we talked about it a little further. I really thought he was joking at the beginning, because I didn't see any particular function that I would be playing, but he then made me feel that I would be welcome

on the tour and that he would like to have somebody along who might
do odd jobs here and there, perhaps make contact with the American
correspondents in the various places we were visiting. It was going to
be a small party, and he would find it pleasant to have me along, he
was kind enough to say.

So I thought it was a magnificent opportunity, and I immediately
made my arrangements to go. I felt I could only be away from my job
for three months, which took in the entire Asian part of the trip, and
that was a part of the world which I'd never visited before, so it was
particularly important to me to see Asia and to accompany Stevenson
there.[6] His trip on into Europe I would greatly have enjoyed sharing
with him, but that was much more familiar territory to me, so I
thought I'd better come on back at that point, and I left the party in
Karachi, with great regret.

[On the tour] Stevenson had a long interview with Prime Minister
[Jawaharlal] Nehru in India. He asked me to sit in on this conference,
and they talked for about three hours without stopping. Here, although
they did not agree on a lot of issues, there was immediately a kind of
natural affinity between these two men. They were on the same wave-
length, you might say. Even though they might disagree heartily on
individual points, they were both talking from the same kind of ball-
park. They understood each other. Now this was just not true of Eisenhower and Stevenson. They did not think in the same way. Their minds
had not been trained in the same way. They didn't use the same kind
of language. The language the two men used in this interview between
Stevenson and Nehru was really amazingly similar. They had the same
kind of phraseology that they used. Nehru was beautifully trained in
the use of the English language and used it almost better than anybody
I know. Stevenson also was quite an artist in that way. The two men
were expressing their views with such wonderful lucidity, each enjoy-
ing the other one very much and each savoring not only what the other
one said but the way he said it. It was a most fascinating interview. I
don't know when I've enjoyed anything more. I was in literally the
enviable position of being the fly on the wall. I was introduced to Mr.
Nehru and said, "How do you do?" and sat down, and that was all.
And here I was, sitting, listening. How I wished I could have had a
tape recorder at that moment.

I sat in for a long discussion with Chiang.[7] [Stevenson] asked me
to come to that little meeting too. I made some notes of that which I
gave him later. I didn't make notes of the conversation with Nehru
because that was so extremely fresh in his mind, I think, but he asked

me to give him a little memorandum of his conversation with Chiang, and once again, I emphasize, I was not a part of the conversation at all. I was simply present.

Chiang gave him quite an ideological lecture: that America must understand that he was going back to the mainland of China and that we must be sympathetic toward this exploit. He reiterated repeatedly that he would not expect any help from the United States as to ground troops. He was sure that he could reconquer the mainland of China by some air support, which would be given to the landing operation, and that within a matter of a few weeks he would so have organized the resistance on the mainland that he would be able to take over the government, and it would go from there. There would be no danger that America would be involved in a land war on the Asian continent.

Now he seemed to want to get this thought across to Mr. Stevenson very deeply. I had the distinct impression that Chiang Kai-shek didn't expect to find Stevenson sympathetic. He was a man who had been much more favored in Congress by the Republican side rather than by the Democratic side, and Stevenson had never been sharply critical, I think, of the China lobby and that kind of thing, but he'd said some things that indicated that he had questions about it, had questions about our continuing support of Taiwan, and I think Chiang Kai-shek thought this was his great opportunity to try to convert Stevenson. Stevenson did not say very much, and it was mostly really a torrent of words coming from the generalissimo.

[Chiang] also was a charming host. He gave us a perfectly beautiful lunch in his private house in Taiwan. In fact, I think it was the best meal I ever ate in my life. I'm very fond of Chinese food. We ate beautifully on that occasion. Stevenson was not very much aware of food. He was often so absorbed in what he was thinking about, or talking about, that he would just eat whatever came on. But after that he did say, "Well, this is one of the most marvelous meals I've ever eaten."

He had a different feeling when we got into what was then still Indochina and were asked to eat two-hundred-year-old eggs. This was served to us as part of a very fine formal banquet, and at that point we came to a tacit agreement that one person in our party would partake of any dish that was served. And it always seemed to fall on me, because I seem to have the digestion of an ostrich, so in many cases if there was some tidbit that nobody else wanted to eat but somebody had to take, I was always the one, and I ate the two-hundred-year-old egg.[8]

[Stevenson decided to pursue the 1956 nomination] certainly in the fall of 1955. It was that far in advance, because I went up to Chicago to talk with him about it at that time, and he discussed with me the possibility of helping to form a volunteer organization which would be working toward the nomination, along with, of course, a more political organization which would be working at the same time, getting delegates lined up and that kind of thing. We then started the volunteer organization in Chicago at the very beginning of 1956—I believe in January—and Jane Dick and I and Archie Alexander were cochairmen of this group, and we were working from then on getting in huge volumes of correspondence and trying to get in touch with his supporters all over the country and getting things organized for him.[9] This, in a way, perhaps, could have been left to fate, because it looked inevitable that he would be the Democratic nominee at that time, but in this instance he wanted to be the nominee. He did not want to see it go to someone else who might try to do it in a different way. He felt that he'd taken the responsibility in '52, and he wanted to continue it in '56, so of course all of us were trying very hard to help him, partly because he wanted it and partly because we were convinced that he'd be the best candidate.

Now one of our great difficulties in that campaign, and I'm sure this is always true of volunteer organizations, was that the pros are quite suspicious of amateurs in politics—volunteers. They think they're a lot of trouble and they suggest a lot of impractical things and that they sometimes divert funds that they could use better to projects that may not be fruitful. And we were constantly battling that and trying to explain to our professional friends that we were not trying to go counter to their views. We were trying to supplement their efforts in ways that they could not do themselves.

I suppose one always thinks about the ending of a campaign. I was in Washington at the time when the campaign closed, and we had that familiar scene of everybody gathering to hear the returns. I was surrounded by people who had been working their hearts out for Stevenson during that whole campaign, and I must say that people were grief-stricken by the loss, but I must again say something that I believe I've said earlier: I didn't find anybody who was disillusioned. I didn't find anybody who was embittered against the American political system because their man had lost. I have a feeling that they were—I hope I'm not overstating this—almost a little ennobled by having taken part in a campaign of this kind, which they were proud of and which they thought had permanent value for the American people.

This was, I hope, some comfort to Adlai himself after these two defeats. It isn't very nice, of course, always to read your name "Adlai Stevenson, twice-defeated Democratic candidate for president," and this was endlessly repeated, and it's a factual statement. But I think the discouragement of that must to some extent have been alleviated by the feeling that he drew from many people that they had gained permanent benefit by the things that he said and did during those campaigns and that everything he put into the atmosphere of American life has stayed there, and in some cases the things that he enunciated have become more important since then, even though they're not particularly identified with Stevenson anymore. They're there. Things are not lost in American political life. That's one of the good things about it. And I think this is something you have to dwell on when you come to the end of a campaign that you have been tremendously wrapped up in. There is a tendency to think all is lost. Was it worth making the effort? Of course it was. I had so many people who came up to me and said, "Aren't you sorry that you spent almost a year working on the campaign?" I just couldn't imagine how I could have been sorry for it, because it had been a tremendous experience for me, and I do think it did something important—win, lose, or draw.

I was not at all favorable to his running again in 1960 for the nomination. I think it was a mistake. He was very much of a divided mind about it, as I suppose everybody realizes, until almost the eve of the Los Angeles convention. I wish he had not allowed himself to be put forward at Los Angeles. I think it was a mistake, and I think it did a little damage to the last years of his life. He then became what seemed like almost a perennial candidate, rather than one who had gone through two campaigns with great dignity and value. I didn't think 1960 was right for him, and I would much have preferred that he take some other role in public life at that point, rather than allow himself to be a candidate almost at the last minute, as he did. Now of course, his candidacy immediately picked up a lot of support in Los Angeles. Gene McCarthy made that fine nominating speech, and there was a lot of excitement in the galleries for Stevenson, but it was so obvious, sitting as I was in the press box, right above the Illinois delegation, that he didn't have the Illinois delegation with him. And a man just can't get a nomination under those circumstances. I thought it was misguided and unfortunate. I had talked to him about this before the convention of 1960 and had urged him to make it clear that he wasn't going to be a candidate, but he didn't. He couldn't quite make up his mind which way to go on that.

I was in Chicago for another meeting—I think it must have been in April of that year—and had a chance to see him, as I always did when I was up there, and went and had a rather long talk with him in his office. I had made up my mind that I ought to tell him how I felt about it, for what little that might be worth, but being such an ardent supporter of his and an old friend, I felt I'd better just expose my point of view to him. He listened, as he always did, with the greatest politeness, but I could see that he was not really ready to make up his mind on the subject. He was still playing around with the idea. He was getting a lot of pressure from some of his other friends and some of his other associates to get in and try to capture the nomination again, and [they were telling him] that this would be an easier race than it had been against Eisenhower, which, of course, was obviously true. It should have been an easier race. I could tell I wasn't really getting through to him with my arguments in this case. Even though he might have been able to win, it would have been a terribly hard campaign for him, again. And as a friend, I guess I was influenced by my feeling that he'd be happier if he didn't again make himself the subject of all the slings and arrows that the candidate has to endure. I thought he'd done his service, and I'd been one of the ones who'd urged him so strongly to get into it in the first instance, but it seemed to me that he'd already done a pretty noble piece of work in being the candidate twice and doing all he had done, and I had the feeling that [in] 1960 the atmosphere wasn't right for another Stevenson campaign.

Quite a number of the people with whom I worked in '56 called me up and said, "Are you getting active? What can we do?" and that kind of thing, and I just had to say that I was not getting into it from that standpoint, that I didn't think we ought to be working for the Stevenson nomination in 1960. I didn't think it would be the right thing to do. And there never really was an organization. It was just a lot of different people moving around more or less on their own, trying to promote a candidacy which didn't really exist. Now this was to some degree true in 1952 also, but then there was this very strong drive to nominate him and a sort of inevitability about it which didn't exist at all in 1960.

I did [urge him to endorse John Kennedy], without success. I tried to follow perhaps several lines of argument. I thought that [Kennedy] was going to get the nomination, to begin with, but that was only a part of it. I did think that Kennedy at that time offered a fresh face in politics, a very attractive political personality. I thought he was, in general, sympathetic to the same principles that Adlai was sympathetic to and that it was time for somebody of his generation, the first one of the twentieth century, to run for president, to get into the campaign and start stirring up the young people and doing all the things that needed to be done. I just thought his time had come in politics, as Adlai's time came in '52 and '56. I also thought that if we had a Kennedy administration that Stevenson could become an extremely important part in that administration and that the combination of Kennedy's talents and Stevenson's talents might have been an extremely effective thing. Now that combination never really fully worked, for reasons that we have been discussing.

I know he had some reservations about Joe Kennedy, because they were ones with which I was pretty familiar, but I don't think at the same time that he felt Jack Kennedy would be so dominated by his father that he wouldn't be able to be a completely independent agent. Bobby Kennedy, too, had gone around a good deal with us in the '56 campaign, as an observer. He almost never was introduced or wanted to say anything or take part in the activities, but he was frequently at meetings and rallies and public appearances of the candidate and obviously, I think, taking mental notes about everything that was happening. It was interesting to see that, and I expect a good many things that Bobby learned during that campaign became available to Jack in 1960.

[In the 1960 campaign I had] no official role at all. We came out in support of Kennedy with our papers, and I did see the candidate several times during the course of the campaign. I was on the campaign train at one point. I met him when he came into Kentucky in the course of the campaign and had a chance to have lunch with him privately and sit down and talk with him. I was on the plane another time. But I had no official capacity at all in the Kennedy campaign. I was simply an interested observer and a supporter.[10]

[After 1960 Stevenson and I had] only rather occasional contact, not nearly as much as I would have liked to have had. He was often very generous about asking my wife and me to come up and stay with him in New York and, in fact, begged us when we were there just to come and use his apartment, saying that he loved to have people there, which I'm sure he did. He was always a pretty lonely man, and I think those were lonely years for him. We did a few times go and stay there. We were always afraid that we would be a bother to him. He was terribly busy, and he was engaged in so many activities, and we were always reluctant to interrupt him in the things he was doing, so we didn't see him as much as we would have liked to do. He came down

and stayed with us several times, and we also saw him once in Barbados when he was staying down there with Marietta and Ronald
Tree.[11] So there were occasional friendly social meetings in which he
was always unusually warm, and he was always thoughtful about
sending little notes, just brief things that he would dash off. He didn't
try to write long letters, and goodness knows, nobody would have expected him to, as busy as he was, but he was awfully good about keeping up with things, and he always showed an interest in our children,
and there was that kind of family relationship which continued right
up to the end.[12]

Chapter 9

Reflection

From Barry Bingham, "Some Reflections
on Forty Years of Journalism,"
Lecture Delivered at the University of Louisville,
17 June 1970

It was four decades ago that I first began working on the Louisville
newspapers. That is a long time in anybody's book. Tonight I want to
share with you a few of the thoughts that rise to the top of my mind as
I reflect on the experiences of those many years.

We thought we had troubled times back in early 1930, when my
newspapering began. Those of us who were fresh out of college found
ourselves in a world that seemed suddenly to have lost all its certain-
ties. The stock market crash had carried down with it the spirit of easy
confidence, the vision of eternal prosperity and perpetual progress
which had lain like a happy enchantment over America.

In 1930, newspapers faced the need of reporting an America that
was suddenly filled with doubts and dangers. Many people were disillusioned with the government and suspicious of politicians. Deep fis-
sures were opening up between classes of Americans. There was fear
and resentment in the land.

Does all of this sound familiar today? I think we are in another era
of quite profound uneasiness. This time it is not the danger of economic collapse that confronts us, but a loss of confidence in ourselves
and in each other which closely parallels the mood of 1930. And like
everything today by comparison with earlier times, our problems are
much broader than of old. As we entered the 1930s, we were seriously
concerned for the welfare of our country. As we enter the 1970s, we
are at least as deeply concerned about conditions in the whole world
as about these here at our own doorstep.

Such times of national strain are always difficult ones for newspapers. Latent antagonisms between the press and government bubble
up angrily to the surface. Readers of newspapers dislike what they see

in the press, and by a process of guilt by association they dislike the medium that brings them such distasteful tidings.

Marshall McLuhan has told us that in the modern world the medium is the message.[1] I think many Americans have embraced the reverse philosophy that the message is the medium. The paper that persists in carrying stories about wars and riots and failures of responsibility in high places is identified with the evils it reports. The ancient Greeks had a phrase for it: Kill the messenger who bears bad tidings.

What has happened to American newspapers in the forty years between these two testing times?

In numbers, they have shrunk by almost one-fourth of the total. They have gained in circulation, though not in full proportion to the population increase. In physical bulk, they have burgeoned because of the development of advertising.

In the matter of quality, any judgment given is bound to be subjective. My personal conviction is that newspapers in general are somewhat fairer and more balanced than they were forty years ago. I believe American newspapers on the average are the most responsible in the world. I believe, at the same time, that they are not as good on any single day as they should be, or as those who produce them know how to make them be.

Let's examine the side effects of the changes I have mentioned in the tumultuous years since 1930.

The shrinkage in the number of daily papers is an economic fact, caused by the rising costs of production. It used to be said that any man with a lot of nerve and a shirttail full of type could start a newspaper. Nowadays, almost nobody is willing to risk the multiple millions needed to start a new paper. Old and famous papers have folded—*The New York World, The Herald Tribune, The Boston Transcript,* to name but a few.

There used to be papers to suit every political taste in a city of any size. When I started to work in Louisville, *The Courier-Journal* and *Times* were in very lively competition with the *Herald-Post.* The fact is that the two ownerships were cutting each other's throats, spending money lavishly on circulation wars and by necessity stinting the real value of the product—the news and feature content of the papers.[2]

Going back another thirty years or so to the turn of the century, there were seven papers published in a Louisville less than half its present size, two of them in the German language. Every reader could choose a paper that supported his own political convictions.

Reporting of events was completely and unashamedly non-objective. You read what you wanted to read, reported in the way you liked to see it reported.

Then came the inevitable march of newspaper failures and consolidations. The *Herald-Post* suddenly closed its doors forever in 1936. *The Courier-Journal* and its sister paper, *The Louisville Times,* which it had created in 1884, were left the only dailies in a growing metropolitan community. For a while, Louisville was the second largest city in the country with only one daily ownership, with Kansas City first. Now by latest count, there are fourteen American cities larger than ours with but one newspaper ownership. Cincinnati, Indianapolis and Memphis are three cities in our general area which have moved into the category people label a "monopoly."

Such a role has placed terrific new pressures on newspaper management. One paper is expected to cover all news events with satisfaction to all kinds of readers. In some monopoly cities, owners have tried to disarm criticism by reducing their editorial pages to such safe actions as praise of motherhood and condemnation of the common cold. In some others, such as a nearby Kentucky community, the owners have sought to satisfy readers by presenting Democratic editorial views in the morning and Republican opinions in the afternoon, or vice versa.

The Louisville papers have tried to follow the traditional line of the free press in America—the presentation of straight and unbiased news in the news columns, along with the expression of vigorous opinion in its historic place, the editorial page. Our efforts to do two difficult things well at the same time have satisfied nobody, including ourselves. I still feel, however, that this is the most honest and constructive way to try to run a newspaper.

The increased bulk of newspapers is another source of difficulty to responsible management. Advertising can be of strong interest to most readers, but it can also overwhelm them with its volume and weary them with its competitive claims.

One thing I think we need to remember about advertising is the part it plays in keeping the price of a newspaper relatively low. If we were to eliminate all advertising from our pages, we would have to raise the price of the daily paper from 10 cents to a quarter, while the Sunday price would double to 50 cents.

Along with this necessary volume of advertising has come a parallel increase in the news coverage a responsible paper feels it must carry. Forty years ago, America was pretending to itself that the outside world was of no great concern to us, and that we needed to know only certain relevant facts about events in our own country. Now a whole front page may be covered with news reports from such distant places as Vietnam, Israel, Berlin and Biafra. It would not serve the public interest for papers to ignore what is happening in those areas, as though the disturbing events would go away if people just didn't talk about them. We Americans need to know about a lot of things, though they disturb our digestion and cut down on our sleep. The theory that ignorance is bliss is not one that can be followed by the citizens of the strongest nation in the world in the twentieth century.

News reports flow into our office every day in a deluge which never subsides. More than a million words of copy reach us daily from every conceivable source. From that flood tide of material, our editors have to divert about one-tenth of the total flow into the pages of our papers. That represents about 100,000 words of printed matter a day, the equal of a long novel. On Sundays, the material we print in the paper is another *Gone with the Wind*.

This process of selection has to be done by editors, I remind you, who are working under the ceaseless pressure of deadlines. They must get the stories placed in the papers, write headlines for them, exercise split-second judgments on sets of problems that are never the same from night to night. Then there is the further difficult effort to get the material set accurately in type and to comb it for last-minute errors. Our papers contain some errors every day, as do all papers I have ever read. We are only a little different in our conspicuous way of acknowledging and correcting them.

I have tried to suggest some of the ways in which journalism has become more complex and hazardous than it was when I came into it as a cub reporter. Here I would mention a significant change in the staffing of papers which I have personally observed.

I started out in what was still the age of *The Front Page,* the rough and tumble era of journalism. Old timers tend to look back on the days of their youth as a golden age, and newspaper people are as sentimental and nostalgic as any I know. It's true that there were colorful characters in the news rooms of four decades ago, Hildy Johnsons in green eye-shades and elastic armbands, demon reporters who knew where all the political bodies were buried, a general atmosphere of excitement and cigar smoke.

The city room of today is a very different place. Many of the newsmen with whom I started out were people of zest and determination, but of very little formal education. Nowadays, the news staff is made up solidly of college graduates, a good many of whom have one or more advanced degrees. In the 1930s the only specialists on the staff were crime reporters, and reviewers of books, plays, and music. A modern news staff has added men and women with special, trained skills in reporting such fields as science, medicine, education, urban affairs, labor, and transportation, as well as all the old special "beats."

These modern, well-educated newsmen and women are just as devoted to journalism as their colorful counterparts of other years. They must be or they wouldn't be in a profession that offers a hard and nerve-wracking life. And I submit that the new breed of journalists are better able to assume the responsibilities of handling information than their forebears because they are better educated and more carefully trained.

Those who attack the news reporting in a paper as intentionally biased or inaccurate are not just making an assault on management. They are accusing intelligent reporters and editors of one of two things: willful irresponsibility in conducting their jobs, or slavish subservience to an ownership that wants to distort the news. Neither charge is easy for people of pride to accept.

I have tried to describe the increased difficulty of running a newspaper now by comparison with the America of forty years ago. In one way, I must indict all of our papers for a failure which ours in Louisville share. I can only plead that we at least have recognized the problem, and are trying with all our hearts to meet it.

Newspapers, to put it briefly, have failed to communicate. Communication is supposed to be our business, yet we have not managed to convey to our readers any clear idea of what we are trying to do or how we are doing it.

This is dangerous to newspapers. They do not lead a charmed life in America, despite the special protection of the First Amendment which we enjoy. There have been shocking evidences of late that a great many Americans don't have much use for the First Amendment, if indeed they even know what it is. They are willing to support free speech only if the speaker says what they believe is right. They will tolerate a free press, as long as it does not print things they think endanger their own comfort, convenience or welfare.

This is of course as yet a minority attitude in America, but it is a growing one. It is dangerous, I say, to newspapers. It is also dangerous to the very existence of a democratic society in America. We saw in this city of Louisville what a movement called "Know Nothingism" produced in the way of murdered citizens, burned churches, and long-lasting bitterness. I think I see signs of a "Know Nothing" philosophy arising again in a prosperous but deeply troubled and divided nation.

What newspapers can do to stem such a disaster is perhaps limited, but it is not unimportant. A loss of confidence in the press is one of the factors that contributes to public frustration. If it goes far enough, it can convince many people that the protection of a free press is no longer in their interest, and therefore expendable.

I am deeply convinced that newspapers need to speak more directly, more understandably to their readers. Our papers in Louisville have tried several methods of communication with admittedly limited success, but with no lessening of effort.

For years we have conducted a truly open letter column in both our papers. Anonymous letters and those which clearly libel individuals are not published. All others we receive appear in print, no matter what views they express. We have to reduce some in length, in order to accommodate the many correspondents who want to be heard. We cannot print a letter every day from the same writer, for the same reason of giving space to the many rather than the few. Almost every day I get letters ending with such a phrase as "I know you won't dare to print this." Those who write such letters must never read the columns we carry each day, filled as they are with sulfurous comments on our newspapers, their policies and their ownership.

A more recent experiment we have tried is the correction of errors, in a conspicuous spot on the first page of *The Courier-Journal*'s second section. These are not retractions, made under threat of legal action. They are open admissions of mistakes we have inadvertently made, some pointed out to us by our readers, others caught by members of our own staff. Oddly, some readers now complain that we are making more errors than ever before. The fact is that we are voluntarily correcting mistakes which every newspaper everywhere contains, and which most readers never even notice until attention is called to them by apology.

This operation relates directly to the work of our Ombudsman. He is the special editor whose sole duty is to hear criticisms from readers and to see that corrections are made when errors are brought to our attention. We were the first paper in the country to establish such an unusual form of reader service. Recently we have had visits from representatives of a dozen newspapers, some famous ones, which want to follow our lead.

The Ombudsman keeps an open line to the public. Sometimes it is clogged with complaints that have nothing whatever to do with newspaper operations, but at least the Ombudsman serves as a safety valve for people who are in danger of blowing their tops. I think we have better papers as a result of his intimate contact with the public.

To sum up my feelings after forty years in journalism, I am no apologist for all of the things the press has done and is doing. I think those responsible for running newspapers have a harder role to play than ever before, but then everybody in a free society has heavier duties now than in less turbulent and confusing times. It just is not easy to be a responsible citizen of a free society today. And the greater power the individual exerts, the heavier is the burden on his conscience. But we cannot falter; we must not despair.

I would like to end by reading you three statements made by prominent men of the twentieth century. Here they are:

"The organization of our press has truly been a success. Our law concerning the press is such that divergences of opinion between members of the government are no longer an occasion for public exhibitions, which are not the newspapers' business. We've eliminated that conception of political freedom which holds that anybody has the right to say whatever comes into his head."

The author of that statement is Adolf Hitler, a totalitarian of the Right.

"Why should freedom of speech and freedom of the press be allowed? Why should a government which is doing what it believes to be right allow itself to be criticized? It would not allow opposition by lethal weapons. Ideas are much more fatal things than guns. Why should any man be allowed to buy a printing press and disseminate pernicious opinions calculated to embarrass the government?"

Those are the sentiments of Vladimir Lenin, a totalitarian of the Left.

"A free press is the unsleeping guardian of every right that free men prize; it is the most dangerous foe of tyranny. . . . Under dictatorship the press is bound to languish, and the loudspeaker and the film to become more important. But where free institutions are indigenous to the soil and men have the habit of liberty, the press will continue to be the Fourth Estate, the vigilant guardian of the rights of the ordinary citizen."

Those are the words of Winston Churchill, who believed in the principles of democracy and practiced them all his life. I will throw in my lot happily with him.

From Barry Bingham, "Does the American Press
Deserve to Survive?" Sigma Delta Chi Foundation
Lecture, Delivered at the University of Wisconsin,
6 October 1970

I have been urging for several years the establishment of local press councils to serve this purpose.[3] I first explored the thought before another Sigma Delta Chi audience in Norfolk back in 1963.[4] Let me very briefly review my proposal.

I would recommend a community press council of perhaps five members, men and women. They should be appointed by some impartial entity such as a journalism school. The members would undertake to read the local papers diligently, as well as four or five other papers, for the sake of making comparisons.

These people would receive written complaints from the public on alleged inaccuracies or acts of unfairness which the newspaper would not acknowledge. The complainants would be called to sustain their arguments in person. The newspaper would have its opportunity to introduce a defense, calling publisher, editor, reporters or others as witnesses. These hearings would be open to coverage by all the news media. At least four times a year, such hearings would be televised on a local station.

The press council would have no legal authority whatever. Its functions would be to render an opinion on each serious and fully documented complaint. The council could not compel the newspaper to publish anything, including news of an adverse decision. But in practice, the existence of several communications media on the local scene would assure newspaper use of such material.

Most of my fellow publishers, I am sorry to say, were cold to the press council idea. It has been tried in recent years in several small communities, thanks to grants from the Mellett Foundation. There may still be other and larger cities that will try the experiment.

Meanwhile, the American Society of Newspaper Editors proposed this year a national press council that would operate under its aegis. The board of directors adopted the idea after long and searching debate. The majority of publishers, I regret to say, were once more strongly opposed, as were many of the editors. The Society is still studying the proposition, but for the time being the momentum seems to have been lost. . . .

And here I come to the most difficult part of the case I want to make for the press's worthiness to survive. I am determined to load some of the burden onto the shoulders of young people who are not even holding newspaper jobs today, but who are aspiring to newspaper careers. I see what many of them are doing on student newspapers, and I am seriously concerned for the future of the profession.

To get right to my thorny point, I am disturbed by the tendency of young people to practice "commitment journalism." It scares me to see how far they have gone toward discrediting the old standard of objective reporting. They dismiss objectivity in the handling of news as irrelevant and even unworthy.

Of course objectivity is a difficult art. Of course it is one which is never perfectly practiced. But to give up the attempt is the surest way to widen the credibility gap between us and the public to Grand Canyon proportions. I don't think anybody will be able to bridge such a chasm in another decade if it is allowed to go on widening at its present rate.

Here I want to add two personal notes. First, I am and have always been a man with a passionate set of convictions. My lifelong fixation about civil rights was nourished rather than suppressed by my southern heritage. My convictions on racial justice have subjected me to abusive post-midnight telephone calls over a long period of years. On foreign policy, I have held to the necessity of trying to understand peoples whose ideologies clash with our own. That conviction has earned me a whole range of unflattering labels, from pinko to outright Communist.

I have always believed in what Wilbur Storey announced as the policy of *The Chicago Times* back in 1861. He called it "a newspaper's duty to print the news, and raise hell." I am as committed to raising journalistic hell against injustice and corruption as I was forty years ago when I started out as a cub reporter. But I have only grown more convinced through the years that in order to enjoy the right to raise hell, we must first perform the primary duty of printing the news.

Back in the 1950s there was a lively battle between those who believed in "interpretive news" and those who thought such a practice would only lead to thinly disguised editorial opinion in the news columns.

I was one of the first, and I am afraid one of the loudest proponents of interpretive news. I argued that it was essential in order to make readers understand the real meaning of news events. I acknowledged the danger of editorial seepage into the undefiled well of news coverage. I contended, however, that any trained journalist would know how to draw the proper line between background information and mere opinion in a news story.

I don't regret having fought for that cause. I still believe in it. I am dismayed today, however, by evidence that many budding newsmen simply deny that any barrier should exist between news and opinion.

From Interview of Barry Bingham by Wilson W. Wyatt, Kentucky Educational Television, 15 May 1975

I was always particularly interested in the American Society of Newspaper Editors.[5] I have had, at times, the title of both editor and publisher. My interests were much greater in the editor side than in the publisher side. In going to publishers' meetings, I sometimes felt their emphasis was so much on bread-and-butter things, about making money, to be frank about it, and dealing with labor unions and things of that kind—all important, but not particularly in my line of interest. Now the editors' meetings always were full of life and vigor, and I've always enjoyed them tremendously and tried to take part in them.

And they always had interesting speakers, and they had a lot of give and take, and I've always felt that every meeting of editors that I went to gave me something that I could use of value. I was at one time chairman of something called the American Press Institute, which is a very fine institution, I think. It's run up at Columbia University.[6] They conduct seminars for newspaper men and women. This is a professional organization altogether. Many people from our newspapers have gone up there on these seminars and have derived a great deal of benefit from them. Young Barry was at one of them very recently. They give you expertise and experience in a group of people who have like problems and like interests to yours. And I think they've done a great deal of good in that way.

I also was active for a good many years, and still am, in something called the International Press Institute, which is, as its name implies, an international body.[7] They have members in sixty-five countries. They are not in the iron curtain countries. They do operate in countries that have some degree of freedom of the press. Now you've got to use that expression *freedom of the press* rather broadly these days, because in so many parts of the world, unfortunately, there are restrictions on press freedom of one kind or another. But in any case, we operate in countries where there is some degree of press freedom. The International Press Institute has been quite influential, I think, through the years, in helping to preserve press standards around the world, protesting against censorship and against closing down of newspapers in several countries where their protest has actually worked and kept these things from happening. It has been personally, to me, a perfectly delightful experience. They meet in some part of the world each year—they have an annual meeting—followed by a little tour in the host country, and some of those meetings and some of those tours have been absolutely fascinating, I must say. One of them—just to give you one example—we met in New Delhi one year when I was chairman, and afterward we were taken on a tour of India, which included spending six days on a train, riding all around in India. There were a hundred of the press people on the train, and we saw a very large part of India from that train, and I don't know when I've had a more interesting experience.

I'm sorry that I keep on being enthusiastic about things. I can't quite get rid of it. And some of this is in the field of foreign affairs: the English-Speaking Union is in that field. I also have been very active in the Asia Foundation.[8] I'm on that board, and we're still trying to do some useful things there. What I'm doing is what I want to do now. That's one of the good things about being retired. You do do the things that you want to do. Maybe you do more of them than you really want to do, but they are in the areas that you are most interested in, and these are things that are still of primary interest to me, and I'm happy to be able to devote what energy I have left to these causes.

Barry Bingham, Introduction of Queen Elizabeth II, New York, 9 July 1976

I am warmly sensible of the honor which has fallen to me today.[9] I am privileged to introduce a guest who commands the admiration, the pride, and the goodwill of every man and woman in this room, and indeed in all the English-speaking world.

May I take advantage of your courtesy by asking you to join me in a brief excursion into the past. I invoke in your minds the month of November in the year 1942. It was a dark period for both Britain and America.

That year had opened to the heavy drumbeat of enemy victories. Singapore fell, and so did Bataan. Famous warships were destroyed at sea; famous fighting units were thrown into combat against daunting odds.

As the year wore on, El Alamein lifted all our hearts to the skirl of Scottish bagpipes at dawn in the desert. Later, the Allied landings at Casablanca set new hope like a torch held at the end of a dark tunnel. But long and painful trials lay ahead of the British and the American people, standing on the ramparts of the world that yet remained free. That winter, I was one of many thousands of Americans in military service in the British Isles. We saw our traditional American holiday of Thanksgiving Day approaching. We knew it would find us far from our own firesides and our families.

Then came an invitation for many of us to attend a Thanksgiving Day party especially for American servicemen. Our host and hostess gave us a most gracious welcome. They were assisted by their two daughters, very young ladies in simple but attractive dresses. The feeling of being so far from home melted away in the warmth of that happy family occasion.

I need hardly tell you that the house in which we were so kindly received was called Buckingham Palace. Our host and hostess were King George VI and Queen Elizabeth. And the older of the young ladies in her schoolgirl party dress was the charming visitor who honors us with her presence today.

At this moment I recall with gratitude that distant Thanksgiving Day in the darkest period of the war. Your visit now to America, Ma'am, seems to me the occasion for another kind of Thanksgiving.

This is the 200th anniversary of American independence. In this significant year, the British sovereign comes to share with us the true meaning of our national celebration.

The bicentenary is a time to give thanks for the ties that continue to draw us and hold us together in mutual respect.

It is a time to give thanks for the principles of law and justice our American founding fathers drew from the ancient well of British freedom. It is a time to celebrate our common heritage of the dignity of man, rooted in the deep soil of the Magna Charta.

It is a time to rejoice in our common use of a rich and noble language. It is a time to treasure the knowledge that English is indeed the language of liberty.

I like to remember a phrase used by Edmund Burke in the House of Commons in 1775. Speaking of America, he said: "My hold of the colonies is in the close affection which grows from common names, from kindred blood, from similar privileges and equal protection. Those are ties which, though light as air, are as strong as links of iron."

May I be permitted a quotation, Ma'am, from one of your own royal ancestors? After the war had ended with the Treaty of Paris in 1783, King George III spoke words of goodwill to the American people: "Religion, language, interest, and affection," he said, "may—and I hope will—yet prove a bond of permanent union between the two countries. To this end, neither attention nor disposition shall be wanting on my part."

It is in that spirit, Ma'am, that we see your visit to America today. Ours is, we believe, a "permanent union" in the sense of enduring good faith between proud and independent peoples.

You yourself are a symbol in a world that needs such talismans. You are a symbol to your own people of all that is strong and true and worthy of respect in the British character. You are also a symbol to us in America—of lasting friendship in a world full of hostility, a symbol of the ties between us that Burke celebrated as "light as air, but strong as links of iron."

At this moment, we Americans join with your British subjects in a spirit of Thanksgiving as we say in unison: "God save the Queen."

From Interview of Barry Bingham by William E. Ellis, Eastern Kentucky University, 2 April 1979

The buck has to stop somewhere. I was at that time the only active member of the family in the newspaper business, and it had to devolve on one person. Now when I say "me," that doesn't mean that I didn't accept a great deal of advice and listen a lot to other people's opinions about these matters, but eventually when the decision was made—Who are we going to support in this race?—I had to make that decision. In most cases I wrote the editorial because I felt that since I was deciding in that direction, I ought to give exactly the reasons as clearly as I could state them why I thought the paper should support that candidate. These were elections, not primaries. We did not [always] endorse in primaries.

I was always talking to members of our own editorial board—our editorial writers. I also talked frequently to people who were covering politics in this state. I always wanted to get their views. Then I talked to certain people on the outside whose political opinions I valued. I would never like to say [who they were]. I don't think it would be quite fair to them, because I often consulted them on a highly confidential basis. I never put it on a formal basis, but I was always talking to friends in various parts of the state about public affairs in this state. You can call it politics. Yes, it's politics, but I was always asking them what their opinion was of the way the governor was handling the job and the way another candidate might be doing it, and this was not a question of polling. I never believed in that kind of thing, but it was just a question of getting their opinion and weighing that when the time came when I had to make a decision. Of course I also read the state newspapers pretty widely in those days and noted editorial comments and news stories there which might be relevant.

I nearly always wrote the first editorial outlining the reasons why we were making that endorsement. Then after that, of course, I didn't write all the editorials by any means. Others would pick up the themes and develop them further, although I continued to write some editorials on what I regarded as the very important and very controversial issues of the campaign. I never wanted to ask anybody who was an editorial writer on our paper to write something that he didn't thoroughly believe in. And since everybody can't possibly think exactly alike about any issue, there were times when I felt the only honest thing to do was for me to go ahead and write it myself. And it was known then to be my work, and anybody who didn't agree was perfectly at liberty to tell me so and discuss it, but I thought I had to make the decision.

Oh yes, there were a few occasions of that kind. You may recall one time when Lisle Baker did not agree with the editorial endorsement that the papers gave to Lyter Donaldson, and he was strongly in favor of Ben Kilgore. He then wrote a piece on our op-ed page saying why he didn't agree with *The Courier-Journal* policy on that subject. This was an unusual instance, but it did exist. Now Lisle Baker was not directly in the news or editorial part of this newspaper, but he used to sit in every day on our editorial conferences, so he was very much a part. He was the kind of person whose judgment I always wanted to have on these matters. He did not agree with my decision in that case, and he was given space to state his case.

You see, in the daily editorial conference we used to discuss what we were going to say about various issues. If somebody else was going to write it, I would certainly see the copy before it got in type. If I didn't see it before it got in type, I never failed to see the page proofs before the page went out. So there was never any question that the thing had not had my knowledge. Now there were times, of course, when I was away from town. I certainly was not here all the time. But I think through the years we developed a system whereby I would get a telephone call if it was something that really needed to be decided. If it was something that was merely following the line that we had already very clearly established, there was no question of having to get my endorsement before something could be written or published. I never believed in being on the other end of the telephone three or four times a day the way some publishers that I know of have done in the past. The old Joseph Pulitzer, for instance, in St. Louis, would spend all summer up in Maine at Bar Harbor, and he was on the telephone several times every day telling people exactly what to do, what to write and so forth. I never wanted to carry it that far. But I certainly was always available.

Oh, I think [having major state and local newspapers] carries more responsibility. I don't see how you can get away from the added responsibility of added size. A bigger newspaper, I'm afraid, just has it. Its circulation is big. Our circulation, particularly on *The Courier-Journal*, has been statewide all these years. Therefore, I think it entailed a decided responsibility in two directions. One was to cover the news of public affairs in this state just as clearly and fully as we possibly could. The other was to make our decisions on editorial matters known as clearly as we could and boldly, courageously, speak them out. So I think the responsibility lay in both directions, and we tried to follow them through the years.

From Letter by Barry Bingham
to John A. Mitchell, 10 April 1970

I am responding to your letter of August 6 to my son Barry, and also to previous correspondence with Norman E. Isaacs, our executive editor.[10] Since I am the person who has had the full responsibility for editorial policy on *The Courier-Journal* during the whole period covered by your study, it is appropriate that I should undertake to discuss our Vietnam position with you.

Let me say first of all that I am pleased by your choice of our paper as the basis for your thesis. I would very much like to see your conclusions, and I trust you will let me have a copy of the completed thesis.

I would have preferred to discuss the subject with you in person, as I believe we might have come to a clearer mutual understanding in an interview of that kind. Unfortunately, my vacation schedule took me out of town just at the time when the subject was raised, and I of course understand your need to return to your teaching duties in Virginia at the conclusion of your summer school session at Morehead.

I would like to preface my further remarks with a general statement about the questions you have posed to us. I have the feeling that you are viewing the Vietnam issue as something rather static and complete, while seeing the editorial policy of the paper toward that issue as one of wide fluctuation. It is perfectly natural that you should look at things this way, when examining the editorials on the subject as a body, from the standpoint of the present status of the Vietnam controversy.

Those of us who have been writing or directing editorials on Vietnam over a period of years, on the other hand, have felt the issue changing very materially as events have progressed. All of us are subject to some extent to alterations in public opinion. Beyond that, the tragic sequence of events in Vietnam, the piling up of casualties, and the progressive evidences that military power (within the limits which all administrations have felt it necessary to set in order to avoid the risk of World War III) is unable to secure a clean-cut solution in Indo-China.

These events have not progressed in a steady order. There have been times when optimistic reports from Vietnam have appeared to have at least a degree of justification. There have been other moments of deep discouragement. A monolithic editorial policy on an issue which has fluctuated so widely might provide a stunning example of single-mindedness. I can certainly claim no such prescience.

My first personal contact with Indo-China came in the spring of 1953. I visited both Saigon and Hanoi, and also Cambodia, at that time with Adlai Stevenson, in the course of a trip around the world which he asked me to share with him after his defeat for the presidency in 1952. I did not try to write about really substantive matters from that journey, as Mr. Stevenson was providing his comments in a series of articles for *Look*. The impressions I received while moving around in that part of the world, however, have undoubtedly affected my thinking to some extent in the 17 years that have since passed.

Now to make what response I can to your specific questions:

[Question 1: It appears that, in 1954, *The Courier-Journal* took a position advocating support of the Radford one-shot air strike program for intervention into Indochina. What motivation lay behind this advocacy of intervention?]

1. I can recall no editorial comment which justified the phrase "advocacy of intervention" in regard to Admiral [Arthur W.] Rad-

ford's proposals. My recollection is that we went along with proposals that we send in air power in 1954 to relieve the desperate situation of the French troops, but without displaying any enthusiasm for the move. I had personally seen the difficulties the French were encountering in Vietnam, their inability to adapt the military tactics of St. Cyr to a guerrilla war, and the discouragements they met in their own policy of "Vietnamization"—the training of Vietnamese cadres to carry on their own battles. I was in the audience at the annual meeting of the American Society of Newspaper Editors in Washington when Mr. Nixon, then vice president, stated as a fact that we were going to send air power to relieve the French at Dien Bien Phu. In the end, that policy was rejected by President Eisenhower, but the vice president made a very persuasive case for it. I held no brief for French political control of Indo-China. I thought they made all their concessions to the independence movement there on the schedule of too little and too late. I was not convinced, however, that the rout of the French troops there would lead to an independent Vietnam, and I feared the future involvement of the United States in a situation in which France had made so many tragic blunders.

[Question 2: In 1955, 1956, 1957, and 1958, *The Courier-Journal* maintained a low level of comment if not a complete silence on Vietnam. Why did this paucity of comment exist? How was this policy of *The Courier-Journal* related to the concurrent policy of Eisenhower?]

2. The "low level of comment" on Vietnam from 1955 to 1958 indicated no preconceived editorial policy on our part, but was a reflection of general lack of sharp concern for affairs in that part of the world. I believe you would find that news columns at least equally reflected this relative absence of interest. We know now that conditions were developing during those years which are still causing us grief and concern. At the time, affairs in Europe seemed of more intense interest, involving more directly the Cold War frictions between the United States and the Soviet Union.

[Question 3: Why did *The Courier-Journal* condone the Dulles anti-Communist hard line in 1954, but condemn the same Johnson policy in 1965?]

3. I cannot accept the statement that *The Courier-Journal* "condoned the Dulles anti-Communist hard line in 1954, but condemned the same Johnson policy in 1965." The question, phrased in that way, is at best a very misleading over-simplification. The paper has always recognized the necessity to deal with the danger of Soviet expansionism, though it has deplored the shallow response of mere denunciation

of "Godless Communism" and the fevered search for Communist agents in every area of controversy in our own country. We have never believed that this is an effective way to meet the real challenge. The policy of "containment" of the U.S.S.R. has had a long history, dating back to the decision of President Truman to give help to Greece and Turkey when they were threatened with a take-over by Communist force. We supported that policy. I spent a year as Chief of the Marshall Plan Mission to France, in an effort to rebuild the economic and moral strength of Western Europe so that the nations there could maintain their freedom. We were willing to accept the general thrust of Secretary [John Foster] Dulles's purpose in mustering Western resources in opposition to the possibility of a Soviet attack, though we were often critical of his methods and of his inflexible, arrogant manner.

To say that the Johnson policy of 1965 was the same as that of Mr. Dulles is a misreading of facts, in my opinion. We supported the Johnson administration's policies in Europe, which was the central focus of the Dulles policies. By 1965, however, the issue of Vietnam had become far more acute. It was on Mr. Johnson's conduct of our operations in Southeast Asia that we became increasingly critical. I would like to point out, however, that there were frequent editorials in which we made a direct appeal to Mr. Johnson to alter some of his positions, to cease bombing raids, to seek a cease-fire, to attempt a major rally of world opinion around a truce in Vietnam. In other words, we did not simply attack him when we thought his policies were going astray. We tried to reason with him, on the constant assumption that he was a sane, patriotic and humane man, though a strong-willed and ambitious one. We never represented him editorially as the blood-thirsty ogre which some other papers made of him.

[Question 4: Of what significance is the inclusion of various syndicated writers on *The Courier-Journal* editorial page? To what extent are their views indicative of *The Courier-Journal* editorial policy?]

4. The use of syndicated material on the editorial page does not indicate either agreement or disagreement with the views expressed. It is simply an effort to present our readers with other expressions from qualified sources, such as James Reston of *The New York Times*. Sometimes the space at the bottom of the page is devoted to a light, humorous column, such as Russell Baker produces. At other times, it is used for Editorial Notebook pieces, contributed by members of the editorial page staff writing under their own by-lines, and with complete freedom to express their personal view. On the opposite editorial page we run a variety of material. Some of it may follow the same line

as our editorials, but it is not selected for that purpose. There is a deliberate selection of the David Lawrence column, however, as a way of exposing our readers to a strongly conservative view, which is on many issues diametrically opposed to our own editorial policy.

[Question 5: How do you account for the shift of editorial opinion in *The Courier-Journal* from conservative with respect to Vietnam to extreme liberal after 1966? Has this shift merely mirrored the concurrent shift of public opinion, or has it led public opinion? If so, why?]

5. Here again I do not go along with the phrasing of the question. I do not see the issue of Vietnam as one which can accurately be described as a liberal-conservative issue. I know many people whose general impulse is decidedly conservative, but who are passionately opposed to continuation of the war in Indo-China. I know people of strong liberal leanings who, though not advocating a policy of seeking military victory by any means available, are nonetheless strongly opposed to any hurried withdrawal from Vietnam. Granting that the editorial position of *The Courier-Journal* has become increasingly critical of our involvement in Southeast Asia since 1966, I submit that such change as has occurred is a reflection of the editorial staff's growing disillusionment with the turn of events there, and our unhappy conviction that the United States is losing men, money, and international influence in the process.

[Question 6: To what extent are the cartoons of Hugh Haynie indicative of *The Courier-Journal* editorial policy? How has the addition of Hugh Haynie to the staff of *The Courier-Journal* affected its editorial opinion, particularly as regards Vietnam?]

6. Hugh Haynie joined the editorial page staff of the paper on December 1, 1958, so his addition came long before the alterations in Vietnam policy which you have observed. Mr. Haynie is an independent voice on the page. He chooses his own subjects and treats them in his own way. His views are in general along the same lines as those of the editorial writers, but he does not illustrate or directly reflect the editorial positions taken.

[Question 7: What determines which syndicated writers appear on the editorial page of *The Courier-Journal* on any given day? Is the paper obligated to publish any or all of the syndicated works of a syndicate to which it subscribes? To what syndicates does *The Courier-Journal* subscribe?]

7. Syndicated material is used on the page on the basis of what is available, fresh and stimulating, and the extent of open space to be filled. We never undertake to run all of the syndicated matter we buy.

Political columnists are never omitted on the basis of disagreement with what they are writing on a given day, but even the best syndicated writers have their days of turning out material that is not up to their highest standards. We believe in being selective on the basis of quality alone. *The Courier-Journal* and *The Louisville Times* subscribed to the following wire services: Associated Press, New York Times Service, Washington Post-Los Angeles Times Service, Chicago Daily News Service. In addition, we buy from various syndicates a wide variety of features—columns, comics, women's page features, crossword puzzles, etc.

[Question 8: To what extent, and in what direction did the change-over from Kennedy to Johnson affect *The Courier-Journal* editorial policy on Vietnam?]

8. The change-over from Kennedy to Johnson did not in itself have any effect that I am aware of in the editorial policies of *The Courier-Journal*. The two men differed widely in style and manner, but Mr. Johnson established his administration on a firm foundation of Kennedy policies. Especially in the field of racial equality, he succeeded in pushing through Congress some of the reforms which Kennedy had espoused but on which he had not been able to get positive action. We have always acknowledged in dealing with Mr. Johnson's Vietnam policies that they derived from earlier policies established by Mr. Eisenhower and to a much greater extent by Mr. Kennedy. In the course of the Johnson years, however, this issue developed to a degree that was not easily predictable when his predecessor was in office. We certainly never said or implied that things took a bad turn in Vietnam simply because Johnson instead of Kennedy was at the helm. Our criticisms of Johnson policy were based on developments that occurred during his administration, at points when we felt that he was making unwise decisions.

[Question 9: Who determines the composition and the topic of staff editorials?]

9. The editorials in both our papers are based on an editorial conference held each morning from Monday through Friday at 10:30 A.M. I preside at this meeting, and in my occasional absences my son Barry takes my place. All writers for both pages attend the conference each day. I run down a list of possible topics which I prepare in advance, offer some of my own views on them, and invite the comments of others present. Later I go around the table and ask each participant to suggest further topics, or to contribute additional comment to those already discussed. These conferences run from approx-

imately 30 minutes to over an hour. They afford an opportunity for lively discussion and debate. Some of the topics are clearly indicated for immediate treatment, while others are thrown into the discussion for a first analysis which is to be followed by further research or which must logically await the development of further events. At the conclusion of this general conference, the editorial page editor of each paper sits down with his own group of writers, assigns specific topics on the basis of the earlier discussion, and plans the outline of the resulting page. All editorials come to me in proof, so that I have a chance to see how they are presented. They have previously been submitted to the editorial page editor, who has read them closely. I sometimes make suggestions on the change of a word or phrase, or the addition of a line of thought.

[Question 10: What effect did the 1963 administrative change-over in *The Courier-Journal* management have on its editorial policy as regards Vietnam?]

10. I assume that you refer to the retirement of Mark Ethridge, who for many years carried the title of publisher of the paper. Mr. Ethridge and I worked in the closest kind of association. He regularly attended the editorial conference, and presided when I was not available. Our own views were very closely parallel on all important topics. He seldom wrote editorials himself, however. It was always my responsibility to establish editorial policy on any subject, which I did in close consultation with Mr. Ethridge as well as with members of the editorial page staff. His retirement removed from our circle a wise and experienced voice, but it did not create a change in our editorial policies.

[Question 11: Looking back over the past fifteen years, what changes in the course of *Courier-Journal* editorial policy do you see?]

11. This question is so broad that I find it difficult to answer satisfactorily. The page has changed as events have developed and issues have emerged. I have never been reluctant to alter the position of the paper on a topic if I believe that conditions have made such a change desirable, or if it appeared that our previous policy was not well founded. It would be a dead page which did not reflect the extraordinary movement and complexity of the past 15 years. I feel, however, that our editorial policies have been governed by one constant attitude—a respect for civil liberties, for responsible government at all levels, for courage in fighting oppression in all its forms, and for an assumption of responsible leadership in the affairs of the world which the strength of the United States seems to me to require.

[Question 12: How does today's *Courier-Journal* editorial policy on Vietnam look to you as compared with that of 1954? (*i.e.,* more liberal, more conservative, or about the same?)]

12. Again I do not agree with the designation of policy on Vietnam as an accurate measure of liberalism or conservatism. I would have to answer this question by saying that our policy is more critical of involvement in Southeast Asia than it was in 1954, more aware of the nature of the problems there, and more deeply concerned with the dangers of a further continuation of our direct involvement.

[Question 13: Among major American newspapers where would you rank *The Courier-Journal* in relation to its editorial policy on Vietnam? (*i.e.,* left, right, or center?)]

13. I again find difficulty in interpreting Vietnam policy in terms of right, left and center. If these categories are to be used, however, I would define our policy in this matter as left of center.

[Question 14: What factors do you feel caused *The Courier-Journal*'s disenchantment with LBJ on Vietnam?]

14. I think this question has been materially answered in response to other queries above. We were affected by the continued accumulation of evidence pointing to the futility of our search for a clear-cut solution in Vietnam. The American reliance on air power as an instrument of deterrence has been sadly compromised by our experience in Southeast Asia. We have not shown the hopeful degree of adaptability to the conditions of a guerrilla war. Mr. Johnson's plans were clearly based on confident predictions made to him by the best military brains at his disposal, and confirmed in many cases by his closest civilian associates. We came to the conclusion as time passed that he was honestly misled. We felt that he was plunging further and further into the morass, as one after another of the promised successes turned into failures.

[Question 15: How have changes on the editorial staff affected the editorial policy of *The Courier-Journal* in relation to Vietnam?]

15. The only significant change in the editorial page staff which took place during the period you have considered was the resignation of Weldon James, and the subsequent addition of William Peeples. Neither of these events entailed a change in our policy on Vietnam.

[Question 16: What prompted the resignation of Weldon James?]

16. The reasons for Mr. James's resignation are clearly stated in a signed piece which we published under his name on the editorial page. I enclose a copy of this document, and one of a note which I wrote for publication on the same day.[11]

[Question 17: What views does Molly Clowes hold on Vietnam, and how do they affect editorial policy on Vietnam?]

17. The views of individual editorial writers are not publicly stated, except by their own choice and at their own time. Miss Clowes edits the page, coordinates the work of the other writers, and plays a very active role in the discussion of all issues. It is not her direct responsibility, however, to formulate editorial policy on major issues.[12]

If you would like to correspond further in order to clarify any of these responses in your mind, I would be glad to hear from you. May I wish you the best of luck with your thesis, which I am sure has entailed a heavy amount of research and effort.

From Interview of Barry Bingham by Dennis Cusick, *The Louisville Times,* 21 May 1984

Perhaps I'd like to start by saying [*The Louisville Times*] is not a reflection of *The Courier-Journal*.[13] It is an entity on its own and was from the very beginning. It's a different newspaper—in my view, a different outlook, a different mandate. That doesn't mean the principles of journalism that both observe are not pretty much the same, but I think we have a different job to do with *The Louisville Times,* quite separate from the job that we try to do with the Louisville *Courier-Journal,* and I've always wanted to maintain that separate identity and make it as obvious as possible. A lot of people don't seem to understand that there are two different newspapers in this building. A lot of people in the community just never have quite understood what the distinction is. I call that a failure on our own part that we never have been able to get that across more fully than we have, or more understandably than we have. You know, we're all in the business of communication, but we don't always communicate very effectively—and in this case, I think, over a period of years. We've never quite been able to get through to our readers what the distinction is between the two newspapers, and yet they look very different. I think they reflect their separate missions rather effectively typographically and other ways, but we don't seem to have gotten the whole story across.

The Louisville Times is much more concentrated in the metropolitan area, and there it has a somewhat different audience. There are, of course, overlaps, but I do think there is a much more distinctly metropolitan audience for *The Louisville Times;* whereas *The Courier-Journal* has got some of that, but it also has got a large rural clientele that has to be considered.

I think [*The Louisville Times* has] got to be a more informal newspaper than *The Courier-Journal*. It's got to be a paper that appeals more readily, I think, to younger, upwardly mobile people than *The Courier-Journal*'s general circulation does. I think "Scene" [a Saturday insert devoted to local entertainment, initiated in 1970] is a very good example of taking hold of that opportunity. "Scene" has been a great success and has, I think, helped to develop this audience that we think is a natural one for *The Louisville Times*. I always am looking for new areas of readership for both of our newspapers, because, as we know, readership of newspapers has not increased proportionately with the development of population in this country. And we need to bring in more readers at all times. We can't rely absolutely on the idea that young people as they grow up are going to become automatically newspaper readers. A lot of them do not do that, but there must be ways in which we can make readership of a daily newspaper more attractive to those people. I think the *Times* has made a special effort on that score with young readers who are coming along.

I don't feel that [the demise of *The Louisville Times* is] inevitable. We realize it's a problem. We have seen afternoon newspapers fall by the wayside in recent years in a sad sort of way, many of them quite outstanding papers, but the fact they were in the afternoon field seemed to be fatal to them. I don't think that's necessarily going to happen in Louisville. In fact, I hope very much that it will never happen here. We've got to do all we can, I think, to sustain the *Times*. There are certain obvious disadvantages in having an evening newspaper these days: the fact that television news has skimmed off so much of the top layer, the cream, of the news. Also, our delivery of an afternoon paper is getting more and more difficult as traffic gets denser. Now Louisville people think we have pretty bad traffic here: of course, it's nothing compared to really big cities. I just don't see how you get out of a big metropolitan city to deliver an afternoon paper at all. It's practically impossible. But Louisville is still small enough so we can do that.

The other reason [*The Louisville Times* has been sustained] is, I think, ownership here has always been determined to keep these two newspapers going. Now in some cities, of course, if you've got different ownership you haven't got that kind of feeling at all. You've got, perhaps, rivalry between them. Here, since they are both owned by the same people, there is the feeling that it is our choice, if we can possibly make it work, to keep both newspapers going permanently, feeling that each has a role to perform that we want to see continue.

That is one of the reasons, I think, too, why a concentration of ownership in one small group of people—in this case, a family—makes it a little bit more feasible to come to decisions of this kind and how to carry them out. If you have a very wide ownership, if we had many stockholders, for instance, out in the community or elsewhere, we might find it much more difficult, I think, to persuade them that it was a good idea to keep on with an afternoon paper when so many of them are going out of business. But here we have that choice to make, and as long as we can make it, that's what we're going to do.[14]

I remember when I first began to be active with the papers here in the early thirties. There was talk about how the *Times* was so dominant and was so much more successful financially than the *Courier,* even talk at that time about a possible merger in which the *Times* would take over *The Courier-Journal.* But that was reflecting a financial situation that seemed to exist then, and I'm glad to say that the two papers have come into more even balance since then.

I think it's definitely healthier. I don't think it's a good idea in any case for two papers to be under the same management that much unbalanced, one way or the other. Remember that that was in the day long before TV and when street sales of the *Times* were much larger because men as they left the office downtown were very much inclined to buy an evening paper on the way home. Also, people sat down and read the evening paper when they got home much more frequently than they do now. It was a different era, and the *Times* enjoyed that prosperity while it went on.

[*The Louisville Times* has more circulation than *The Courier-Journal*], I suppose, partly because it is a local newspaper, and I think local readers like to read the paper that has a strong local flavor. And the *Times* has got that. We've always wanted to maintain that. Also, it has features that are very attractive, I think, to readers in this particular locality, and we try to keep the tone of it something that would be appealing to readers here. I think the broader aspect of *The Courier-Journal* makes it, perhaps, a little less personal than the *Times.* I've always had the feeling that the *Times* has a distinct personality in the community, which I like to think will always be there. . . .

I would hope that we've carried good information about many local causes. Of course, on the editorial page we have supported many local causes, but I would like to think, also —quite aside from that sort of advocacy, which I think is important on an editorial page— we have tried to enlighten readers on the facts about a good many local situations that have occurred. I think particularly about the situation that arose in connection with integration here. I date back to the time when we were much concerned about integration, not just of the schools, which came along rather normally, but of the parks, the swimming pools, the restaurants, all of the movie theaters, all those things. The *Times,* I think, did a pretty good job of trying to explain to the community here what was happening in that case. Now that was a local story. That was a *Times* story, as I always saw it. And I hope the *Times* was effective, not just in making a special plea for that kind of thing, but in acquainting people with what the facts were.

[That was in the] 1950s, and that was a big and fundamentally a *Times* story. Other developments, such as the revival of the downtown area of Louisville, which I think is beginning to come together now in a rather striking way, fundamentally, I think, is a *Times* story, again. It's something that I think the *Times* has helped to shape and helped to inform people about.

[When remembering personalities] let's think fundamentally of Tom Wallace, who was the editorial page editor of the *Times.*[15] He was just called editor, but he really was editorial page editor. A most unusual personality, a man with a very strong Kentucky background, a tremendous environmentalist long before it was popular to be that kind of thing, but a man at the same time who had such a strong interest in the rest of the world that he was a principal factor in the Inter-American Press Association. He used to go to meetings in Latin America regularly. A very broad-gauge person, who gave the *Times'* editorial page, I think, not only a strong local character but also gave it, perhaps, a broader outlook than most city newspapers have. He's one of the people I would definitely identify, and very much, as a *Times* man. Then, coming on after him, was Russell Briney, who was a remarkable person, who was first on the *Times* and later on *The Courier-Journal,* so he served in both capacities.[16] Of course, other executives such as Mark Ethridge, who's so fondly remembered here, served for both newspapers, but he always had a strong interest in *The Louisville Times.* He used to find time, no matter how busy he was, to drop by and talk to people on the news staff, which was very much appreciated, and of course, the people he ran into were very often *Times* people who were here. And I think that personal touch that he always maintained was very important to Mark personally, because he'd been a newspaperman all his life, and he loved the business, and he loved to be in contact with people who were working in it, not just the executive level.

I go back to the time when Al Aronson was managing editor of the *Times*. He was the first managing editor that I worked under. Now he died a good many years ago, and there aren't many people on the staff, probably, who would remember Al personally as I do.[17] He was known as a rough, tough boss. He was considered a really hardfisted, hard-nosed newspaperman who demanded a great deal from his staff. I felt that I learned a good deal from him because Al did not spare the rod on me when I was first working for him. He made it clear that a good deal was going to be expected of me, and I needn't think that I could get away with anything as the boss's son, as I then was. Aronson was a rather old-fashioned newspaperman's newspaperman, but a good man, I think, for a local newspaper, because he knew his community well and worked it hard and always believed, as I did, in the very great importance of local news in the *Times*.

I think the thoughts I've tried to express about what I've always wanted the *Times* to be were pretty clearly in my mind from the beginning, particularly since I had started out on the *Times*' news staff and had a pretty strong feeling about that. But I did realize that I was going to have responsibility for two newspapers of very different character. I didn't regret that for one minute, because I felt the different character was one of the things that was most interesting about the job here.

Another thing that many people used to say to me was "You know, many of your readers are Republicans. Many are Democrats. Why don't you have one Democratic newspaper and one Republican newspaper?" as Lexington did for many years—they were quite distinct in that way. I just could not see how I could be that schizophrenic. I didn't see how I could be a Republican in the morning and a Democrat in the evening, or vice versa.[18]

The *Times*' seventy-fifth anniversary issue was one of the ones that was a big event in the life of this newspaper, and I think it was quite well celebrated then. I have not gone back to the files to read the material that came out at that time, but I remember it as being pretty definitive. And some of the history there more clearly, I think, reflected the history of the community as it had developed during those years. And we've tried always to stay close to this town of ours, through all of its ups and downs, and that's what I always want to see the *Times* do.

From Interview of Barry Bingham by William E. Ellis, Eastern Kentucky University, 2 April 1979

We are much more a part of the mainstream of the United States than we were thirty or forty years ago. This was, in many ways, a backward state. The physical evidence of it was that we didn't have any roads and that we were called the detour state. Do you remember when that phrase was used all over the country, that we were the detour state? Because you had to detour around Kentucky. You couldn't ever get through here, so that tourists who were trying to get south, or east, or west, or wherever they were going, had to go around Kentucky. Because the roads here were so terrible the Automobile Association would say, "Take a detour here and go around through Tennessee" or Ohio or Indiana or whatever it may be. This was psychologically true. The state was cruelly divided into sections, by the fact that we had bad roads, and we had all these toll roads and toll bridges. We had very poor communication between various parts of the state. This made the state fragment its power a great deal. It meant that factions in the state were stronger than they needed to be. I think Kentucky has gained a lot since then.

We haven't gone nearly as far as many of us would like to see in education. I begin to think that we're going to make some progress on that at last—partly because of the infusion of more money, but partly because of this system which is just starting today, by the way, of testing the results in selected grades in the public schools. Now that in itself is not going to perform any miracles, but at least for the first time we're going to have some idea of what these boys and girls are really achieving in public school. How backward or how forward are they? If they are backward, if they are behind national averages, we've got to do something about bringing them up. And just spending more money is not going to do it. We're going to have to have remedial reading classes. We're going to have to have a great deal of remedial work done in order to bring them up to the national average, as I think we must do for the future of this state. Beyond that, we've got to look much more, I think, to how people are being taught in the first instance. We ought not to have to do as much remedial work as we do in Kentucky schools. The children ought to be taught better in the first instance so that you won't have to go back and correct so much. But that's a long argument which I suppose people have very different views about it, but it seems to me so obvious that we've got to spend more money at the very beginning and see people get more education at the start so they can proceed from there, instead of going back and spending a lot of money on remedial work in colleges even. You get college students who are not capable of doing satisfactory work and have to be taught reading and writing. This to me is so horribly wasteful, not only of money but of human talent. We're handicapping those people so badly.

All right. I think Kentucky is improving on that. I think Kentucky is a state that is becoming increasingly a two-party state, and I think that probably is an advantage. A state that leans so heavily to one party or the other, whichever it may be, tends to get stagnant politically. Now this state is getting more and more evenly divided, and I think probably this is a good thing for us. It's going to mean that both parties are going to have to be a little bit more responsible in order to win public support. That's good. The state is marvelously placed for many things. Industrial development. Tourist development. We have a state name, Kentucky, that would be worth a billion dollars a year in public advertising. There is something about the name and the Old Kentucky Home and the atmosphere and the color of this state that is a tremendous advantage to us that we couldn't possibly buy. You just can't purchase things of that kind. We've got it naturally. We've never taken full advantage of a lot of these things, but I think we're now beginning to come around to it. Another thing mentioned earlier that I'd like to stress again—I think the old division between the city and the country in Kentucky is disintegrating, and I'm very happy to see that. Part of that may be the influence of television. Everybody always wants to blame everything bad on television, and it does do some bad things, I'm afraid. But the effect of TV on making people more alike and making them understand each other better, in rural areas as well as urban areas, I think, has been favorable. And I think it's high time somebody had a good word to say for this aspect of television.

There are some areas where industry has grown rapidly, and you can see the evidence of it, but in general this is still a state that has rather light industrial development. Many of us are concerned now about nuclear development all down the Ohio River valley, which I think we've got to be very careful about. Many people have talked for years about the Ruhr of America, as though this were altogether a desirable thing. It could perhaps bring a great deal of employment into this state, but I think we've got to consider what else it might bring in in the way of pollution and perhaps actual danger to populations living near these nuclear plants.

However, talking about the changes in Kentucky that I've seen, just driving around the state can be a revelation. When I used to drive through Kentucky—and I've always enjoyed doing it—you saw so many run-down farms thirty, forty, fifty years ago. You saw so many houses with no paint on them. You saw barns falling in. You saw a lack of agricultural equipment in many rural areas which was obviously causing problems. You drive around Kentucky now, and you see a lot of prosperity. Now people still haven't got as much money as they'd like to have, but there are a great many people in Kentucky that are getting on pretty well these days. The rural areas especially seem to me to show a very distinct improvement in tone over the way it used to be years ago. If it's only the question of a fence having been whitewashed or a barn propped up and put back in order, you see this kind of thing as a symbol. You see a lot of good, prosperous herds of cattle around on the fields and pastures in Kentucky, and this usually means that things are going better. I think the old problem of what's to be done about the tobacco economy is still to be faced, but I think we're beginning at last to think about what crops can be brought into Kentucky and will substitute for some of the cash value of tobacco, which has always been so appealing to Kentucky farmers. We're going to have to find, I think, some other crops which will bring in that kind of cash inducement which makes tobacco so appealing and yet at the same time be less subject to the winds of change than tobacco.

From Interview of Barry Bingham by the Staff of the Poynter Institute for Media Studies, 4-5 April 1985

I'm always very much concerned about foreign affairs, and I think we're facing a very difficult period ahead of us in foreign affairs, in which our country, it seems to me, is not going in the right direction on some important issues, such as Central America.[19] I'm very much concerned about the continued spread of atomic weapons around the world, and I'm afraid that the present efforts to hold down on weapons in Geneva may have exactly the opposite effect. I think we may be faced with a tremendous proliferation of weapons, a big weapons buildup on the part of the Soviet Union as well as the United States. I can't help but see that as really a possible disaster in the truest sense for the human race. If the United States and the Soviet Union cannot find some way to work out this very difficult problem, I cannot foresee anything but disaster for our children and grandchildren in the next generation. I think it's ruinous. Now there is no simple solution, no simple answer to that kind of question. It's tremendously broad, tremendously complicated. I think a newspaper does owe it to its readers to try to inform them just as fully as possible on such an issue as that. To take a vigorous editorial stand, as I say, but also to give them all the information you possibly can from all sources in the news columns.

For years we've pursued a policy of putting, perhaps, more foreign news into our daily papers than the public would necessarily want or ask for. I think if you only gave your readers exactly what you think they are asking for, you would probably have such a heavy budget of comics and sports that you would have hardly anything else in the newspaper. That, obviously, is not quite acceptable. We've always given them, I think, a little more of foreign news than, perhaps, they think they would ask for. However, you've got to make it understandable to them. There's no use in throwing foreign news at readers if they really can't understand it or don't really want to read it at all. You've got to make it as palatable as possible. And I think that is a very neat trick. It's got to be very well written. It's got to be varied. It's got to be understandable to readers. And we've tried awfully hard through the years to do that. Some people have wondered why we use so much foreign news and so much national news, as distinct from local news. We've tried to give it a balance all the way through. And it's not a balance, as I say, that you can ever quite measure, but it's a balance that we have in mind all the time and that we always think about.

Some people think that a newspaper simply ought to reflect its community. I don't see that that would be possible, even if you thought it was a good idea, because you don't really know what everybody is thinking in a community. Suppose a newspaper tried to reflect exactly what you think people think on a certain issue, and then their opinion would change in another year or so. You would have to change the policy again, and that would be impossible.

I suppose the race issue was the one that created the most stir in Louisville and the one that created a lot of adverse reaction, let's face it. We always felt that racial fairness was not only the right thing morally but that it was in the long run the only way a community could thrive. I derived my feeling about this, I'm quite sure, from my grandfather Bingham, who fought all the way through the Civil War, came back to a ruined economy in North Carolina in 1865, and one of the first speeches he made to a group there was saying the black people of North Carolina are going to have to be educated. We cannot have a small, or a large, black minority in this state that is illiterate and that has no part in running the whole state as it should be run. Now that was, I think, a very advanced position for a man who had been a Confederate officer all the way through the war. And I always felt that that was the right tradition for us to follow in the newspapers here. It did get us some pretty bad criticism at times. We had lots of telephone calls in the middle of the night. And I always kept my name in the book, so people could call me up if they wanted to. At three or four o'clock in the morning, I often got abusive calls, and nine out of ten of them were based on our race policies, or how they perceived our race policies. And in many cases, of course, they would end up by saying, "You're just a Communist sheet, and this is a southern edition of *The Daily Worker,*" and that kind of thing. That was the syndrome we're all unhappily familiar with, that if you don't agree with somebody, you call him a Communist. And we did get a lot of that. However, I do think some achievements were made in Louisville, *somewhat* as a result of our papers' policies. At least I hope we had something to do with it. This was the first city in the South which integrated its public schools. And it was considered a notable enough event in that case for the superintendent of schools to be called to Washington to be interviewed by President Eisenhower and congratulated because this change had been made without really upsetting the community or creating any horribly bad episodes.

I think newspapers have got to feel accountable to their readers every day, every hour. It's something we cannot possibly dodge, because if we try to get away from it, we're simply going to lose the readers. They've got to feel that we're serving their interests, and we've got to keep working at that. There's this great question now that the media simply is not regarded as trustworthy or reliable or important, to a great many readers. We've got to get away from that. One way *The Courier-Journal* and *The Louisville Times* faced this problem was to put in an ombudsman. This was the first one in the country in a daily newspaper. This is a full-time official, whose whole duty is to take complaints and criticisms from readers and to make corrections where they're indicated. Make them promptly. Not just legal corrections, but corrections that need to be made so that the reader can feel that he has gotten a fair treatment. I had hoped, in the beginning, that this would improve our image of fairness quite considerably. It hasn't gone quite as far as that, I think, but I believe it's made people believe that we're a little more responsive to criticisms, when they are justified criticisms.

I think, certainly, that more attractively presented newspapers are a part of the wave of the future. I think newspapers have been rather dreary-looking through the years, as a matter of fact, not just because they were black and white, but because their type dress was often very old-fashioned and very unattractive. We've tried to make our papers attractive, visually, through the years by the way we've used type and layout. I do think that for the future, color is going to be more and more important in newspapers. Just think of the days in television when we thought black-and-white television was a miracle in itself, and now almost nobody is satisfied with anything but color television. I guess that's the same way we are going to go in newspapers.

From Barry Bingham "Time and the River Have Changing Currents," *The Courier-Journal,* 2 December 1959

It is plain that time is very unevenly distributed among the members of the human race. Children have too much of it, and most adults have far too little. And, like sleep, it is impossible to hoard it up when we have it in excess supply, to hold as a reserve against the days when we will need it badly.

Most of the familiar figures of speech about time were obviously coined by people on the downward slope of life. "Time flies" is a statement that is sometimes true, but often utterly false. It was an elderly Robert Herrick who urged his young readers to "gather ye rosebuds while ye may, old time is still a flying."

To those who can summon the moods and memories of their own childhood, the thought of time suddenly stretches out like pulled taffy. Instead of hurrying by, the hours of childhood often limped past on maddeningly slow feet. Of course this pace was most irritating in the weeks before Christmas, and before the end of the school year. But the phenomenon exists in every day of childhood. A child's afternoon simply has more hours in it than an adult's.

There were summer afternoons in my childhood that were as slow as molasses, as though they were too thick with sunshine to flow more swiftly. I can remember lying on the ground, out near Cherokee Park, and watching the activity that took place in the long grass. There was a warm smell of pink clover from a nearby field, like a soft accompaniment to the muted sights and sounds.

The world of ants is surely an adult world, full of purposeful bustlings to and fro, ticking with the pulse of responsibility. But there are other small creatures moving in the greenery with a pace that is slowed to a child's long afternoon. The grasshopper makes sudden, prodigious springs from blade to blade, but between leaps he takes plenty of time to survey the little green universe around him. The bee may be busy gathering honey, but his hum is the drowsiest of sounds. Birds skim swiftly through the air, yet they have leisure to come back over and over again to the same leafy bough, or to examine with timeless intensity a bit of bright glass that catches the sunlight. The shadows of the trees move with an unhurried rhythm like the movement of the waves on a deserted, sun-drenched beach.

An adult, plumped down on the grass for a couple of hours on a hot afternoon, would fidget himself to death. He would be bothered about the ants crawling on his clothes. He would keep looking at his watch. He would probably wish for a portable radio "to make the time pass," or even some work from the office to finish up.

There is an idea that the members of a simpler civilization than ours have more time on their hands for the joys of leisure. I'm not sure that this isn't just a sentimental notion. There was an early American saying: "Time is something that we ain't got anything but." That is a pleasing thought, but the people who lived on the early frontier were so busy keeping alive that they could seldom have known a moment of leisure. We imagine a winter evening in a pioneer cabin, when the family sat together in unhurried companionship. The chances are, however, that the mother would be weaving or sewing with all her might, the father working on his gun, and only the children could swim about for a few moments in the warm limbo of pure idleness.

Maybe something could be done about arranging a more even distribution of time among age groups today. Nearly all adults feel an urge to escape from what Matthew Arnold called the "sick hurry" of modern life. That is surely why some people make a retreat at the Abbey of Gethsemani, and why others search feverishly for a hobby that will make them oblivious for a little while to "time's winged chariot hurrying near."

H. G. Wells used to write about a time machine, capable of rearranging the hours, the days, and even the years. Maybe somebody could invent a device that would give grown-up Americans some of the extra hours they were so eager to discard when they were very young.

I'm afraid, however, that such an invention would not really serve. The truth is that people, when they grow up, lose their talent for the use of long, slow, idle hours, just as they lose their first teeth and the summer freckles of childhood. If given those surplus hours, they wouldn't know what to do with them.

We are all at one with John Quincy Adams, who noted that "my stern chase after time is like the race of a man with a wooden leg after a horse." Something inside us keeps ticking like a time bomb, and with increasing age the spring gets wound up tighter and tighter. Time for most of us is a fugitive that has run back into the stillness of our childhood, where we can never return to drag it out again.

It may be the best thing to give in to the process, and try to make some good use of it. There is a lot of sense in this old saying: "Let time, which makes you homely, make you sage."

Barry Bingham, "Lines For A Bequest," 1984

These are for you, my unknown heir,
These eyes that served me long and sweetly,
To view a life we cannot share,
No longer mine, but yours completely.
Use them to watch my joyous sights,
Autumnal gold, green blush of spring,
High diamond stars on winter nights,
White sparkling snow, glossy blackbird's wing,
Visions to Adam fresh unfurled,
In their first shining clarity,
Wedding my dear, familiar world
With wonders I shall never see.[20]

Remarks by Barry Bingham, on the Reopening of the Brown Hotel, 12 January 1985

Ladies and gentlemen, I am unabashed in saying how delighted I am to be here tonight. This isn't just a great occasion as it is for everybody. It's a special one for me, because as Tom Simons told you, my father was in this same position in 1923 at that first opening.[21]

Now, I have a proposal for you. I'm thinking already about the one-hundredth anniversary of the hotel in 2023. You know that isn't just a science fiction movie. It will be a real year, I guess, and I just may not be available for a return engagement on that occasion, but I have a candidate. I have a grandson who'll be glad to take his place on this platform on that occasion, and I'm already preparing him for it. I'm giving him all the training that he'll need so he'll know just how to handle himself. And I've got plenty of time to get him ready—he's only two years old. I'm going to tell him about all of the wonderful things that we know of about this hotel. I'm going to tell him about the wonderful old days, dancing to those fine orchestras up there in the Crystal Ballroom, about the Benedictine sandwiches the ladies used to have in the Tea Room, and especially about the Mint Juleps in the English Grill. And oh yes, those Hot Brown sandwiches in the Bluegrass Room—something nobody has ever quite been able to reproduce in all their golden glamour. He'll hear about all that. You see, all of us are awash in nostalgia tonight—all us older people. I think nostalgia is the hottest product in America today. I think it's only a question of time until somebody finds a way to bottle it and put it out as Old Nostalgia, and everybody will want to buy it.

But I don't want to talk about the past tonight. I really want to talk about the future, because that's what my grandson will be concerned with. Now you know this hotel was, at the beginning, as act of faith on the part of J. Graham Brown. That's why it was built, as an act of faith in this community of ours. Twice when he was building the hotel, he added additions to it, and he said, when asked why he was doing it: "Because I have confidence in Louisville." That was his reason—and a darned good one which proved to be correct. At some later date, there were some problems financially with the hotel, as there are with many. A bank threatened to foreclose, and here was Graham Brown's answer: "Go to hell." It was so typical of him. I can see him right now scuttling through this lobby. You know, he was a small, compact man, absolutely charged with energy and determination. We used to laugh a little bit and call him the Wizard of Oz, because he looked very much like the Wizard of Oz as he hastened around. But beyond that, there was a reason for it. He really saw Louisville as the Emerald City, as a place where anybody who remembers the Oz books knows, anything in the world could happen. That's what Graham Brown felt about this town.

From the very beginning this hotel was legendary, and it began to gather legends around it. One of the legends you've all heard was that a fish was caught in this lobby by Elmer the bell captain. Now I saw that fish. I cannot lie to you. I did not see it swimming. I saw it on the wall. It was there on a plaque; and where is that fish now, I ask you?

The only thing I miss in the magnificent decor of this hotel is that wonderful stuffed fish. It should come back.

When my father was speaking at the earlier occasion, he said: "Success is never an accident. It is a result of courage, character, judgment, and hard work." I add one more word to what he said: it's also a result of vision. And those are the characteristics that Graham Brown had *par excellence.* They're the same qualities, I submit to you, that have been shown by another generation of people here in Louisville, not all of whom are natives of this town. They have shown these same characteristics, and that vision especially, in rebuilding and reconstructing this magnificent showplace that we're standing in tonight. So now I'm going to tell you that I think this is not only exciting in itself: it's a part of a still bigger project, the Broadway Renaissance. So the whole thing is spreading out from this magnificent center we're in tonight.

Let me ask you, ladies and gentlemen, to join me in a toast. Would you please raise your glasses. I am proposing a toast to the Brown Hotel of the past, so fondly remembered, the Brown Hotel of the present, of which we are all justly proud, but most of all, to the Brown Hotel of the future. I know it will be a very, very bright one. Let's drink to it.

From Interview of Barry Bingham by William E. Ellis, Eastern Kentucky University, 24 September 1987

[In November 1916 Barry Bingham's father married Mary Lily Kenan Flagler (1867-1917), widow of financier Henry M. Flagler (1830-1913). When she died eight months later, the Kenan family initiated an investigation, which exonerated Judge Bingham of any wrongdoing. The results of an autopsy were never made public, however, and rumors persisted. When David Leon Chandler dredged them up in his book *The Binghams of Louisville,* adding the twist that Judge Bingham had also infected Mary Lily with syphilis, Barry Bingham was incensed.]

The only reason that I got up this great documentation was to try to just protect my father's memory as far as I could against these perfectly ridiculous, irresponsible charges.[22] So I got all the material together that I could. As you know, Macmillan decided not to publish the book, but I guess it's going to be published elsewhere. I hear there is another publishing house that apparently is planning to bring it out in January, but I don't really know whether that's true or not.[23] That's the word that has come to me. I know that Chandler, the writer, has been peddling it elsewhere. When Macmillan decided not to publish, they did make a statement that Chandler was free to seek another publisher, if he wanted to do that. And that is what he has done.

He came to see me, saying that he was representing *People* magazine and wanted to do a little interview with me about the sale of the papers—nothing whatever about my father and Mary Lily Kenan, any of that.[24] Then, after he had been talking to me for a few minutes, it began to be obvious to me that he was not talking about the sale at all. He was talking entirely about things that had happened when I was twelve years old, about my stepmother's death and all that, which of course I had no personal memory of, or couldn't have.

It was right after the Flagler book. I hadn't seen the Flagler book at that point, but he told me he had written a book about Mr. Flagler, and he later on told me he was planning to write a book about my father and Mary Lily. But in the beginning I had understood that this was nothing in the first place but an interview with a magazine correspondent, and no book was mentioned whatsoever. That's the way it developed. That was my only direct conversation with him—in my old office. Then, rather to my surprise, a lady came in, and it was his wife. She also joined us, and I hadn't known she was coming, but the two of them, then, I talked to for a little while. I tried then to answer their questions as best I could, but I made it clear to them that many of the questions they were asking were things I couldn't possibly know about, because they were events that had happened in my childhood, or even earlier.

He starts out so obviously, in his book about the Binghams of Louisville, with a thesis that he then builds up with what he regards as information on the subject. He makes everything fit the pattern. That's the way the book was constructed. And I'm glad that a really reputable publishing house, such as Macmillan, felt that they just did not want to publish that material in that form.

The first point that I made [to Macmillan] about the Chandler book on Flagler was the book contained nothing in the way of an accusation against my father, but the jacket had that very overt statement that he was very probably the person who had killed Mary Lily. And this, of course, I thought was unconscionable, particularly since I had never known a jacket blurb which had an entirely different point from what the book itself had. That's what that one did. And I protested that, to begin with, to Macmillan, but I could get no satisfaction on that at all. They just made it clear that this was in the interest of selling the book and selling the next book that came along, which Chandler was going to do for them. [The Flagler book] is a pretty slipshod kind of job. There are lots of things in there about people's motives and what they were thinking at the time, and all that sort of thing, that I don't think a respectable biography goes in for.

We had no way to know, of course, what the Chandler book would contain, but as soon as I got some information about some of the charges being made in the book, I thought the time had come when I had to take action. I immediately got in touch with our attorneys and started the process on that.

I just heard about [my father's remarriage] from my aunts, with whom I was living at that time, and it sounded all right to me. It was several years after my mother died. I was really too young to have any view of what it would be like. And if I thought he would be happy with it, I would have been glad for that. I was only with [my father and stepmother] at that one Christmas, in 1916, when they were back here at the Seelbach Hotel. I think they were there several weeks, while they were looking around for a house. [They rented] Lincliffe. The Belknap family were the owners of it. Lincliffe is further down the River Road. The property on which we now live is about two miles further out, at Glenview. The big house there was built in 1912 [1910-11], I think, and the house in which we are now living was built in 1916 for Mary Churchill Humphrey—built by her parents, Judge Humphrey and his wife, who lived on the other side of the hill there. They built it for her. It was an interesting thing. She had been living in Italy for some years. She was something of an expatriate American, and she loved living in Europe and was very happy in Italy, but of course, World War I drove her back to this country. And her parents decided the thing to do was to give her a little Italian house in which she would feel comfortable, right on the Glenview property, and that's how that started. It's a little Italian villa, I guess.

Glenview started around what they called the Fincastle Club.[25] Some people had what they considered summer cottages out there. That was really the beginning. It seems a little odd now, but it was considered something of a summer resort for people who lived downtown in Louisville, and they went out there and spent some of the hot months in cottages out there. Then, later on, people began to build homes there, and the Ballards built two houses on that property out

there, one on each side of the road.[26] Then Judge Allen and various
others built their homes out there.[27] So it developed from that. Further
back into Glenview are much more extensive real estate developments, with many houses on smaller lots. But the big ones were the
ones that really started out there.

After my father was married to Mary Lily, he found that she had
a will which she had made prior to their marriage, and he realized
from his legal experience that that would not be a valid will, since she
had remarried after it was signed. So he persuaded her to do what they
call "republish" the will, which is to revalidate the will, really, establishing what she had originally intended with her will. Otherwise,
if that had not been republished, he would have had a right to half of
her real property, and he persuaded her that was not what he thought
should be done. Then, in return, more or less, I think, for that, she
decided that she wanted to make a special provision for him and dictated this codicil to Mr. Davies.[28]

I always called him Uncle Will, as we did in the family. He was
such a friend of my father's.[29] He was a delightful, genial gentleman,
of the southern old school, a most attractive person, with a wonderful
sense of humor. He was very well known and well liked in the Louisville bar community here—very respected. [He and my father were]
very close friends all the way from their college days on. And then,
they did join in a law firm here in Louisville. Oh, my goodness, when
I was in my childhood, I used to be over at the Davies house frequently. He had four children, who are more or less the age of my
family, and we all saw a lot of each other.

I don't know [why they dissolved their law partnership]. I think
there may have been reasons why they felt they could go on independently, but there was never any bad feeling between them or any disagreement that I ever knew about. There was no breach whatsoever,
because those were the years when I continued to see so much of Uncle Will and his family. They lived on Ransdell. Funny enough, I was
passing that house last night. I remember it so well. It's now the house
of the president of the University of Louisville.

I've been aware of [the rumors that have circulated since Mary
Lily Bingham's death], vaguely. When you are a child, you just can't
comprehend things of that kind. And I remember just knowing about
them in general—that this was a disagreeable episode in my father's
life. That's about all I ever knew about it. I knew it caused him grief.
I think he would have been most reluctant to see his wife's alcoholism
exposed publicly. You know, in those days that kind of thing was not

nearly so much talked about as it is now. And it was, I think, undoubtably the cause of her death. And neither he nor the Kenan family wanted to see that exposed to public view.

He didn't know of her alcoholic problem until after they were married, and then he was suddenly confronted with this, what was unfortunately a sort of cyclical habit of taking much too much to drink and really being out of herself for several days. He tried very hard to get her to undergo treatment and tried to work that out also through Dr. Young by getting her to go to the Hopkins or somewhere else to have treatment. She was unwilling to do that.[30]

I knew that political opponents of his—and he had political opponents, of course, as anybody has who is in public life—did make use of this. I remember, of course, the event when his confirmation was up before the Senate, and these things were brought back up. But they seemed to have been brought up by people who were so obviously politically motivated, I didn't think it could have had too much validity in people's minds.

[One who brought it up was Abraham Flexner.] The Flexner family had been a very well-known family, particularly in medicine, and Abraham Flexner is the man who is credited as being sort of the father of the modern medical school. He was the one who felt that there were a great many medical schools in this country, many of which were just very inferior. He began the movement toward consolidating those schools and putting them on a higher basis and, therefore, had a very good reputation in that way. Unfortunately, and I never knew anything about this, really, until all this matter came up, he and my father had had a disagreement about a boys' school here that Dr. Flexner at that time had been associated with. My father had entered my brother in the school, then found that Dr. Flexner was not taking any part in it at all, and had objected to that, so there was a disagreement between them on a perfectly trivial matter of that sort, which had nothing to do with what later happened between them.[31] But unfortunately, Dr. Flexner apparently felt that my father had been unfair to him in that and then took what would appear to be a really rather bitter revenge against him.

One of them, whose name came up pretty prominently in those hearings, was Congressman Jack May, who had been pretty strongly opposed in the editorials of the newspaper, I have now learned.[32] This again was long before my day. They may have been critical of him, and he was therefore, I think, taking a shot at my father because of that. It's the old theory that you really can't fight the newspaper or city hall, but there are ways that people try to fight back, and if they can't do it directly, they do it indirectly. In that case, he really tried to do it through character assassination. Those are the ones who spring to mind, right away. There were a few other people who, I think, may have indulged in the gossip here in Louisville, and perhaps elsewhere, but nobody else, that I knew of, who took such an overt part in this procedure as those people did.

Dr. Ravitch [a dermatologist] I just knew when I was a child, and I went to him a couple of times as a doctor. He moved away from Louisville a long time ago, and I've never heard of him or seen him since.[33] [My father] was under treatment for [eczema] for years. I think it was an allergic problem, similar to the one that I have and that I've had all my life, really. In my case, it turns into asthma and hay fever. In his case, he did suffer very repeatedly with attacks of eczema.[34] And he took treatment for that and did the best he could to counteract it, but we don't even know how to deal with those things very well now, and I'm afraid there was really very little that could be done for him at that time. That's why he went to [Dr. Ravitch]. But he also did go to Johns Hopkins to be investigated for this problem.

[Aunt Sadie] used to have an outbreak that they called nettle rash in those days, which was another form of allergy, and she would have terrible outbreaks of the skin, and she was under treatment for the same kind of thing. I think it all came from the same ancestor, whoever he may have been. We all have it. I'm happy to say that none of my children has inherited it, which is unusual. I thought, undoubtedly, that at least one of my kids would have had it. And so far, our grandchildren don't seem to be subject to it. My father, also, at that time, not only had these attacks of, really, not shingles, but a rather similar type of thing, and he had really blinding headaches that came on, more or less in conjunction with that.

**From Interview of Barry Bingham by Carmin Pinkstaff,
Bonnet Productions, North Junior High School,
Henderson County, Kentucky, 15 June 1987**

The one that we had before was called the Bingham Enterprises Foundation. The purpose of that was to give to good causes 5 percent of our pretax earnings of all of our family corporations, and for a number of years we did do that, and we hope we did some good with it. At the time when these properties were sold, that had to come to an end, because that 5 percent of earnings, of course, was no longer available. My wife and I have since then started a small fund—it's not a foundation, it's a fund really—in which we are expending some money on what we regard as very important causes. The top priorities with us really are education, and the arts, and mental health. And for those three things we are trying to do the very best thing we can. We are confining our gifts, our pledges, to our own area, here. There are so many good causes all over the country, and indeed, all over the world, that we get letters about or telephone calls from friends. If we scattered out over all that field, we wouldn't be able to do enough to have any effect. We hope that here, in our own community, in our own area of Kentucky and southern Indiana, we can have some effect, and we want to do that while we are still around to watch the results.[35]

There are still places I'd like to go. I'd like to go to Kathmandu, in Nepal. I've never been there. My son has been there and thought it was wonderful and fascinating, but I've been to a lot of other places that I'm glad I went to at the time I did. My wife and I went to Afghanistan a few years ago, and we couldn't go there now, of course. It would be impossible for Americans to travel there. I went as a member of the board of the Asia Foundation, which had an office there and was doing some good work in Afghanistan. We had a fascinating time. I think it is the most beautiful country I ever saw in my life, and very rugged and very admirable. And those people have withstood siege and occupation for many years and always held out. I hope they're going to hold out again.

I enjoy traveling. I've done a lot of it in connection with my newspaper work. I was once the chairman of the International Press Institute, which had meetings in countries all over the world, and I loved going to those meetings.

It's nice to think that I haven't lived so long without having some purpose yet to be served. Nobody knows how long anybody is going to live. Even very young people don't know that, of course. But when you get to my age, you've got to think about what can I do with whatever is left of it. And there are things I still would love to see done, and I'm going to try to do as many of them as I can while I'm still around. And I have the wonderful support of my wife on all these things. We agree on the things we're trying to accomplish, and we're working together on them.

From Letter by Barry Bingham to William Keller, M.D.,
29 November 1987

I would rather be talking to you about this matter, as a dear old and supportive friend, which you have always been.[36]

It may be easier for both of us to do it this way at the moment, however.

Bill Blodgett has diagnosed me as having a brain lesion about a half inch in length.[37] The diagnosis of malignancy seems to be certain, though we will seek confirmation and advice at Massachusetts General in Boston without delay.

The possible courses of action seem to be surgery or a start on radiation. Bill has felt that exploratory surgery would be unsafe and possibly counterproductive because of the location of the tumor, in a narrow aperture far back at the base of the brain.

Dr. Lawrence Borgis at Mass. General has a somewhat different opinion, however, from what he has learned by telephone from Bill. He feels that there would be a rather short and direct entry to the affected area. None of this can of course be decided until examinations at Mass. General and full consultation. I am flying up at 1:30 Monday, carrying the X-rays from Norton.

Mary is going with me, though it is not easy for her as she is just recovering from a kidney infection which caused a fever of up to 103 degrees. She has been free of the fever for three days, but is naturally a little weak and less able to control her emotions than she would normally be. You know her, however, for the strong and selfless person she has always been, and is at this trying moment. Bill has started me on Decadron pills, one every six hours. The cortisone seems to be taking effect as a mood elevator, and I am having no side effects.

This all came on pretty suddenly. I had had some hoarseness, loss of voice, and minor breathing problems back in Chatham last summer. More recently, I became conscious of a loss of balance and difficulty with depth perception. I played tennis as recently as November 10, but cut myself out of the doubles game then until I could find out what was going on.

Bill gave me a full physical, finding no physical changes of note, but listening to my description of symptoms. He felt that they might just derive from the aging process as I move through my 82nd year, but ordered the brain scan to see if anything turned up. And this little sneaker did turn up.

As you know, I have had a long and interesting life, with sad episodes more than counteracted by many blessings. It did not surprise me that age would at last catch up with me, but the suddenness of the change appeared unexpected. I have had a kind of warm and mellow Indian Summer of late, with many of the things I had wanted to accomplish coming to fruition. I have had the incomparable blessing of a happy and enduring marriage.

I am not signing off. I feel that something may be done through surgery, or alternatively through radiation. I will count as always on your unfailing support for both Mary and me.

Notes

Chapter 1. Childhood

1. Mary Henrietta Long (1842-1922), the daughter of Dennis Long (1816-93) and Catherine Elizabeth Young Long (1818-1900), married Samuel Adams Miller (1839-95). Dennis Long had established one of the largest foundries for the production of cast-iron pipe principally for municipal gas and water systems. He also produced steamboat engines and machinery and was instrumental in obtaining the financing for Louisville's Big Four Bridge, the construction of which his son-in-law Samuel Miller nearly completed. Miller had been a store clerk, had served on the Louisville general council, and had been a miller before becoming a partner in Dennis Long and Company. He suffered from recurring depression, and in late 1894 he went with his family to Asheville, North Carolina, to seek relief. It was there that his daughter Eleanor Everhart Miller (1871-1913) met the instructor in Greek and Latin at the Bingham Military School, Robert Worth Bingham (1871-1937). On 2 February 1895, while awaiting Eleanor's arrival in Asheville after a brief trip, Samuel Miller threw himself under a train and committed suicide. According to his obituary, he was president of Dennis Long and Company, the East End Improvement Company, and various municipal water companies and was also a bank director.

2. The stone house with a polychromed mansard roof was built by John Watts Kearney about 1874 and purchased by the Millers in 1885.

3. Charles Harvey Joiner (1852-1932) was born in Charlestown, Indiana. He began to paint formally in 1874. He later maintained a studio in Louisville and was encouraged by the journalist and humorist Irvin S. Cobb to "stick to that light effect," which became characteristic of his paintings of autumn woodlands.

4. *The Courier-Journal* reported: "Anyone in Louisville who didn't see the comet last night must have been asleep or just too stubborn to look at the clear western sky. It was there, nucleus, nebulae and all four tails" (26 May 1910). The comet reappeared in April 1986.

5. *Sputnik I,* the world's first artificial satellite, was launched on 4 October 1957.

6. Eleanor Miller Bingham's brother, Dennis Long Miller (1875-1914), married Lucy F. Young (1873-1929). They had no children.

7. Robert Norwood Bingham was born on 15 April 1897. His name was later changed to Robert Worth Bingham, Jr. He attended the Bingham Military School and graduated from Louisville Male High School. He attended the University of Virginia and Tulane University. He married twice and was survived by Felice Desmit Bingham when he died at their residence in Genoa, Nevada, on 30 December 1965.

Henrietta Worth Bingham was born on 3 January 1901. She graduated from the Louisville Collegiate School in 1920, attended Stuart Hall in Staunton, Virginia, and matriculated at Smith College. She lived in England from 1923 to 1936 and then returned to raise horses on her Harmony Landing Farm, now a country club, near Goshen, Kentucky. She moved to Connecticut in 1948 and later moved to New York City, where she married B.F. McKenzie. They were divorced. She died on 17 June 1968.

8. Lots 28 and 29 at the end of Douglass Boulevard in the Douglass Park Subdivision were purchased for twelve thousand dollars by Mary Henrietta Miller in 1902 and were conveyed for one dollar to her daughter Eleanor Miller Bingham in 1905 (Jefferson County Deed Book 572, p. 131, and Book 625, p. 239). The Binghams began construction of a house designed by the architectural firm of Hutchings and Hawes. They continued to live with Mrs. Miller until the house was completed in the summer of 1907. When Robert Worth Bingham purchased a residence, later known as Melcombe Bingham, from Mina Breaux Ballard in 1919, Ballard obtained the Cherokee Park property and immediately sold it to Giles VanCleave (Jefferson County Deed Book 905, p. 585). It burned down on 28 February 1926.

9. Alma Kellner, age eight, was last seen alive at the altar of St. John's Church on 8 December 1909. Her disappearance triggered a nation-wide search. See *The Courier-Journal,* 25 January 1935.

10. William E. Ellis, Ph.D., professor of history at Eastern Kentucky University, interviewed Barry Bingham six times from 1978 to 1987 and published several articles on Robert Worth Bingham and his family, including "The Bingham Family: From the Old South to the New South and Beyond," *The Filson Club History Quarterly* 61 (Jan. 1987): 5-33, and "Robert Worth Bingham and Louisville Progressivism, 1905-1910," *The Filson Club History Quarterly* 54 (April 1980): 169-196.

11. Eleanor Miller Bingham died on 28 April 1913. She was forty-two years old.

12. Sadie Alves Bingham was born on 10 February 1867. She attended Peace Institute with her sister, Mary Kerr Bingham, who was born on 6 November 1865. It was through his sisters that Robert Worth Bingham met Mary Lily Kenan, also a student at the institute, who became his second wife. Sadie Bingham married Major Robert Temple Grinnan, who became cosuperintendent, with Colonel Robert Bingham, of the Bingham Military School. They had no children, and he died in 1915. Mary Kerr Bingham married Major S. Reid McKee, who taught science at the Bingham Military School in Asheville, North Carolina, and became superintendent upon Colonel Bingham's retirement.

Chapter 2. Education

1. The school established in 1911 on Douglass Boulevard near the Bingham home was the Louisville Country Day School. Its headmaster was Ira William Davenport (1863-1938), who had been associated from 1901 to 1910 with John Letcher Patterson in a school on Third Street. Patterson also was dean of the University of Louisville's College of Arts and Sciences. He died in 1937 at the age of seventy-six. While Patterson pursued full-time university activities, Davenport developed the "country school for city boys." Such schools were then a national movement.

2. James Howell Richmond (1884-1945) was born in Ewing, Virginia. He attended Lincoln Memorial University and graduated from the University of Tennessee in 1907. He taught in Texas, Tennessee, and Kentucky. He was elected state superintendent of public instruction in Kentucky in 1931. In 1935 he announced for governor but withdrew. He became president of Murray State University in 1936 and remained in that capacity until his death.

3. Nancy Lee Frayser (1874-1924), a nationally recognized educator and children's storyteller, was born in Louisville and educated at Hampton College and the Teachers College at Columbia University. Although a dedicated classroom teacher, she wrote frequently and lectured widely.

4. Charles Rowland Peaslee Farnsley (1907-90) was an innovative mayor of Louisville from 1948 to 1953. He served in the Kentucky House of Representatives (1936-40) and the U.S. House (1965-66). He was a particular friend of the Louisville Free Public Library and the local orchestra and was instrumental in the creation of the Fund for the Arts. In 1954 he established the Lost Cause Press, which provides comprehensive collections of Americana on microfiche to research libraries around the world.

5. Archibald Thomas Robertson, Jr. (1906-65), the son of a professor at the Southern Baptist Theological Seminary, graduated from Louisville Male High School and was a classmate of Barry Bingham's at Harvard. He worked for *The Courier-Journal* before becoming an editor and author.

6. Cary Robertson (1902-75), Archie's brother, was Sunday editor from about 1930 to 1966. During that period the magazine took on color and prominence. Cary had begun as a police reporter in 1925 and was briefly the night city editor. After the Richmond School, he attended Louisville Male High School, Wake Forest College, and the University of Virginia.

7. Richard Wilson Knott (1849-1917), a native of Frankfort, Kentucky, had worked for *The Courier-Journal* before helping to start *The Evening Post* in 1873. He would edit and eventually own the *Post*. Knott was also owner and publisher of *The Home and Farm*, a bank director, and a recognized expert in finance. He helped draw up the city charter. He had been a Democrat and then an Independent before 1900. Knott's papers supported Robert Worth Bingham in his campaigns.

8. Margaret Menefee Todd (1876-1950), the daughter of Richard Jouett Menefee and Elizabeth Speed Menefee, was married to James Ross Todd. She was once president of Children's Hospital, to which the Todds gave the

Equitable Building. She also served as Kentucky chair for the Women's Organization for National Prohibition. The Todds lived at Rostrevor, a villalike house they built about 1910. The New York firm of Carrère and Hastings designed the house, as well as the Bingham amphitheater.

9. Robert Bingham (1839-1927), a graduate of the University of North Carolina, was teaching before the Civil War in the school founded in 1793 by his grandfather William Bingham. He was captured at South Anna Bridge in Virginia by Union forces and imprisoned at Johnson's Island, Ohio. He returned to combat, and his wife, Delphine Worth Bingham, was later presented his company's tattered flag. The couple had four children, including Robert Worth Bingham.

10. The Wilderness Road Book Shop was principally the enterprise of Henrietta Bingham and Edith Callahan. It was soon sold to George Fowler and moved into the Brown Hotel, where it was later run by Morton V. Joyes. Joyes closed the store in 1958.

11. His thesis for distinction was entitled "The Heyday of English Sentimental Comedy."

12. *Brown of Harvard* was performed in the spring of 1926. The playwright was the nationally known author Foxhall Daingerfield (1887-1933), who was reared in Fayette County, Kentucky, and graduated from Transylvania College and Washington and Lee University. During World War I he organized the Liberty Theater at Louisville's Camp Taylor. In the winter of 1926 Barry Bingham played the central figure of Harlequin in an adaptation of Gozzi's *The Love of the Three Oranges*.

13. Nathan M. Pusey was born in Council Bluffs, Iowa, in 1907. He served as president of Harvard from 1953 to 1971. John Phillips Marquand (1893-1960) was a Harvard-educated short story writer and Pulitzer Prize-winning novelist who depicted upper-class life and frequently the "Harvard Man."

14. Edward Grey (1862-1933) had been foreign secretary and in 1919-20 served as ambassador to the United States.

15. Allen Taylor Caperton (1810-76), the son of Hugh Caperton, a representative from Virginia who owned Elmwood, was educated at the University of Virginia and graduated from Yale University. He studied law in Staunton and practiced while serving in the Virginia legislature. He served in the Confederate Senate from Virginia and briefly in the U.S. Senate from West Virginia.

16. Edith Dee Callahan (1897-1983) was the daughter of Julia Cahill Callahan and Patrick Henry Callahan. They were not related to Americus Franklin Callahan, who married Eleanor Miller Bingham's sister, Katherine. In 1902 A. F. Callahan invented and patented the window envelope. His brother James Callahan was in the grain business and built the Louisville, Harrods Creek and Westport Railway (the interurban to Prospect) that ran below the Callahan family house, Rock Hill, east of Mockingbird Valley Road.

P. H. Callahan (1866-1940) moved from Cleveland to Louisville and joined the Louisville Varnish Company. He was active in Catholic affairs, politics, and Prohibition, and he strongly supported Roosevelt.

Edith Callahan was a lifelong friend of Barry Bingham's, and in 1949 she had architect Louise Leland design a house that was built on a piece of Bingham property in Glenview. When Miss Callahan died, the Binghams purchased the house.

17. Francis Slocum Parks (1905-30) was an aspiring writer when he died from an automobile accident. His death had a profound effect on Barry Bingham.

18. The wedding took place on Tuesday afternoon, 9 June 1931, at St. James Episcopal Church in Richmond, Virginia. Mrs. Bingham's matron of honor was Mrs. Thomas Roderick Dew, and her bridesmaids were her sisters Mrs. John Wilson Brown III, Mrs. Robert Nelson Page, Mrs. W.L. Lyons, Jr., and Miss Harriette Caperton, as well as Mrs. John Hagan. Mr. Bingham's best man was Robert M. Carrier, Jr., and his groomsmen were H. Warren Buckler of Baltimore; John C. Reuter of Cambridge; Eduardo Andrade, Samuel R. Peale, and Rodney Fiske of New York; Edwin Earle of Los Angeles; and Thruston Ballard Morton, Floyd T. Smith, W.L. Lyons Brown, and Kim Babcock of Louisville.

19. The stuccoed cottage, which has become known as the Little House, was built in 1916 for Mary Churchill Humphrey by her parents, Judge and Mrs. Alexander P. Humphrey, who owned the property. The site had been the location of the Fincastle Club, a compound of summer homes clustered around a clubhouse, which the Humphreys later acquired. When the Fincastle Club (named for the Virginia county that included Kentucky) was disbanded, Judge Humphrey and Charles T. Ballard bought the other summer houses. The Ballards' Holiday House was replaced in 1910-11 by a more permanent dwelling they called Bushy Park. Judge Bingham purchased this property in 1919 and renamed it Melcombe Bingham. Judge Humphrey lived in Fincastle until he died in 1928. Judge Bingham then acquired the property, razed Fincastle, and replaced it with an amphitheater designed by the prominent New York architect Thomas Hastings, whose firm also designed Louisville's Memorial Auditorium.

Barry Bingham moved into the Little House in 1930. In 1933 it was substantially enlarged by architect W. S. Arrasmith to accommodate the Binghams' growing family. Mary and Barry Bingham moved into Melcombe in 1942 and returned to the Little House in 1971.

20. Barry Bingham published frequently in *The Harvard Advocate*. In the May 1925 issue his short story "White Carnation" appeared. A passage signaled his intent: "They sat down on a hard wooden bench, and he began to talk in a low, quick voice that made Molly realize that he was telling her of something that lay very close to his heart.

" 'I'm writing a novel, Molly,' he began, 'or at least I want to write one. I know I could do it, because I have lots of ideas and lots of enthusiasm, but it simply can't be written unless I can make it just the sort of thing I want it to be. It's got to be as vital and vivid as life itself, and as devoid of sex as clear water or mountain snow.' "

Chapter 3. The Family Business

1. Barry Bingham wrote an Editorial Notebook piece on Anna Logan ("Aunt Ruth") Hopper, dated 1 August 1962. She died on 6 April 1960.

2. In 1912 the newspapers moved from their building opened in 1876 on the southeast corner of Fourth and Green (now Liberty) streets into renovated quarters in the former Post Office and Custom House on the southwest corner of Third and Liberty streets. The old post office, designed by E.E. Williams, was built in the 1850s. The Haldemans, the founders of the newspapers, leased it out as warehouse space and intended to raze it once it was replaced by the Fireproof Storage Company next door.

3. Robert Worth Bingham purchased the newspapers' stock held by W.B. Haldeman, his sister, Isabelle M. Haldeman, and Henry Watterson on 6 August 1918. The signing of a contract to purchase the minority interest owned by the Haldemans' brother, Bruce, was announced in *The Courier-Journal* on 31 July 1919. On 30 April 1920 Judge Bingham became the sole owner of the newspapers and their properties.

The purchase price was not revealed, but Watterson deposited $186,000 in the National Bank of Kentucky on 6 August. He had held 12.5 percent of the stock. Therefore, Judge Bingham's purchase of controlling interest cost about $1,057,328. Adding in Bruce Haldeman's minority interest, reportedly $418,500, the total cost of the newspaper companies was $1,475,828.

4. Henry Watterson (1840-1921) became editor emeritus of *The Courier-Journal* when sale of the newspapers was announced on 6 August 1918. He had been editor of *The Courier-Journal* since its formation in 1868, and the newspaper had just received a Pulitzer Prize for two 1917 editorials. Watterson had been a journalist before serving in the Confederate army. After the war he worked in Cincinnati and Nashville before coming to *The Louisville Daily Journal*. He was a member of the U.S. Congress (1876-77). His fiery editorials made *The Courier-Journal* a major voice in the South. His retirement was disclosed on the editorial page of 2 April 1919. The announcement blamed a conflict in "his views, opposing the League of Nations, and those of *The Courier-Journal,* favoring the proposal."

5. Credo Fitch Harris (1874-1956) was a newspaperman and novelist before Robert Worth Bingham asked him to establish a radio station. On 18 July 1922 WHAS became Kentucky's first station to broadcast. Harris assisted in the start-up of NBC and then switched WHAS to a CBS affiliation in 1933. He was the great-uncle of Jane Morton Norton and her brothers, Thruston and Rogers Morton.

6. See Terry L. Birdwhistell, "WHAS Radio and the Development of Broadcasting in Kentucky, 1922-1942," *The Register of the Kentucky Historical Society* 79 (Autumn 1981): 333-353.

7. J. Emmett Graft was the first radio operator and engineer at WHAS.

8. The Fireproof Storage Company on Liberty Street was part of the newspapers' complex centered in the old Post Office and Custom House at Third and Liberty streets. It had been built by the Haldemans in 1907 and was part of the real estate purchased by Judge Bingham in 1918.

9. "Baby Eyes" and "Midnight Melody" were published in 1930 by WHAS.

10. George Barry Bingham, Jr. (b. 1933), graduated from Harvard University and served in the U.S. Marine Corps. He worked for CBS for one year and NBC for three years before returning to WHAS. When his brother Worth died in 1966, he moved to the newspapers, becoming editor and publisher in 1971. After the Bingham enterprises were sold, he published a newsletter concerning media ethics. He is married to Edith Wharton Stenhouse Bingham, and they have four children: Philip J. Francini Bingham and Charles Willing Francini Bingham, from Mrs. Bingham's previous marriage, and Emily Simms Bingham and Mary Caperton Bingham.

11. Nathan Lord was an executive with WAVE. Frederick Craik ("Fritz") Lord was chief political writer for *The Louisville Times* from the mid-1930s until his retirement in 1962. He had been managing editor of *The Herald-Post* before its demise in 1936. Their sister Juliet Lord was Barry Bingham's receptionist for many years.

12. The daughter of Louisville monument maker Michael Muldoon, Aleen Lithgow Muldoon Hilliard Bingham (1877-1953) was the widow of stockbroker Byron Hilliard when she married Robert Worth Bingham in 1924. She was active in Bundles for Britain and the preservation of Stratford, Robert E. Lee's ancestral home in Virginia.

13. Robert Worth Bingham (1932-66) graduated from Harvard University and served in the U.S. Naval Reserves. He worked on newspapers in Minneapolis and San Francisco before returning to the family newspapers in 1960. Worth Bingham was assistant to the publisher and was destined to succeed his father, but in 1966 he was killed in a freak automobile accident while vacationing in Nantucket. He was survived by his wife, Joan Stevens Bingham, and their two children, Clara York and Robert Worth, Jr.

Mary and Barry Bingham had five children: Robert Worth, George Barry, Jr., Sarah ("Sallie") Montague, Jonathan Worth, and Eleanor Miller.

14. Ulric Bell (1892-1960) was a reporter, as well as a city and Sunday editor, before becoming *The Courier-Journal*'s Washington correspondent. In Washington he was a president of the Gridiron Club and the National Press Club. Bell also served as press adviser to Secretary of State Cordell Hull in the early 1930s and was active from the beginning in the Fight for Freedom organization. When World War II started he was assistant director of the Office of Facts and Figures, and he then became deputy director of the Office

of War Information. He later worked in Hollywood, and as executive assistant to the president of 20th Century-Fox.

15. The Gridiron Club was the most famous of the newspaper clubs. Its membership was limited to fifty. Ulric Bell was elected in 1926.

16. George W. Norris (1861-1944) represented Nebraskans in the U.S. House for five terms (1903-13) and for five in the Senate (1913-43).

17. Alben Barkley (1877-1956) was elected to the Senate again in 1954.

18. The *Eala* was chartered to the Department of Commerce for one dollar a year when Judge Bingham was appointed ambassador to Great Britain. Because he could not obtain insurance to cover its use by the government, the ninety-three-foot yacht was sold to Mrs. Robert Busey of Miami in 1936.

19. Pineland Plantation was a quail preserve near Albany in Baker County, Georgia, consisting of some 17,000 acres in fee simple and 5,500 acres under lease. Judge Bingham began purchasing the property with W.W. Davies in the early 1920s, and it was sold after the Judge's death. Early visitors for hunting were Lee Miles, Irvin Abell, M.D., Bishop Woodcock, Adolph Reutlinger, and Hugh Young, M.D. Barry Bingham once recalled: "I myself made a number of visits during Christmas vacations from college, and later. Our regular routine was to get up for an early breakfast featuring broiled quail wrapped in bacon, and served with grits. We would then start out for a day's hunting with my father's pointers and setters. We usually took a picnic lunch, which we would enjoy in the sunshine at some shady spot along a creek, or in the edge of a pine woods.

"The plantation was managed at that time by a man named Jack Milward, originally of Lexington, Kentucky, who spent full time there. The dogs were handled by Herbert Fischel, who came down from Indiana during the hunting season.

"After hunting all day, we would return to the lodge for a leisurely supper. Afterward we would sit around an open fire and talk or play bridge until bedtime. The plantation was a wonderful place for both sport and relaxation.

"There was a famous day when a field trial took place at Pineland and over 100 coveys of quail were found" (Letter to Geraldine Clemmons, 3 March 1977, Northwest Florida Regional Library, Bonifay).

20. Urey Woodson (1859-1939), a newspaper editor and publisher in Owensboro and later Paducah, was a fixture on the Democratic National Committee and at Democratic conventions. He was present when Goebel was sworn in as governor on his deathbed. His biography of Goebel, *The First New Dealer,* appeared in 1939.

21. The City Fusion party was formed to drive Tammany out of power. Its chairman was Louisville transplant Ben Howe (1868-1946), who was Judge Bingham's close friend and early business partner and was city buyer when Bingham was mayor. His son, Laurence Lee Howe, was a professor of history at the University of Louisville.

22. Michael Albert Powell's 1980 M.A. thesis for George Washington University was titled "Robert W. Bingham: United States Ambassa-

dor to Great Britain, 1933 to 1937." In late 1983 he was in the process of revising it into an article.

23. Robert Worth Bingham forged the tobacco cooperative movement after the burley market collapse in 1920. He personally guaranteed one million dollars of the initial loan to establish the cooperative fostered by lawyer Aaron L. Sapiro (1884-1959), a leading attorney in the field. James C. Stone of Lexington was elected president and general manager. After initial successes, the cooperative began to feel external as well as internal pressures. Large tobacco buyers were able to regain control as growers became dissatisfied with the future-payment system. Bingham intended only to put the cooperative in place, and by the mid-1920s the movement had faltered from lack of internal combustion. See William E. Ellis, "Robert Worth Bingham and the Crisis of Cooperative Marketing in the Twenties," *Agricultural History* 56 (Jan. 1982): 99-116.

24. After early successes, Aaron Sapiro had a checkered career. When Henry Ford's weekly, *The Dearborn Independent,* carried a series of articles considered anti-Semitic, Sapiro sued the auto manufacturer for one million dollars. He accused Ford of damaging his reputation by publishing that a Jewish conspiracy was trying to gain control of American agriculture. Sapiro was later indicted for trade racketeering in Chicago and then for bribery in New York. He was acquitted but subsequently was disbarred.

25. Another area was farming—cooperative marketing and crop control. Shortly before his death, Judge Bingham wrote Barry Bingham, reiterating his positions. Judge Bingham recalled: "On the 1st of September 1931, Mr. Roosevelt asked me to go to Albany to see him. At that time, at least, Col. House, Cordell Hull, Louis Howe and I believed that he would be nominated and would be elected President. He knew about my activities in behalf of the farmers of the country and he surprised me then, as he has surprised me often since, by the vast amount of knowledge he had on the subject. At any rate, when I told him that crop [control] was the very fundamental basis and root of any hope for agriculture, it needed no argument from me to convince him. He had already and quite independently arrived at the same conclusion. . . .

"I must go back and tell you of the campaign by *The Courier-Journal* and *Times* which carried Kentucky for the League of Nations in 1920. Day after day we printed the truth about the League and the Covenant. Day after day we printed the actual Covenant of the League, including Article I. We supplied all the country newspapers with material, set up, which most of them printed. To the end, despite the overwhelming Republican victory in the nation, Kentucky returned a small majority for the League. Our support then was not for Cox, but for the League. Our support now should not be primarily or necessarily for the President, but for the principle of crop control, for the salvation of the farmers of the nation. More than half of the people of our country are directly dependent upon the price of agricultural products, and the welfare of the balance is indirectly, if not directly, so affected. All other methods designed to improve agriculture have failed. Hoover sank five hundred million dollars of the taxpayers' money in an absolutely futile effort to bolster prices, which did nothing but increase production, and wound up with five-cent cotton and five-cent tobacco and fifteen-cent corn." (18 Aug. 1937, Robert Worth Bingham Papers, Manuscripts Division, Library of Congress).

26. WAVE went on the air, as an NBC affiliate, on 30 December 1933. George W. Norton, Jr., was president; Nathan Lord, former day city editor of *The Courier-Journal* and editorial writer for *The Herald-Post* was manager. Norton had purchased the station, which had been WLAP, from CBS with the understanding that it would discontinue that affiliation. WLAP was started in 1929 by Dinwiddie Lampton and was sold to Ralph L. Atlass of Chicago in 1931 before being purchased by CBS.

In 1933 station WFIW had applied to the Federal Radio Commission for permission to move from Hopkinsville to Louisville and had a promise of NBC affiliation if permission was granted. When Norton brought suit to block the move, testimony revealed that he had learned from Barry Bingham that WLAP was for sale. Bingham was then working for WHAS. The suit was dropped when WFIW agreed to be purchased by WLAP. Evidently, Judge Bingham aided Norton in the purchase. WLAP thus received the NBC affiliation and changed its call letters to WAVE.

According to a letter from Barry Bingham to his father, there had been discussion for months "of the possible consolidation of WHAS and WAVE under an open identity of ownership, which would mean sharing the same studios and making many other savings in operating expenses" (12 Nov. 1935, Robert Worth Bingham Papers, Manuscripts Division, Library of Congress.)

Chapter 4. Transition

1. Even before the 1932 election some speculated that Judge Bingham would serve either as secretary of the navy or ambassador to Great Britain. After the election he was considered for secretary of state, and he met with the president-elect in Warm Springs and New York City. *The New York Times* reported on 24 February that he would be the envoy, and he was named ambassador on 13 March 1933.

2. This cablegram is in the Robert Worth Bingham Papers, Manuscripts Division, Library of Congress.

3. The cablegram from the ambassador was not retained. The Herald-Post Company had filed bankruptcy in late 1930. The morning *Louisville Herald* and the evening *Louisville Post* had been consolidated in 1925 after James B. Brown had purchased both. *The Herald-Post*'s morning edition was discontinued in 1927. The newspaper in receivership was sold to John B. Gallagher of Chicago in 1931. He sold it to the Girdler Corporation of Louisville in May 1933. Publication terminated in October 1936.

4. Emanuel Levi (1880-1963) had been vice president and general manager of the newspapers since 1925. He left in 1936 to publish the Hearst newspapers in Chicago. In 1938 he resigned and returned to Louisville.

Levi was a law graduate of the University of Virginia (1908) and the University of Louisville (1909). He was an associate in the firm of Kohn, Bingham, Sloss and Spindle, which became Bingham, Sloss, Tabb and Mann when Aaron Kohn died in 1916. Kohn's son-in-law Stanley E. Sloss was designated by Judge Bingham to be the managing editor of the newspapers, but he died just after they were purchased. Arthur Mann died in the same week of October 1918. The Judge's longtime friend Arthur Peter (1872-1960) joined the firm, which later became Peter, Heyburn, Marshall and Wyatt. Levi left the firm in 1921 to become an assistant to Judge Bingham at the newspapers.

5. Howard Wesley Stodghill (1885-1969) became circulation manager of the newspapers in 1921 and business manager as well in 1925. He left in 1936 to be circulation director of the Hearst newspapers and publisher of *The Atlanta Georgian-American*. From 1939 to 1964 he worked for the Philadelphia *Evening Bulletin*. With Emanuel Levi, he started the Independence Life and Accident Insurance Company in 1934. He served as board chair from 1945 to his death. The Bingham newspapers offered an insurance policy for a new subscription, a practice that Barry Bingham discontinued, considering it a conflict of interest.

6. Edward Asher Jonas (1863-1951) was a native of London, England, and a graduate of University College, Oxford. He was editor and publisher of *The Henderson Journal* before becoming an editorial writer and columnist for *The Louisville Times, The Louisville Herald,* and *The Courier-Journal*. He had broad interests and published and lectured widely. His books include *A History of the Republican Party in Kentucky* (Louisville: John P. Morton Co., 1929) and *Matthew Harris Jouett, Kentucky Portrait Painter* (Louisville: J.B. Speed Memorial Museum, 1938).

7. Judge Bingham helped George W. Norton, Jr., purchase a radio station. See Chap. 3, n. 26.

8. Robert Worth Bingham graduated from the University of Louisville School of Law in 1897 and joined the law firm of Pryor, O'Neal and Pryor. In 1899 he formed a partnership with a friend from North Carolina, William Watkins Davies. His appointment as Jefferson County attorney took effect on 1 January 1904, and he defeated Lafon Allen in November to complete the term. He was reelected in November 1905, but when those local elections were overturned, he was appointed mayor of Louisville. He served from 29 June until 11 November 1907. He ran as a Republican for the Kentucky Court of Appeals in November 1910 and was defeated. On 11 January 1911, however, he was appointed chancellor, Chancery Branch, First Division, Jefferson Circuit Court. He sat until after the November 1911 election. In November 1917 Judge Bingham was defeated by James F. Grinstead for a seat on Jefferson County Fiscal Court.

9. The bipartisan ring or combine was a loose grouping of racing, coal, whiskey, and railroad interests that influenced elections and government but operated outside political parties. It functioned into the early 1930s.

10. Robert Worth Bingham was confirmed as London envoy on 22 March 1933. A farewell dinner was held in Louisville on 5 April. Ambassador Bingham and his wife both went to Johns Hopkins Hospital in Baltimore for medical treatment under the direction of Hugh Young, M.D., and did not sail for London until 10 May.

11. Norman L. Johnson was an associate editor and editorial writer for *The Louisville Times* for many years. His wife, Josephine, was librarian for the newspapers.

Chapter 5. Taking Charge

1. Hugh Rodman Leavell (1903-76) became director of health in 1934. He was a graduate of the University of Virginia and Harvard University School of Medicine. He was honored for his dedicated work during the flood. Later he studied at Yale University and was on the faculty of Harvard's School of Public Health.

2. Barry Bingham wrote a series of articles on mental health that appeared in *The Courier-Journal* between January and April 1937. The articles were reprinted in a pamphlet, *They Can Be Cured.*

Barry Bingham had written Robert Worth Bingham on 18 November 1936: "I am going up to Frankfort to take a trip with Happy [Chandler] tomorrow through the Feeble Minded Institute and the Deaf and Dumb asylum. The day I spent with him at the Frankfort Reformatory and the Eastern State Hospital for the Insane was gruelling, but extremely interesting, and I am going to get him to take me to all the State institutions. He has never seen them before himself, and they are impressing him greatly. I want to get him to go through the Children's Home Society when he is down here to inspect Lakeland" (Robert Worth Bingham Papers, Manuscripts Division, Library of Congress).

3. The meeting was actually held in the spring of 1936. See memorandum of Robert Worth Bingham, 14 March 1936, Barry Bingham Papers, the Filson Club, Louisville. Mark Ethridge (1896-1981) was named vice president and general manager in 1937 and publisher in 1942. He became chairman of the board in 1961 and retired in 1963, accepting the position of vice president and editor of *Newsday.* He taught in the School of Journalism at the University of North Carolina from 1965 to 1968, and his personal papers were given to the university's Southern Historical Collection. He was married to the prolific author and humorist Willie Snow Ethridge (1900-82), who also contributed frequently to the newspapers.

4. Harrison Robertson (1856-1939), a native of Murfreesboro, Tennessee, was hired by Henry Watterson. His first column appeared on the editorial

page of *The Courier-Journal* on 7 January 1879. He worked with Watterson on the editorial page and wrote the editorial in which *The Courier-Journal* bolted from the Democratic party in 1896 and let William Jennings Bryan and his free silver languish. He was honored by Judge Bingham for fifty years of service in 1929 and by Barry Bingham for sixty years in 1939. He was replaced by Herbert Agar.

5. James C. Hutto died in 1986 at the age of seventy-nine. The Alabama native joined *The Louisville Times* after working on *The Birmingham Post*.

6. The Editorial Notebook feature began on 4 December 1956, and it alternated with the syndicated columns of Joseph and Stewart Alsop. The announcement of the introductory piece by John Ed Pearce commented: "We hope readers will like this new feature on the page. It is frankly an experiment, and we know of no other paper which has tried anything just like it."

7. The undated, soft-covered book contains fifty-three pieces, the latest written in 1961.

8. John Ed Pearce was born in Norton, Virginia, but he has spent his adult life in Kentucky, first as editor of *The Somerset Journal* and from 1947 to 1986 as an editorial writer and then a feature writer for *The Courier-Journal*. Since 1986 he has continued to write a Sunday column for *The Courier-Journal* as well as *The Lexington Herald-Leader*. Barry Bingham thought that John Ed Pearce was the newspapers' best writer, even considering Henry Watterson. Pearce has had a particular interest in Kentucky politics, the state's park system, and the Kentucky Oral History Commission, which he helped establish. His books include *Seasons* (Louisville: Cherokee Books, 1983), *Divide and Dissent: Kentucky Politics, 1930-1963* (Lexington: University Press of Kentucky, 1987), and *The Ohio River* (Lexington: University Press of Kentucky, 1989).

9. Tarleton Collier, who died in 1970 at the age of eighty-one, was an Alabama native and a graduate of Auburn University. He came to *The Courier-Journal*'s editorial staff in 1942 and retired in 1958. While in Kentucky he took part in a range of civic and welfare causes. He also wrote verse and was an authority on baseball.

10. Louis F. Dey was art director for *The Courier-Journal* and *The Louisville Times* for many years.

11. Lisle Baker, Jr. (1903-84), a native of Monticello, Kentucky, was a Frankfort banker before joining the Bingham newspapers in 1936 as secretary. He was named treasurer in 1937, vice president in 1942, general manager in 1949, and executive vice president and general manager of the Bingham companies in 1961. He retired in 1968 but remained on the board of directors. He was active in local cultural and civic affairs and was a member of the Kentucky Council on Higher Education.

William Purcell Dennis Haly (1875-1937) was a protégé of Governor William Goebel's and was appointed adjutant general by Goebel's successor, Governor J. C. W. Beckham, whose political fortunes Haly actively supported. General Haly also supported Woodrow Wilson and held positions with the Internal Revenue Service. He was an adviser to Judge Bingham and helped establish the Burley and Dark Tobacco Growers' Cooperative Association. He was a progressive and a strong supporter of President Roosevelt's. In 1936 Haly became president of the Fireproof Storage Company, which Judge Bingham controlled. He oversaw its liquidation a year later. Haly died from pneumonia contracted during the 1937 flood in Louisville while serving as deputy provost marshal under his protégé, Mayor Neville Miller.

12. Barry Bingham's letter to his father is in the Robert Worth Bingham Papers, Manuscripts Division, Library of Congress.

13. In *Heroes, Plain Folks, and Skunks: The Life and Times of Happy Chandler* (Chicago: Bonus Books, 1989), Chandler recalls a meeting with Judge Bingham: "The deplorable condition of Kentucky's roads greatly agitated Judge Bingham. There were few paved highways, and the rural roads were dusty in summer and quagmires in winter. 'What you ought to do,' Judge Bingham said, 'is hire the best highway engineer in the country.'

" 'Why, Judge, I can't do that!' I reminded him that the state constitution placed a 'cap' of $5,000 a year on the salary of any state official except the governor, who received $6,500. 'I can't hire a really top engineer for five thousand.'

" 'Find the man. Pay him what he asks. I'll make up the difference. It will be between you and me.' . . . 'It wouldn't be smart' I responded, 'to make a secret out of this arrangement. Better that I just announce what you are willing to do. I'll give it a try' " (111-12).

Chandler hired Thomas Cutler, a University of Kentucky graduate who had developed an outstanding record as roads commissioner in Missouri, for twelve thousand dollars per annum. In his book, Chandler concludes that "Judge Bingham donated the extra $7,000 a year through my term. And his family, after the Judge's death, kept up the arrangement for a number of years" (111-112).

14. When the Ballard County native John Howard Henderson died in 1945 at the age of fifty-one, his obituary stated that he "was considered by many one of the greatest political reporters in the history of Kentucky journalism, knowing more of the lore and personalities of Kentucky politics, and more of the theory and practice of Kentucky Government, than any other man of his time." He had worked for *The Courier-Journal* since 1923. He was Frankfort bureau chief from 1926 to 1940, when his editorial column, "I Say What I Think," appeared three times a week. As bureau chief, he continued his investigative reporting.

15. See Walter L. Hixson, "The 1938 Kentucky Senate Election: Alben W. Barkley, 'Happy' Chandler, and the New Deal," *The Register of the Kentucky Historical Society* 80 (Summer 1982): 309-29.

The Courier-Journal reported on 14 June 1938 that Barry Bingham "said after a White House visit today [13 June] that he had talked over with President Roosevelt 'things in general, including Kentucky Politics.' Bingham declined to tell reporters details of his talk."

16. President Roosevelt came to Kentucky to campaign for Alben Barkley in his Senate primary race against Governor Chandler. In Covington on 8 July 1938, Chandler managed to position himself between FDR and Barkley in the back of an open touring car.

17. In *Heroes, Plain Folks, and Skunks,* Chandler states: "It began simply enough. Judge Bingham pushed me as early as 1936 to go up against Alben Barkley. 'He must be removed from the Senate,' Judge Bingham told me. 'He is a cipher in Washington. He is a bad influence. He is not serving the interests of the people of Kentucky.' . . . So Judge Bingham had made it crystal clear to me that he wanted to unseat Barkley.

"Then, unfortunately—in just a matter of weeks after we had finally agreed that I would challenge Old Alben—the Judge passes from the scene. I am deprived of his wise counsel and the extremely potent and critical support of his newspaper. His son, Barry Bingham, Sr., is a strong and loyal supporter of Roosevelt policies.

"So I know if Roosevelt asks Barry, Sr., for help in the Senate race, *The Courier-Journal* will go all out for Barkley.

"I felt I must go on, even though the reigning god of national politics tries to dissuade me, asks me to wait and promises to look out for me later" (134-35).

18. Making no headway in his campaign against Barkley, even after the FDR incident, Chandler reported on 25 July that he had been made ill by water laced with poison provided in a pitcher during a radio broadcast from the Kentucky Hotel in Louisville. The chief of police scoffed at the accusation and a grand jury could find no evidence for it.

Chapter 6. World War II

1. For a study of the interventionist movement, see Mark Lincoln Chadwin, *The Hawks of World War II* (Chapel Hill: University of North Carolina Press, 1968). The warhawks were initially centered in the Century Group, so named because the group met in the Century Association, the New York club for men prominent in the arts and sciences. The small band of Century Group leaders included Ulric Bell and Herbert Agar, who both held responsible positions with *The Courier-Journal.*

According to Chadwin, in Chicago in mid-July 1940 the well-placed columnist Joseph Alsop, "had been enlisted in the warhawk's work in a meeting in the suite of the Louisville *Courier-Journal* during the Democratic convention. Here Herbert Agar, Ulric Bell, and Barry Bingham had asked him to obtain from both British and American sources in Washington as much data as he could pertaining to the situation of the British, their material needs, and their chances of repelling the imminent Nazi invasion" (81).

Out of the Century Group grew the Fight for Freedom Committee. Chadwin states, "In 1941, some, like Dorothy Thompson and Barry Bingham, were willing to stump the country on behalf of the Fight For Freedom" (27). He also mentions that Barry Bingham continued to pay Ulric Bell's and Herbert Agar's salaries and expenses, "despite the fact that they were spending nearly all of their time working for the Fight For Freedom" (178).

2. Barry Bingham, "Shall We Go to War?" in *Defense for America,* ed. William Allen White (New York: Macmillan, 1940), 35-44.

3. Wilson Wyatt states in his autobiography, *Whistle Stops: Adventures in Public Life* (Lexington: University Press of Kentucky, 1985), that he felt compelled to support Lyter Donaldson because Donaldson was backed by Governor Keen Johnson, who had been helpful to Louisville during the most recent session of the General Assembly (25).

4. *Parade* would continue to offer its weekly supplement as a replacement for *The Courier-Journal*'s own Sunday magazine. As the cost of producing a local magazine far exceeded the purchase of *Parade*'s generic package, *The Courier-Journal* would realize the difference.

5. Veteran correspondent Richard L. Stout recalled for *The Christian Science Monitor* that "even at the start of the affair, there had been a kind of anticlimax. Lt. Comdr. Barry Bingham, the naval public relations officer, had summoned six of us into his SHEAF office in London: Cecil Carnes, *Saturday Evening Post;* Edward A. Candy, *Gaumont British News;* Thomas Wolfe, NEA; Bill Schadel, CBS; William Heinz, *New York Sun;* and me, and opened the great drama with the banal phrase, 'Gentlemen, this is it.'

"I ask myself even now would I—would Shakespeare—have started a thing off with anything quite as trite? It meant that we were security sealed from then on. That was May 31, 1944. Tom Wolfe asked plaintively, couldn't he send a message to his draft board, which had just refused him an appeal for deferment? Commander Bingham said no" (7 June 1974).

Barry Bingham commented to Malcolm Bayley on 11 July 1974 that his recollection was slightly different. He recalled saying, "Gentlemen, this time it really is it!"

6. The letter is in the Arthur and Elizabeth Schlesinger Library on the History of Women in America, Radcliffe College, Cambridge, Mass. Mary Caperton Bingham's letter to Barry Bingham regarding her meeting with President Roosevelt is also in that collection of Bingham correspondence.

7. Samuel Spafford Ackerly, M.D. (1895-1981), a Yale graduate, came in 1932 to teach at the University of Louisville and to head the child guidance clinic. He has been called the father of psychiatry in Kentucky, and with his arrival the mentally ill began to receive more humane care. Aided by the Binghams' initial contribution in 1944, one million dollars in private and public funding was raised to build the Norton Psychiatric Clinic, which opened in 1949. In 1971 the clinic was renamed the Bingham Child Guidance Clinic. The Mary and Barry Bingham, Sr., Fund helped endow the Ackerly Chair in the School of Medicine at the University of Louisville in 1989.

8. George Washington Norton, Jr. (1902-64), was a Yale graduate and a Harvard-trained lawyer who practiced in the firm of Humphrey, Crawford

and Middleton before serving in World War II and then devoting his full time to the radio broadcasting business at WAVE. He was active in civic and cultural affairs. He was married to Jane Lewis Morton Norton (1908-88), an artist also active in local cultural affairs.

9. Andrew Wallace Duncan (1912-87) received a law degree from the University of Virginia in 1935. He practiced in his native Louisville until 1957, when he became administrative assistant to Senator John Sherman Cooper.

10. The initial contribution toward the erection of the wing housing the Norton Psychiatric Clinic was made by Barry and Mary Bingham in memory of Barry's father, Robert Worth Bingham, on 28 December 1944.

11. Weldon B. James (1912-85) was educated at Furman University and at Harvard, where he was a Nieman Fellow. He was a United Press correspondent in China and Spain before working as bureau chief in London for *PM* and, in his early days in the Marine Corps, he shared a flat with Barry Bingham. He joined *The Courier-Journal* in 1948, after serving as far eastern editor for *Collier's Magazine*. He was again on active duty from 1950 to 1952 and served as press secretary for the chair of the Democratic party during the 1952 campaign. After leaving *The Courier-Journal* in 1966 in protest of its dovish position on Vietnam, he worked for the Marine Corps and the National Credit Union Administration.

12. Sibyl Colefax was an interior designer who began work in 1933 and in 1938 became associated with John Fowler. She retired after the war, and Nancy Lancaster, a niece of Lady Astor's who had been married to Ronald Tree, purchased the business.

Alexander Humphreys Woollcott (1887-1943) was a writer, dramatic critic, and radio commentator. *The Letters of Alexander Woollcott,* edited by Beatrice Kaufman and Joseph Hennessey, was published by Viking in 1944. Before the war Woollcott had visited the Binghams in Louisville, and they had spent a weekend at Woollcott's Vermont place. Mrs. Bingham once took him to the Abbey of Gethsemani near Bardstown, Kentucky.

13. Norris Houghton is an author, educator, stage director, and founder of the Phoenix Theater in New York. He was Bingham Professor at the University of Louisville in 1979-80. John Mason Brown introduced him to Barry Bingham in London in the winter of 1943-44. Houghton's autobiography, *Entrances and Exits,* was published in New York by Limelight Editions in 1991.

14. John Hersey's first novel, *A Bell for Adano,* set in a Sicilian village during World War II, won a Pulitzer Prize for fiction in 1945.

15. Jane Morton Norton's *Blackbirds on the Lawn,* was published in New York by Coward-McCann in 1944.

16. Barry Bingham roomed with Roger Straus, a partner in the book publishing firm of Farrar, Straus and Giroux. Bingham was on the firm's board for many years. It was the only board of a commercial enterprise on which he served.

17. *The Courier-Journal* had moved into the old Post Office and Custom House at Third and Liberty streets in 1912.

18. Standard Gravure Corporation was incorporated by David B.G. Rose, R.W. Ramsier, and George M. Able on 23 June 1922. It was located at 220-228 South First Street, and D.B.G. Rose was listed in the 1923 city directory as president. In 1924 Rose also headed the Standard Printing Company at the same address. In 1925 Emanuel Levi was listed as head of Standard Gravure, while Rose remained head of Standard Printing. In 1926 Standard Gravure moved to 716 West Breckinridge Street.

Standard Gravure printed a high-quality sepia section for the Sunday *Courier-Journal,* as well as some poster art. In 1938, after years of experimentation, the first four-color work was printed. After World War II, Sunday magazines—locally edited and printed in color—evolved into distinctive and popular newspaper inserts. By the 1970s only nine rotogravure plants existed in the country, producing sixty-two magazines. Standard Gravure printed more than twenty weekly magazines (numbering some fifteen million copies) and also printed *Parade* magazine. *The Courier-Journal* discontinued publishing its own Sunday magazine with the 7 April 1991 issue. It had been initiated on 19 April 1942.

19. Powel Crosley began broadcasting in Cincinnati with a five-hundred-watt station in 1922. His was the first station in the country to broadcast with a five-hundred-thousand-watt transmitter.

20. WHAS-AM and WAMZ-FM were sold to Clear Channel Communications of San Antonio, Texas, on 10 June 1986 for $20.1 million. WHAS-AM, one of twenty-four clear-channel radio stations in the country, ranked first in the Louisville market.

21. WHAS-TV, Channel 9, began broadcasting on 27 March 1950. It was estimated that twenty-five thousand television sets had been installed in Louisville since WAVE-TV went on the air in November 1948.

After two years of experimentation, W9XEK went on the air on 30 January 1946. It became WCJT and was the first commercial FM station in Kentucky.

22. WHAS-TV was sold to the Providence Journal Company on 30 May 1986 for $85.75 million. It ranked first in the Louisville market during prime time.

23. Barry Bingham prepared two series of newspaper reports from Germany. The first appeared daily in *The Courier-Journal* from 4 November through 11 November 1946. The second appeared on 24, 26, 28, and 29 December 1947 and 2 and 3 January 1948. They were reprinted in a booklet, *Problems of Germany.*

Chapter 7. Chief of Mission

1. Paul Gray Hoffman (1891-1974) rose within the Studebaker Corporation from auto salesman to chairman of the board. After serving as admin-

istrator of the Economic Cooperation Administration, he was associated in various capacities with the Ford Foundation and the United Nations.

2. Barry Bingham's correspondence from that period, dealing not only with the ECA but also with the family and newspaper matters, has been preserved as a record group in the Filson Club.

3. Henry Richardson Labouisse (b. 1904) was a Harvard-trained lawyer and a Princeton graduate who had been connected with the Department of State since 1941, particularly with the U.S. embassy in Paris.

4. Joseph Bryan III (b. 1904), of Richmond, Virginia, was preparing *The Windsor Story* (New York: William Morrow and Company, 1979) with Charles J. V. Murphy. He used Barry Bingham's account to set straight "a scandalous story" that "began to circulate in the Windsors' world in late 1951" (549).

5. Gardner Cowles (1903-85), nicknamed Mike, was a Harvard graduate who headed the Des Moines *Register* and *Tribune* and Cowles Communications, which included *Look* and *Family Circle*. Fleur Fenton Cowles was a magazine editor and painter.

Chapter 8. With Adlai Stevenson

1. John Luter (b. 1919) was a print and media correspondent before joining the Columbia University School of Journalism. He was employed by the Oral History Research Office to conduct over a hundred interviews, sponsored by grants from the National Endowment for the Humanities and friends of Adlai E. Stevenson.

2. Barry Bingham wrote the lead editorial for *The Courier-Journal* for Sunday, 10 February 1952: "Stevenson and Eisenhower Offer Us Most: Proposing two candidates who could give us a campaign on a decent level, and assure integrity and high ability no matter which party wins the election." He probably preferred Paul Hoffman to Eisenhower, but the former Marshall Plan cohead had declined to be mentioned as a candidate.

3. Stevenson had known Wyatt for some years and in 1947 recommended him to Trygve Lie as assistant secretary-general of the United Nations. He also suggested Barry Bingham. Wilson Watkins Wyatt (b. 1905) graduated from the Jefferson School of Law and was admitted to the bar in Louisville in 1927. In 1935 he became a partner in the firm of Peter, Heyburn, Marshall and Wyatt, with responsibility for handling the litigation of the Bingham newspapers. Judge Arthur Peter had been in Judge Bingham's old firm. After a term as mayor of Louisville (1941-45), Wyatt was housing expediter in the National Housing Agency. In 1947 the firm of Wyatt, Grafton and Sloss was formed. Robert Sloss was the son of Judge's Bingham's former partner Stanley E. Sloss. In 1982 Wilson Wyatt was a founding partner in Kentucky's largest law firm, Wyatt, Tarrant and Combs. He has remained a civic leader. In 1985 the University Press of Kentucky published his autobiography, *Whistle Stops: Adventures in Public Life.*

4. Earle Clements resigned as governor of Kentucky in November 1950, having been elected to a six-year term in the U.S. Senate.

5. Elijah Parish Lovejoy (1802-37) was a schoolteacher, Presbyterian preacher, and newspaper editor. He moved to once-prosperous Alton, Illinois, in 1836 and edited the *Observer* as an abolitionist organ. While defending his press, he was shot and killed by a mob.

6. For a good summary, see Barry Bingham, "With Adlai in Asia," in *As We Knew Adlai,* ed. Edward P. Doyle (New York: Harper and Row, 1966), 188-98.

7. Chiang Kai-shek (1887-1975) was the Chinese Nationalist leader who led a successful incursion against the Communists, taking charge of the government and military in 1928. Civil war again broke out during World War II, and by 1950 Chiang and the Nationalist government, bolstered by U.S. aid, had taken refuge on Taiwan. The conversation notes Barry Bingham made afterward from memory are published in Walter Johnson, ed., *Visit to Asia, the Middle East, and Europe, March-August 1953,* vol. 5 of *The Papers of Adlai E. Stevenson* (Boston: Little, Brown and Co., 1974), 63-66.

8. Barry Bingham wrote a series of eight articles between late March and early June 1953 for *The Courier-Journal* describing his country-by-country observations.

9. Jane Warner Dick is married to Edison Dick, a former executive with the A.B. Dick Company. They were longtime friends and political supporters of Adlai Stevenson's from Lake Forest, Illinois. Jane Dick was national vice chair of the Volunteers for Stevenson in 1952 and cochair in 1956.

Archibald Stevens Alexander (b. 1906), a Princeton graduate and a Harvard-trained lawyer, had been state treasurer of New Jersey and was twice a candidate for the U.S. Senate.

10. Barry Bingham was offered the post of ambassador to Great Britain by John Kennedy. Stevenson called at the behest of the president-elect in late 1960. Although Barry Bingham relished the honor of following his father's path, he recoiled at the huge personal financial cost necessary to help operate the embassy, and he realized that his sons Worth and Barry were to commence working for the family companies in Louisville. He also declined subsequent appointments to Paris and Rome. (See letters from Mary Caperton Bingham to Harold F. Johnson, 19 Jan. 1961, and to Edward White, 22 Feb. 1961, designated to be given to the Filson Club.) David K. E. Bruce was appointed ambassador to Great Britain. Marie Brenner in *House of Dreams: The Bingham Family of Louisville* (New York: Random House, 1988) states: "The president-elect, Bingham told his family, had promised him another chance at the Court of St. James's in 1964" (262). According to Mary Caperton Bingham, no such discussion occurred. David Bruce did write presidential adviser McGeorge Bundy on 14 December 1964, strongly advocating Barry Bingham for the post in Paris, should it become vacant. (National Security File, Lyndon B. Johnson Library, Austin, Texas).

11. Marietta Endicott Peabody Tree (1917-91) held various positions with the United Nations, including one as U.S. representative to the Trusteeship Council with the rank of ambassador. An adviser to Adlai Stevenson, she was walking with him in London when he collapsed and died.

Arthur Ronald Lambert Field Tree (1897-76) was born in England of American parents. His grandfather was Marshall Field. He studied at Columbia University and served in Parliament for fifteen years. From 1949 the Trees lived in Barbados as well as New York.

12. Adlai Stevenson was survived by three sons, including Adlai Stevenson, Jr., who married Nancy Anderson, daughter of the Binghams' good friends Mr. and Mrs. Warwick Anderson, who also resided in Glenview, Kentucky.

Chapter 9. Reflection

1. Herbert Marshall McLuhan, Ph.D. (1911-1980), Canadian communications specialist and educator, wrote numerous books, including *The Medium Is the Message* (New York: Bantam Books, 1967).

2. Robert Worth Bingham and Lawrenceburg, Kentucky, native James Buckner Brown (1872-1940) went head-to-head on various fronts in the 1920s. Brown had been appointed president of the Board of Sinking Fund Commissioners by Mayor Bingham in 1907. He began to assimilate banks, eventually organizing the powerful holding company Banko-Kentucky Corporation. It failed in November 1930. In 1924, however, Brown purchased both the morning *Louisville Herald* and the evening *Louisville Post*. The morning edition of *The Herald-Post* was soon forgone as Brown lined up against *The Louisville Times* in the afternoon and both Bingham papers on Sundays. *The Herald-Post* went into receivership in December 1930 and in 1931 was sold to John B. Gallaher of Chicago, who sold it to the Girdler Corporation of Louisville in 1933. The newspaper suspended operation in October 1936.

The circulation schemes culminated in 1927, when *The Herald-Post* ushered in Chief Thunderwater to adopt Louisville children into the Mohawk Indian tribe. *The Louisville Times*'s dashing of Thunderwater as a bald Indian from Cleveland known as Pete Sands brought on suits for five hundred thousand dollars against the Bingham papers. The suits were dismissed.

3. Barry Bingham had been honorary president of the society of professional journalists, Sigma Delta Chi, in 1956-57. His lecture was published in *The Quill* in January 1971.

4. Barry Bingham's keynote speech to Sigma Delta Chi's fifty-fourth annual convention, entitled "A New Responsibility of the American Press," was printed in part in *Editor and Publisher* on 16 November 1963.

5. The American Society of Newspaper Editors was fifty years old in 1974 when it published *Read All about It!* by Alice Fox Pitts, "with

contributions by scores of eminent editors." Barry Bingham contributed "Our Association with International Organizations," revealing his knowledge and interest. He served on the ASNE board and was active in the organization, especially in the late 1960s, when *The Courier-Journal* and *The Louisville Times* executive editor Norman Isaacs was its president.

Barry Bingham reiterated his stance in his letter to R.W. Cole of New Albany, Indiana, on 18 November 1969: "I have long occupied the position of a gadfly in the newspaper industry because I have constantly called attention to the failures and weaknesses of the press. I have led a movement to start local press councils in cities all over the country, which would give readers an opportunity to air their complaints about their newspapers. I am presently engaged in trying to set up a Public Grievance Procedure within the American Society of Newspaper Editors, again to give readers a chance to make charges against the press when they feel that the canons of good journalism have been violated.

"As you can see, I am no automatic defender of the communications media. I have also said on many occasions that I think television should make a much clearer distinction between straight news reporting and editorial comment. . . .

"Whenever you see evidence of bias in straight news reporting in our papers, I would be grateful to you if you would point it out to me. You may disagree heartily with our editorials, but I ask you to credit us with honest opinions in the section of the paper devoted to opinion, just as I credit you with all sincerity in the opinions you express."

6. The American Press Institute was founded in 1946 as a center for the continuing education and training of print journalists. In 1974 it moved from Columbia University to new headquarters in Reston, Virginia. Barry Bingham chaired the organization from 1963 to 1966.

7. The International Press Institute began operation in 1952 to promote press freedom and free access to information and to improve the practice of journalism and understanding among journalists. The first IPI assembly Barry Bingham attended was in 1958. He became very active and was chair from 1964 to 1966.

8. The Asia Foundation was founded in 1954 to assist Asians in the further growth and development of their own societies. Barry Bingham was a trustee from 1958 to 1988.

9. The introduction was made at an English-Speaking Union luncheon in New York City. Barry Bingham chaired the organization in the United States.

10. John A. Mitchell was a graduate student in history at Morehead State University. His adviser, Edmund Hicks, contacted Norman Isaacs about an interview. Mitchell's thesis title was "The Editorial Policy of *The Courier-Journal* as Concerns Vietnam: 1954-1969." When Mitchell sent a list of seventeen questions on 9 July 1970, Barry Bingham, Sr., was called upon to respond.

11. On Weldon B. James, see chap. 6, n. 11.

12. Molly Clowes (Mrs. Willy Walsh), a native of Birmingham, England, began working for *The Courier-Journal* in 1936 as a reporter. She later became a feature writer and then a writer on the editorial page. She was editorial page editor (the first woman to hold such a position on a major daily) from 1966 until 1971, when she retired at age sixty-five.

13. This transcript was prepared by interviewer Dennis Cusick and sent to Barry Bingham.

14. *The Louisville Times* operation was merged into *The Courier-Journal* on 16 February 1987.

15. Tom Wallace (1874-1961) was chief of *The Louisville Times*'s editorial page and then editor (1930-48) and finally editor emeritus (1948-59). He had worked on the editorial staff of *The Courier-Journal* under Henry Watterson. Before that he had served as the *Times*'s Frankfort and Washington correspondent and had worked for other local newspapers.

16. Russell Briney (1901-66) attended the University of Virginia and joined *The Courier-Journal* as a reporter, covering the Scopes trial. He was promotion manager before joining the editorial staff of *The Louisville Times*. He became chief editorial writer for *The Courier-Journal* and then editor of the editorial page. His wife, Melville Otter Briney, also worked for the newspapers, and in 1955 *The Louisville Times* produced a book of her articles, *Fond Memories: Sketches of Old Louisville*.

17. Albert Y. Aronson (1886-1957) attended Indiana University. He became a reporter for *The Courier-Journal* in 1907 but soon moved to *The Louisville Times*. He covered city hall and then became assistant telegraph editor before becoming city editor in 1919 and managing editor in 1923.

18. Barry Bingham had faced this exact dilemma in 1934, when his father's newspaper executives had proposed that Judge Bingham purchase the old *Herald-Post* and operate it as a Republican newspaper. He then threatened to resign (see chap. 4).

19. Since 1985 the Poynter Institute for Media Studies in St. Petersburg, Florida, has videotaped distinguished personages in American journalism and produced thirty-minute edited tapes in its NewsLeaders series. The unedited tapes are also available for research at the institute, named for Nelson Poynter of the *St. Petersburg Times*.

20. Barry Bingham felt deeply that people should bequeath vital organs for transplant, as he had done. He wrote the poem "Lines For A Bequest" to signal his own commitment. It was drafted in Palermo, Sicily, on 11-12 September 1984 and was later sent to Ann Landers, who had long worked for wider acceptance of the practice. She reprinted the poem in her column in November 1984.

21. Thomas C. Simons was chair of Capital Holding Corporation, a civic leader committed to the redevelopment of downtown Louisville, especially the Broadway area, and a strong supporter of the Louisville Free Public Library. He died in 1988 at the age of fifty-nine.

22. *The Binghams of Louisville* centered an unprovoked and unwarranted attack on Barry Bingham's father, Judge Robert Worth Bingham. Chandler's account is supported with twisted facts, contradictions, fabrications, and untruths. Barry Bingham, incensed by Chandler's characterization of his father, prepared for the author's publisher, Macmillan, a memorandum, dated 15 April 1987, listing the factual errors upon which Chandler had erected the gross deceit. Upon receiving the memorandum, Macmillan declined to publish the book. Unfortunately, *The Binghams of Louisville* was subsequently brought out by Crown Publishing Company.

Chandler raised the specter that Mary Lily Kenan Flagler Bingham had had syphilis and was murdered. This and Chandler's negative characterization of Judge Bingham would color other books, even though his book was refuted.

Three other books would follow. In 1988 Random House published *House of Dreams: The Bingham Family of Louisville,* by *Vanity Fair* writer Marie Brenner. In reading Barry Bingham's oral history interviews conducted by Mary D. Bobo for the University of Louisville, Brenner ran across the fact that the Binghams' wartime correspondence had been deposited in the Schlesinger Library at Radcliffe College. There she found the gold mine of letters that were the basis of her focus on the incredibly strong and enriching relationship of Mary and Barry Bingham. But in the usual slick and trendy *Vanity Fair* style, Brenner embroidered the subject with her particular brand of psychobiographical detail, leaning heavily upon Chandler in the historical sections.

On the heels of *House of Dreams* came the gospel according to daughter Sallie Bingham in *Passion and Prejudice: A Family Memoir* (New York: Alfred A. Knopf, 1989). She begins: "In re-creating my past, I asked questions about the world that once encased me." The answers to her questions reflect the highly personal, idiosyncratic perspective of a devout feminist.

New York Times reporter Alex Jones was assigned to prepare a feature piece documenting the circumstances leading to the decision to sell the Bingham companies. "The Fall of the House of Bingham" appeared in the *Times* on 19 January 1986 (ten days after the decision to sell was announced), and it would win a Pulitzer Prize for Jones. He then approached Barry and Mary Bingham with a concept for a book with which they were quite comfortable—one that would concentrate on their flagship newspaper, *The Courier-Journal,* and its long and leading role in southern journalism. They lent support and encouragement to the project, and because of this blessing, the undertaking was viewed (and proclaimed) as the authorized version. What was five years in the making turned out to be anything but what the Binghams had envisioned. The authors, Alex Jones and his wife, Susan Tifft, would claim they never intended to focus on journalism, as they rehashed an old story and trashed each person in it. The book's title, *The Patriarch: The Rise and Fall of the Bingham Dynasty,* would lead one to believe that some illumination would be cast upon Barry Bingham, Sr., but such is not the case.

This dim characterization of an ineffectual and sly vacillator certainly does not match the man pictured by thirty-nine friends in *Remembering Barry Bingham* (Louisville: Privatly printed, 1990). Barry Bingham would be the first to agree that that is as it should be. But *The Patriarch* lacks journalistic balance and fairness, as well as an understanding of regional or local history and culture.

See Samuel W. Thomas, "Let the Documents Speak: An Analysis of David Leon Chandler's Assessment of Robert Worth Bingham," *The Filson Club History Quarterly* 63 (July 1989): 307-61.

23. Crown Publishing Company issued *The Binghams of Louisville* in December 1987.

24. "Family Feud . . . the fourth in a series about families divided by money and power" written by Eric Levin and reported by David Chandler, appeared in the 2 June 1986 issue of *People*.

25. In the late 1870s the narrow-gauge Louisville, Harrods Creek and Westport Railway made the bluffs east of Louisville along the Ohio River accessible, especially for summer homes—including the Fincastle Club. John E. Green made part of his Glenview Stock Farm available for this purpose. In 1900 Judge and Mrs. Alex P. Humphrey converted the clubhouse into a summer dwelling, which eventually became their permanent residence. It was replaced by the Bingham amphitheater in 1929.

26. Charles T. Ballard maintained a summer cottage known as Holiday House. In 1910-11 he had John Bacon Hutchings design and build a permanent residence, called Bushy Park, which was sold to Robert Worth Bingham in 1919. Judge Bingham changed its name to Melcombe Bingham, and in 1942 it became the residence of Barry and Mary Bingham. Across the ravine Ballard's brother and partner in the family flour mill operation, Samuel Thruston Ballard, built a clapboard house designed by W. J. Dodd in 1900. It burned in 1906 and was rebuilt in stone. In 1976 the house was razed and the tract subdivided.

27. Major Charles J. F. Allen had John Bacon Hutchings design Allenwood (now Eleven Hearths) in 1897, and the house was built just west of the Ballards'. His son Judge Lafon Allen built a Tudor Revival-style house (1911-13), designed by John Bacon Hutchings and his son E. T. Hutchings, appropriately called Glen Entry. Credo Harris, S. Thruston Ballard's brother-in-law, who would put WHAS into operation for Robert Worth Bingham, built a house with Spanish Revival overtones in 1914 on the river bottomland near the interurban station.

28. Mary Lily Kenan Flagler Bingham left Judge Bingham five million dollars in a codicil to her will.

29. William Watkins Davies was a native of North Carolina and a classmate of Judge Bingham's at the University of North Carolina. He began practicing law in 1892. After the Spanish-American War he moved to Louisville, where the firm of Bingham and Davies was established. In 1900 Davies married Sarah Coonley, the granddaughter of Louisville plow manufacturer B.F.

Avery. After Bingham and Davies was dissolved, Davies practiced alone and then with R.L. Page and W.W. Downing. He moved to Canaan, Connecticut, in the late 1920s and died there in 1945.

30. This is confirmed in a letter from Dean William H. Welch, M.D., to William G. MacCallum, M.D., dated 26 September 1917 (Johns Hopkins University Medical Archives, Baltimore). Also, Judge Bingham, when writing his daughter, Henrietta, on 22 November 1922 about her brother Robert's alcoholism, stated: "You know I tried hard to help poor M.L. [Mary Lily] and in that connection made a real study of the disease and I know now a great deal about it from a scientific standpoint" (Bingham Papers, Filson Club).

31. *The Courier-Journal* reported on 17 March 1933 that Senator Arthur Robinson of Indiana "had a telegram from Dr. Abraham Flexner, New York City, asserting that to confirm Bingham [as ambassador] would be a 'scandal and a disgrace.' " Flexner's run-in with Bingham had occurred in 1905, when Bingham helped solicit more students for Flexner's school at 210 Ormsby Street, which Robert W. Bingham, Jr., attended, only to find that Flexner intended to depart and pass his students on to another principal for a fee.

Abraham Flexner (1866-1959) was born in Louisville and educated at Johns Hopkins University (A.B., 1886), Harvard University (A.M., 1906), and the University of Berlin (1906-7). He later received a host of honorary degrees, from which he derived his doctoral title. He worked for the Carnegie Foundation and the General Education Board in New York City and was director of the Institute for Advanced Study. He wrote books, mostly on education, including a significant early report on the lack of uniform quality in American medical schools.

32. Andrew Jackson May (1875-1959), a lawyer from Floyd County, served in the U.S. Congress from 1931 to 1946. He was allied with John Young Brown, Sr., and was the uncle of William H. May, the politically active head of Brighton Engineering.

33. Michael Leo Ravitch (1867-1947) was born in Russia and educated at the University of Moscow and the Central Medical College in St. Joseph, Missouri. In 1895 he moved to Louisville. For a short time he practiced in Lexington. A specialist in dermatology, he was on the staffs of Michael Reese Hospital, Chicago, and Jewish Hospital, Louisville. Ravitch wrote *The Romance of Russian Medicine* (New York: Liveright, 1937). He moved from Louisville to Chicago about 1922. After briefly living in Hollywood, he retired in New York City, where he died.

34. Mary Lily Kenan Bingham also suffered from attacks of eczema, and that is probably why she saw Dr. Ravitch after she married Judge Bingham.

35. In June 1986, Mary and Barry Bingham made a simple list of the projects they favored for substantial funding. The primary recipients of the fifty million dollars already given away have been in the fields of higher education, performing arts, community development, and mental health.

36. William Keller, M.D., died in 1990 at the age of eighty-three. He had chaired the psychiatry department at the University of Louisville School of Medicine. His pursuits ranged from automotive safety to the theater. He was a longtime friend of Barry Bingham's.

37. William Blodgett, M.D., graduated from the Columbia University College of Physicians and Surgeons in 1944. He specializes in internal medicine.

Index